Apple Watch Series 5

Beginner to Advanced
A Complete Guide

Cathy Young

Look Inside

- **watchOS 6 includes a bevy of new features and apps.** Chapter 1 covers the new Watch App Store, Calculator, AudioBooks, Find People, Podcasts, Noise, Cycle Tracking, Voice Memos, and dozens of new watchOS 6 features. Each topic has locations for detailed instructions.

- **The Apple Watch Series 5 uses the ECG app to record an electrocardiogram.** iOS 12.1.1 added blood pressure monitoring and irregular rhythm notifications. Look at Chapter 9 for instructions for using these apps and settings.

- **Learn how to check your fitness progress** utilizing your Heart Rate Recovery data, Activity Trends, and Health Highlights, as discussed in Chapter 9.

- **If you have a hard fall, your Apple Watch will call for help.** See Chapter 2, Guide to Basics.

- **Set up a shared grocery list and add items with your digital assistant.** Everyone in your family can tap their wrist (or iPhone) to view and check off items on your family's grocery list. Use Siri, Alexa, Google Home, or Microsoft Cortana to add items to your grocery list. Chapter 7 covers setting up iOS family sharing and a shared iOS reminder list. The steps for creating IFTTT integrations include how to link iOS reminders and digital assistants.

- **Learn how to set up custom app notifications.** Chapter 3 demonstrates Calendar Alerts, Mail VIP alerts, Map driving alerts, Workout reminders, and more.

- **Any app could include Apple Watch "Complications" for your watch face**. The LoseIt! app tracks daily calories, Pedometer shows steps today, and the Decibel complication monitors environment noise levels. We'll show you how to add these and dozens of other complications to your customized watch faces. In Chapter 4, we'll also explore the new watchOS 6 complications for AudioBooks, Calculator, Cellular Strength, Rain, and Voice Memos.

- **Explore over 100 third-party apps in Chapter 7, including IFTTT.** When a manufacturer doesn't have an Apple Watch app, chances are they do have IFTTT integrations. Chapter 7 looks at Logitech Harmony, eBay, and Twitter IFTTT widgets. We also cover creating your own IFTTT applets and multi-step IFTTT Maker apps.

- **The Mickey or Minnie Mouse watch face will announce the time, and watchOS 6 includes "Speak Time."** See Getting Started, "Sounds and Haptics" in Chapter 2. Personalize this watch face with "Magic Guide to Disney World." Chapter 4 Watch Faces has all the details on watch faces, and samples with suggested apps and configurations to try out.

- **Use Apple Pay & Apple Wallet on your watch.** Send money with Siri messages, pay a cashier, or tap your watch to approve that transaction you're completing in Safari on your Mac. Chapter 6 also explains the PassKit framework and how to add cards to your Wallet app.

- **Apple Apps, like Siri Shortcuts, are thoroughly covered in Chapter 6.** Siri Shortcuts are the embodiment of a personal assistant. Record a personal phrase, pick your apps and tasks, and Siri does the rest. There are details and practical examples that demonstrate this exciting technology.

- **Unlock your Mac whenever your Apple Watch is in range.** Chapter 8, Day to Day has the details on "Continuity" features like Handoff and Auto Unlock.

- **In Chapter 7, learn how to control iTunes or an Apple TV with your Apple Watch.** Now that watchOS6 supports streaming audio directly to your Apple Watch, you can listen to live music and sporting events at any time.

- **Use your Apple Watch as a camera remote control** to take photos with your iPhone. Chapter 5, Watch Apps, has the info.

- **The Science of Haptics uses wrist vibrations to deliver alerts or notifications.** Apple Taptic Engine examples utilizing haptics include Map apps that gently vibrate the Apple Watch on your wrist to indicate an upcoming turn. When "Taptic Time" is enabled with watchOS 6, your Watch taps out the time on your wrist. Check out details in Chapter 10, Accessibility.

Table of Contents

Look Inside   **1**

Preface   **25**

1. Introduction   **27**

1.1 What is the Apple Watch?   **28**

1.2 Apple Watch Series 5   **29**

1.3 watchOS 6 and iOS 13   **31**

New Apps   32
Updated Apps   33
New Features   34

1.4 What's Next?   **35**

2. Setup & Getting Started 37

2.1 Force Touch 39

iPhone Touch Gestures 41
  Swipe Left or Right on an Item to See Options* ... 41
  Swipe Down to See Search Options* 41
  Swipe to See a Text Entry Box on iPhone* 41
  Rotate with Two Fingers on iPhone* 42
  iPhone: Swipe to Go To the Next Step* 43
  Copy Between Apps on iPhone* 44
  Two-handed Gestures on iPhone* 44

2.2 Human Interface Guidelines 44

2.3 A Quick Look at Watch Controls 48

2.4 Turn On or Wake 49

2.5 Charging the Watch 49

2.6 Turn Off 50

2.7 Pair Your Watch & iPhone 51

Your Apple ID 52
Sign in with Apple 53
iPhone Setup 54
Networks: Bluetooth and Wi-Fi 55
  iPhone Wi-Fi Setup 56
  Bluetooth 56

2.8 Rename Your Watch 57

2.9 Setup Cellular Service 57

2.10 Passcode & Security Features 58

Change Apple Watch Passcode Options 58
Wrist Detection 59
Clear Website Data 59
Turn on Find My Watch 60
Find Your Apple Watch 60
Two-Factor Authentication 60
Allow iPhone Access When Locked 62
Accounts & Passwords Settings on iPhone 62

*Share an iPhone Password over AirDrop** 62
*iCloud Keychain on iPhone** 63

2.11 **The Display** **63**
*iPhone Display** 63

2.12 **The Home Screen** **64**
Apple Watch - Grid or List View 64
 Switch Between Grid or List View 65
Delete Apps From Your Apple Watch 65
Reset Apple Watch Home Screen Layout to Factory
Default 65
*iPhone Home Screen** 66
 *iPhone Home Screen Status Icons** 68
 *Arrange Apps in Folders on your iPhone** 69
 *Rename Folders on your iPhone Home Screen** 69
 *Delete an App on your iPhone** 70
 *iPhone Home Screen Layout Factory Default** 70
 *Add Web Pages to Your iPhone Home Screen** 70

2.13 **Side Button & Dock** **70**
Add an App to the Apple Watch Dock 72
Reorder the List of Apps in the Apple Watch Dock 73
Remove an App from the Apple Watch Dock 73
*iPhone Dock** 73
 *Delete Apps on the iPhone Home Screen** 74
 *Move Apps on the iPhone Home Screen** 75
 *Add an App to the iPhone Dock** 75
 *Find an iPhone App** 75

2.14 **The Digital Crown** **75**
Explore the Digital Crown 76
Switch Between Apps 76
Gradually Wake Your Watch 77

2.15 **Control Center** **77**
Rearrange Icons in the Apple Watch Control Center 78
Apple Watch Control Center Icons 78
 Cellular 78
 Wi-Fi 78
 Airplane Mode 78
 Battery 79
 Find My (iPhone) 79
 Flashlight 80
 Do Not Disturb 80
 Silent Mode 80

Theater Mode 80
Walkie-Talkie 81
Water Lock 81
Audio Output 82
Control Audio Volume 82

*The iPhone Control Center** 82
*Change the Order of iPhone Controls** 84
*Add or Remove iPhone Controls** 85

*iPhone Control Center Icons** 85
*Airplane Mode** 85
*Dark Mode** 85
*Audio Output** 86
*Wi-Fi** 86
*Bluetooth** 87
*QR Code Reader** 87
*Text Size** 87
*Magnifier** 87
*Lock the Screen (Orientation)** 87
*Do Not Disturb** 88
*Display Brightness** 88
*Volume** 88
*Mute** 88
*Timer** 89
*Notes** 89
*Camera** 89
*Home Control (Smart Home)** 89
*Hearing** 89
*Accessibility Control** 89
*Apple TV Remote** 90
*Screen Mirroring** 90
*Guided Access** 90

2.16 Heart Rate Sensors & Electrodes   90

2.17 Band Release Buttons   90

2.18 Display & Brightness   92

2.19 Sounds & Haptics   93

Haptics 93
Adjust Volume 94
Cover to Mute 95
Haptic Alerts 95
Silent Mode 95
Do Not Disturb 97

2.20 Change the Time Shown   **97**

2.21 iPhone Today View*   *98*

   Add a Widget to iPhone Today View*   *98*

2.22 iPhone App Switcher*   *99*

   Close an Unresponsive iPhone App*   *100*
   Switch Between iPhone Apps*   *101*

2.23 iPhone Lock Screen*   *101*

   Allow iPhone Access When Locked*   *101*
   iPhone Notifications*   *101*

2.24 Apple Resources   **102**

2.25 What's Next?   **102**

3. Basics   **103**

3.1 General Settings   **104**
   iPhone General Settings*   *105*
   About*   *106*
     RENAME YOUR IPHONE*   *106*
   iPhone AirDrop Settings*   *107*
   iPhone Handoff Settings*   *107*
   iPhone Language and Region Settings*   *107*
   iPhone Storage*   *107*
   Background App Refresh on iPhone*   *108*
   iPhone Keyboard*   *108*
     IPHONE TEXT REPLACEMENT*   *108*
   Reset iPhone*   *109*
     RESET IPHONE HOME SCREEN LAYOUT TO FACTORY DEFAULT* *110*

3.2 Configure Medical ID in the Health App   **110**

3.3 Configure Emergency SOS   **110**
   Enable Emergency SOS on your Watch   111
   View Medical ID or Call Emergency Services   111

3.4 Automatic App Install   **111**

3.5 Watch Orientation (Wrist)   **112**

3.6 Wake Screen — 112
Gradually Wake Your Watch — 113
Lift Your Wrist to Wake Your Watch — 113
Return to Last Activity on Screen Raise — 114
Auto Launch the Now Playing App — 114

3.7 Nightstand Mode — 115
Set an Alarm — 115

3.8 Language and Region — 116

3.9 Siri — 116
Your Contact Card — 117
View and Rerecord Shortcut Phrases on the iPhone* — 117
*iPhone Siri Spotlight Search** — 117

3.10 Privacy & Location Services — 117

3.11 Screen Time: Content & Privacy Restrictions — 119

3.12 Apple ID & iCloud — 119
iCloud — 120
Name, Phone Numbers, E-mail — 121
Password & Security — 121
Subscriptions & Purchase History — 121
Family Sharing — 122
ENABLE FAMILY SHARING — 123
ASK TO BUY — 123
Your Apple Watch Device Info — 123
Turn on Find My Watch — 124
iCloud Keychain — 124
iCloud Backup — 124
iCloud Photo Stream — 125
Find People, Share My Location — 125
Share a Reminder List — 125
Share Calendars — 126
*Apple Pay Setup on iPhone** — 126

3.13 Accessibility — 127
Accessibility Shortcut — 128
VoiceOver — 129
Zoom — 129

*Accessibility Settings on iPhone** 130
*Accessibility Shortcut on iPhone** 130
READ SCREEN CONTENTS OUT LOUD ON IPHONE* 131
VOICEOVER ON IPHONE* 132
ZOOM ON IPHONE* 132
SUBTITLES ON IPHONE* 132

3.14 Continuity & Handoff **133**
Requirements 133

3.15 Enable Screenshots **134**
Take a Screenshot 135

*3.16 iPhone Share Sheet** 135
Reorder Extensions* 137
Add or Remove Extensions* 137

*3.17 Rename iPhone File or Folder** 137

*3.18 iPhone Keyboard** 138
Numbers* 138
Emoji* 138
Install Other Keyboards* 138
Switch iPhone Keyboards* 140

*3.19 iPhone Text Editing** 140
Entering Text* 140
Selecting Text* 142
Moving Text* 148
Predictive Text* 149
iPhone Shortcut Bar* 149
Text Replacement* 150
Dictation* 150
DICTATION COMMANDS* 151

3.20 What's Next? **152**

4. Watch Faces **153**

4.1 Update Your Watch Face **158**

4.2 Exploring Interactive Watch Faces **158**

Astronomy 159

4.3 Changing the Watch Face Style 160

Delete a Watch Face 161

4.4 Customizing a Watch Face 161

4.5 The 'My Faces' Screen 162

Organize Your Watch Faces 163
Reorder Watch Faces 163

4.6 Complications 164

Add a Complication to Your Watch Face 166
The Favorite Complication 167
ADD OR REMOVE A FAVORITE CONTACT 167
Remove Complications 168
Complication Not Showing on iPhone 168
Edit Complications 169
Navigating Complications 169

4.7 Customized Samples 170

Astronomy 170
Breathe Watch Face 170
Color 171
Cooking and Kitchen 172
Disney 172
Kaleidoscope 174
Motion 174
Fire, Water, Liquid Metal, and Vapor 175
Siri 176
Stocks 177
Timelapse 177
World Traveler 178
CONFIGURE THE WORLD CLOCK TIME ZONES 179
ADD WORLD CLOCK COMPLICATION 179
Your Photo 180
CREATE A PHOTO ALBUM ON YOUR IPHONE 180

4.8 What's Next? 181

5. Notifications   183

5.1 Status Icons   184
5.2 Open the Notification Center   186
5.3 Turn App Notifications Off   187
5.4 Change Notification Delivery   187
5.5 Enable Haptic Notifications   188
5.6 Enable the Notification Indicator   189
5.7 Customize App Notifications   189
Mail Notifications   190
Set Mail VIPs   190
Map Notifications   191
Message Notifications   191
Troubleshooting Message Notifications   192
Workout Reminders   192
Calendar Notifications   193
5.8 Adjust Alert Volume   193
5.9 High or Low Heart Rate Alerts   194
5.10 Troubleshooting Notifications   194
5.11 What's Next?   195

6. Watch Apps   197

6.1 Install & Delete Apps on your Apple Watch 199
The Apple Watch App Store   199
Search for Apps to Install   201
Remove Apps   201
Remove Apps from the Home Screen   201
Remove Apps Using iPhone Storage   202
6.2 Alarms   202
Add an Alarm   203
Turn Alarm Off or Snooze   203
Delete an Alarm   203

6.3 Apple Pay & the Wallet App 204

Ask Siri to Send Cash in a Message 206
Safari Apple Pay and Apple Watch 206
Pay a Merchant on Your Watch 207
Add Cards and Passes to Apple Wallet 207
Add Bar Code Tickets with Pass2U 209
Activate Credit Cards on Your Watch 211
Reorder Cards in the Wallet 211
Transit Cards 211
Status of the Apple Pay System 212

6.4 Audiobooks 212

6.5 Books 214

Buy Books 214
Organize Books in Collections 214

6.6 Breathe 214

6.7 Calculator 215

6.8 Calendar 215

Display Calendar Month View 216
Add a Calendar Event 216
Customize Calendar Notifications 216
Integration with Third-Party Calendar Apps 217
Calendar Sync Issues 218

6.9 Camera Remote 219

Screen Time: Content & Privacy Restrictions 219
Camera Remote and Timer 219

6.10 Clock 220

Configure the World Clock Time Zones 222
Add the World Clock Complication 223
Monogram 224

6.11 The Compass App 224

6.12 The iPhone Contacts App* 225

Your Contact Card 226
Animoji 226
Enable Emergency Bypass 228

6.13 Cycle Tracking 228

Log Data   229

6.14 Emergency SOS, Fall Detection, & Medical ID
                                                                                229

Configure Medical ID in the Health App   230
Configure Emergency SOS   231
View Medical ID or Call Emergency Services   231
Enable Emergency SOS   231

6.15 Find People   232

Share Your Location with a Friend   233
Find a Friend   233
Notifications When a Friend Arrives or Leaves   234
Which Device Determines Your Location?   234

6.16 The Heart Rate App   234

Heart Rate Recovery   235
View Heart Rate Data   235

6.17 The Home App   236

Configure Rooms and Devices for Apple Watch   237
Home Automation   238
Apple HomeKit Automation Platform   239
Invite People to Join Your Home   239
Automation   239
Configure Rooms and Devices   240

6.18 Keynote   240

6.19 Mail   240

Read and Reply to an e-mail   241
Delete an E-mail   241
Set Mail Options   241
Search the iPhone Mail Inbox   242
Mail Settings - Inboxes on your iPhone*   242
Mute an e-mail Conversation on your iPhone*   243
Format Bar on iPhone*   244
Flag Style on iPhone*   244
Forward, Mark, Notify Me, Move, or Delete an e-Mail on
your iPhone*   245
Set VIPs on your iPhone*   246

6.20 Maps   246

Navigation 248
Map Notifications 248
Search 248
Collections 249
Find an Address for a Contact 250
'Search Here' and 'Transit Map' 250
Parked Car 251
*Maps on iPhone** 252

6.21 Messages, Digital Touch, & Apple Pay 253

Create a Message 254
Read a Message 254
Reply to a Message 255
Animoji 255
Scribble 257
Dictate 257
Create an Audio Clip 257
The Default Type of Audio Response 258
View a Message Timestamp 258
Options 258
Smart Replies 258
Message Alerts 259
Use Apple Pay to Send & Receive $ 259
Digital Touch 260

6.22 Music and the Now Playing App 261

Play Music 261
Add a Workout Playlist 262
Use Audio Output With Apple Watch 263
Shuffle, Repeat, Source and Output 263
Change Volume With the Digital Crown 263
Download Music to Your Apple Watch 264
Check Available Space 264

6.23 The Noise App 265

6.24 Phone 267

Make a Call 267
Emergency Phone Call 268
Answer a Call 268
Decline a Call 268

Transfer a Call to Your iPhone   268
Call a Favorite Contact   269
    Add or Remove a Favorite Contact   270

6.25 Photos   **270**

6.26 Podcasts   **271**

6.27 Reminders   **272**
Add a Reminder or Show Completed Reminders   273
Enable Family Sharing   274
Share a Reminder List   274

6.28 Remote Control   **274**
Add Apple TV   275

6.29 Siri   **275**
What Can Siri Do?   276
Enable Siri on Your Watch   277
Enable Siri on Your Apple Watch   277
Enable Raise to Speak   278
Ask Siri a Question   278
Siri Shortcuts   278
    Suggested Shortcuts   279
Teach Siri about You   280
    Your Contact Card   280
Siri Phrases   280
Siri Doesn't Respond   281

6.30 Siri Shortcuts   **281**
Create a Shortcut   284
Suggested Shortcuts   285
Favorite Shortcuts   286
Waze   286
Suggested Shortcuts   286
View and Rerecord Shortcut Phrases   286

6.31 Stocks   **287**

6.32 Stopwatch   **287**
Laps   288

6.33 Timer   **289**

6.34 Voice Memos   **289**

6.35 Walkie-Talkie   **290**
Invite a Friend   291
Start a Conversation   291
6.36 Weather   **293**
Example of Weather in Motion   293
6.37 Web Browser   **293**
6.38 What's Next?   **294**

7. Third-party Apps   295

7.1 Calendar and Reminders   **297**
7.2 Grocery and Cooking Apps   **297**
Grocery   298
ADD ITEMS TO THE LIST   298
ENABLE FAMILY SHARING   299
SHARE THE LIST WITH YOUR FAMILY   299
USE IFTTT TO LINK iOS AND ALEXA   299
7.3 Entertainment   **300**
7.4 Games   **301**
7.5 Health and Fitness   **302**
7.6 IFTTT   **305**
Create IFTTT Widgets for your Apple Watch   306
Create Your Own IFTTT Applets   307
Combine Several Actions   308
7.7 Photography and Video   **308**
7.8 Productivity   **309**
Drafts   310
Add a Custom Drafts Action   311
Edit or Delete an Action   312
7.9 Schools   **312**
7.10 Smart Home   **312**
7.11 Sports and the Great Outdoors   **314**
7.12 Travel   **316**

7.13 Water Sports   **317**

7.14 Weather   **317**

7.15 What's Next?   **318**

8. Day to Day   **319**

8.1 Add Bluetooth Accessories   **320**

Hearing Aids   321

8.2 Charging Stands   **322**

8.3 Find Your Apple Watch   **322**

8.4 Find iPhone   **323**

8.5 Handoff and Continuity   **323**

Handoff From Apple Watch to iPhone   324

Requirements   324

Enable Handoff on your Mac   325

Enable Handoff on your Apple Watch   325

8.6 Remote Control   **325**

Apple TV   325

iTunes   326

8.7 Unlock Your Apple Watch   **326**

8.8 Unlock Your Mac   **326**

8.9 Theater and Sleep Mode   **327**

Silent Mode   327

8.10 Watch Bands   **328**

8.11 Upgrade Your iPhone   **329**

8.12 Pair Your Watch to an iPhone   **329**

8.13 Update watchOS   **330**

8.14 What's Next?   **330**

9. Health and Fitness 331

9.1 Basic Settings 333
Motion & Fitness 333
Location Services 334
Heart Rate Alerts 334
Setup the Health App 334

9.2 The Health App 335
Your Health Account 335
YOUR HEALTH PROFILE 336
EDIT YOUR PERSONAL INFORMATIONAL 336
WHEELCHAIR MODE 337
CONFIGURE MEDICAL ID IN THE HEALTH APP 338
PRIORITIZE DATA SOURCES 338
Health Data Backups 338
The Health Data Screen 339
View Heart Rate Data 341
Add Lab Records 342
Explore Recommended Apps 342
Export Health Data 343

9.3 The Activity App 343
Set Activity Settings 344
Share Activity with a Friend 344
Enable Sharing 344
Accept a Sharing Request 345
View Your Friend's Progress 345
Enable Activity Sharing Notifications 346
Move, Exercise, & Stand Rings 346
MOVE RING 346
EXERCISE RING 347
STAND RING 347
Change the Move Goal 347
Trends 348
Challenge a Friend 350
VO2 max Metric 351
Hearing Metrics 351
History, Weekly Summary & Details 351
WORKOUT AND ACTIVITY HISTORY 351
WEEKLY SUMMARY OR ACTIVITY DETAILS 352
Activity Reminders 352

Manually Add a Workout or Activity 352

9.4 The Heart Rate App 353

9.5 The ECG App 354

9.6 GymKit 355

9.7 The Workout App 356
Running Auto Pause 357
Metrics 357
Start a Workout 359
Set a Goal 359
Add to Your Workout 360
Track Your Progress (View Metrics) 360
Listen to Music While You Workout 360
Watch a Podcast or Tune in a Show 360
Pause Your Workout 360
End Your Workout 361
Name Your 'Other' Workout 361
Workout and Activity History 361

9.8 Sample Workouts 362
Running 362
Swimming and Water Sports 363
TURN ON WATER LOCK 363
Yoga 363
Workout Playlist 364

9.9 Additional Workout Apps 364
Explore Apps 366

9.10 What's Next? 367

10. Accessibility 369

10.1 Accessibility Shortcut 370

10.2 The Taptic Engine 371
Enable the Notification Indicator 371

10.3 Customize App Notifications 371

10.4 Vision 372

VoiceOver 372
  Set the Reading Rate 373
Zoom 374
On/Off Labels 374
Grayscale 374

10.5 Workout App **374**

10.6 Hearing **375**

10.7 Bluetooth Accessories **375**
  Hearing Aids 376

  Control your MFi Hearing Aid 377

10.8 Messaging **378**

10.9 The Walkie-Talkie App **378**

10.10 iPhone Voice Control* *378*
  Add Custom Words on your iPhone* *380*

10.11 What's Next? **380**

11. Troubleshooting **381**

11.1 What's Wrong? **383**

11.2 Apple Pay Not Working **383**
  Check the Status of the Apple Pay System 384

11.3 Battery **384**
  Check Your Battery 385
  Battery Not Charging 385
  Check Cellular Data Usage 385
  Remove Favorite Apps From the Dock 386
  Turn on Grayscale 386
  Turn Off Notifications 387
  Power Reserve 387
    Turn on Power Reserve 387
    Turn off Power Reserve 387
  Turn Off Siri 388
  Turn Your Watch Off and Back On 388

11.4 Calendar & Contacts **388**

11.5 Complications   389

11.6 Can't Connect to iPhone   389

11.7 Connectivity   390
Am I Connected to Cellular?   391
Am I Connected to Wi-Fi?   391
Global Cellular   392
Wi-Fi Won't Switch to Cellular   392

11.8 Digital Crown Not Responding   393

11.9 Force Restart   393

11.10 Forgotten Passcode   393

11.11 Home Screen Views   394
Switch Between Grid or List View   394

11.12 How Much Space is Available   394
How Much Total Space is Available   394

11.13 Mickey Doesn't Announce the Time   395

11.14 Notifications   396
Troubleshooting Message Notifications   396

11.15 Reset, Restore & Backups   397
Turn Your Watch Off and Back On   398
Backups & Restore   398

11.16 Screen Settings   398
Reset Home Screen Layout to Factory Default   399

11.17 Siri Doesn't Respond   399
Check if the Siri System is Available   400

11.18 Walkie-Talkie App   400

11.19 Watch Not Responding   401

11.20 Watch Will Not Wake   401

11.21 watchOS Version   402

11.22 Weekly Summary 402

11.23 Why is My App Not Showing on My Watch? 403

Screen Time: Content & Privacy Restrictions 403

Conclusion 405

Visual Index 407

Index 415

Preface

The visionary Apple Watch is, at last, poised to take on the world in the Apple Watch Series 5! Whether you are new to Apple products, an expert, or somewhere in the middle, this book is designed to make it easy to find what interests you. I want you to feel comfortable with all aspects of your watch in an environment that encourages you to learn painlessly at your own pace. My goal is to help you enjoy the wonder of discovering your Apple Watch. Along the way, I want to:

- Teach you how to use all the features of your Apple Watch. I say "all." As far as I know, I found every darned one of them, but don't sue me if I missed one.

- Demonstrate the cool and awe-inspiring features of the Apple Watch. These aren't random tips and tricks. Rather, I have showcased them in a way that lets you find them while exploring a particular feature or topic.

- Help you find what you want, when you want it. The organized and detailed Table of Contents includes more than 200 topics. Skip around to your heart's content.

- Inspire you with over 100 third-party apps. A few of the categories include entertainment, productivity, sports, photography, and games. We'll also cover integration platforms like IFTTT, which opens up the possibility of unlimited applications.

- Focus on the engineering and Apple platforms behind the Apple Watch. The physical device includes the heart rate monitor, accelerometer, gyroscope, and Apple's Force Touch technology. Behind the scenes, learn how Apple is partnering with businesses to extend their HealthKit, HomeKit, and GymKit platforms to enhance your experience for years to come.

- List 30 Common Troubleshooting and Maintenance Suggestions.

While you can use your Apple Watch with watchOS 6 and later without your iPhone nearby, the Apple iPhone is an integral part of your day-to-day experience. In case you are new to Apple's smartphone and iOS mobile operating system, I've included several topics covering the iPhone setup, screens, and gestures. Those topic headings have an asterisk and special formatting, so you can quickly skip them if you aren't interested.

As a final selling point, I make an intentional effort to avoid a few of my pet peeves – and those pertain to incomplete instructions. I frequently see directions such as "tap to go to settings," but they leave novice users asking, "tap where?" In another example I read, the instructions mentioned a workout playlist and how to enable it – but assumed nothing went awry (and something ALWAYS goes awry). I intend to cover those bases for you. And if I do, by chance, make the mistake of omitting a critical detail anywhere in this book, know that I was probably distracted by my Apple Watch telling me to get moving or to breathe. I apologize ahead of time; it wasn't intentional.

Are you ready for the Apple Watch experience? Let's get started.

1. Introduction

In this chapter we discuss

What is the Apple Watch?
Apple Watch Series 5
watchOS 6 and iOS 13
What's Next?

Apple provided an interesting backstory when it unveiled the first Apple Watch. For those who recall the two-way wristwatch sported by Dick Tracy in the 1946 comic strip, this story will sound familiar. The animator, Chester Gould, visited the workshop of inventor Al Gross, who had a two-way radio wristwatch. Gould asked Gross for permission to use the idea in his comic strip; and, thus, inspired the Apple Watch.

Gross was a true visionary. His patents for a garage door opener, cordless phone, and cell phone expired long before they became household objects. His ideas, however, for a beeper and Citizens Band (CB) radio system became hugely popular. His ground-to-air radio revolutionized communication during World War II.

When Apple first released its watch, I couldn't wait to try one. Although well-engineered, the first Apple Watch wasn't quite what I was expecting. There wasn't a lot of support from third-party apps, no cellular service; and considering the steep price tag, I decided to try again on a future version.

A few years went by, and I bought another watch that had a cellular option so I could listen to music on the go. This time I had the opposite problem. This Apple Watch had too many features and apps. Although all the answers were available on the Internet, I had neither the time nor the patience to research them. Frankly, what I wanted was a personal help desk that I could call at a moment's notice. I think my solution to the problem was inspired. I gave the watch to my daughter with the understanding she would teach me how to use it in the future.

Fast forward to the arrival of the Apple Watch Series 4. I admit my daughter did help me through what I consider the hand-holding period. That first week or two, I only wanted to receive calls and messages, listen to music, and set up a cool watch face. There was some teasing involved, but we both enjoyed the process. I took copious notes for future reference. I confess to having a bad memory, so I compensate by organizing and cross-referencing notes like a crazy person. Those notes, lovingly edited by my husband, evolved into the first book in this series. Based on the reviews I decided to continue on with this book on the Apple Watch Series 5.

1.1 What is the Apple Watch?

At its simplest level, the Apple Watch is a digital timepiece with features and applications similar to a smartphone. When combined with an Apple iPhone, your Apple Watch Series 5 is an extraordinary tool, adapted to your preferences and lifestyle. Apple apps are free, and third-party apps are available for download from the Apple Store for a nominal amount – if not also free.

The Apple Watch is designed in part to improve your health. Forget workout or fitness apps for a moment. Fall detection, International emergency SOS, heart rate monitoring, and the ECG app are part of the health lineup. The "Breathe" or "Forest-Stay Focused" apps promote mindfulness. Recent research into the neuroscience of mindfulness shows deep breathing reduces stress and has long-term health benefits. The workout and fitness apps are impressive. Your health goals, moreover, get a huge boost from these Apple Watch features.

Receive messages, stream music, and use Apple Pay or Siri with your Apple Watch. These features are not dependent on your iPhone when you purchase Apple Watch models that include built-in cellular. Keep in mind; however, cellular models require an airtime contract.

The Apple Watch supports several faces that you can customize to your heart's content. Pick the apps you want on your watch and then decide how to arrange them. In Chapter 4, we discuss app "complications" for your watch face. A complication example is a small icon or text that represents an app like your calendar or calorie counter.

Apple has a unique and defined iOS terminology in its "Human Interface Guidelines." These guidelines are not just terms for the interface icons, tab bars, sliders, and switches. We humans come into play here because we're the ones swiping, tapping, and probably cursing a bit as we learn the Force Touch Technology (FTT). Touch gestures are used to navigate to these areas, and I have outlined them in the next chapter.

1.2 Apple Watch Series 5

The Always-On Apple Watch Series 5 is the latest generation of the Apple Watch. You can choose to enable or disable Always-On, and there is an option to Hide Sensitive Complications. While the Series 4 represented a fundamental redesign and re-engineering of Apple Watch, the Series 5 moves forward once again with an always-on watch face. The Series 5 Magnetometer relies on a magnetoresistive permalloy sensor to detect magnetic north. The new Compass app and updated Maps app both use the sensor to show the direction you're facing. The watch ships with the watchOS 6 mobile operating system which encompasses the logistics of how the Apple Watch works. The Series 5 has a 32GB storage capacity, compared to 16GB storage capacity in the Series 3 (Cellular) or Series 4 models.

Chapter 1

The S4 64-bit dual-core S5 processor ships with the Series 5, while the Series 4 came with the S4 64 bit dual-core processor. The S4 and S5 processors are up to two times faster than the Series 3 dual-core S3 processor. The Series 4 and Series 5 watches use Bluetooth 5, which has more speed, better range, and lower power consumption when compared to Bluetooth 4.2 in the Series 3.

Both the Series 4 and Series 5 have 40mm and 44mm cases. The Digital Crown in the Series 4 and Series 5 models includes haptic feedback with the sensation of incremental clicks; haptic feedback is not available in the Series 3 Digital Crown.

The built-in rechargeable lithium-ion battery uses magnetic charging and lasts up to 18 hours. The power-saving Bluetooth 5 and Low Temperature Poly Oxide (LTPO) display are two of the reasons for the longer battery life, along with unique power-saving features of the X5 processor.

- Stainless steel is heavier and has a shiny appearance, while the aluminum has a matte finish.

- The crystal sapphire glass on the stainless steel model resists scratches better than the Ion-X glass on the aluminum model.

The microphone location is on the other side of the watch, away from the speaker. This microphone location reduces echo noise for better sound quality compared to the Series 3. Audio volume is also 50% louder than the Series 3, to accommodate the walkie-talkie app introduced in watchOS 5.

The heart rate monitor, improved accelerometer, barometric altimeter, and gyroscope are ideal for health and fitness apps. The accelerometer can differentiate between a walk and a run and enables features like "Running Auto Pause" to identify when you're taking an exercise break.

The Series 4 and Series 5 models have a black ceramic back with a sapphire crystal and electrical heart rate sensors. The Series 3 does not have an electrical heart rate sensor. Radio waves easily pass through the front and back for better cellular service. The Series 5 case comes in aluminum, stainless steel, titanium, or ceramic. Titanium is 45 percent lighter than stainless steel with twice the strength. The space black titanium finish has a diamond-like coating.

Silver and Space Gray colors are available in both the Series 5 and Series 3, and the Series 5 also has a Gold color. The Titanium comes in Space Gray or Titanium colors, and the Ceramic case is white. Series 5 also has Nike and Hermès options with unique colors.

The Apple ECG app arrived with watchOS 5.1.2 and iOS 12.1.1 on the Series 4 model. The app provides heart rate monitoring similar to an electrocardiogram (EKG). The FDA granted the app the De Novo classification in the U.S. for the ECG and atrial fibrillation detection features. The ECG app works by measuring your heart rate on your wrist while you touch the opposite hand to the electrode in the Digital Crown, creating a circuit.

If the Apple Watch detects a significant, hard fall while you're wearing your watch, it taps you on the wrist, sounds an alarm, and displays an alert. If you do not respond to the prompt, your watch will automatically contact emergency services.   Recently, Dr. Sumbul Desai said falls are one of the most common reasons to go to the ER across all age groups. We all can benefit from the fall detection feature.

1.3 watchOS 6 and iOS 13

The watchOS 6 operating system encompasses the logistics of how the Apple Watch works. The watchOS supports your interaction with your Apple Watch - tapping, swiping, and controls.

This engineering is elegant and simple to use, and provides Wi-Fi and Bluetooth connectivity, pairing to your companion iPhone, and app updates from the Apple Store. The iOS version of your iPhone works in conjunction with the version on your Apple Watch. For example, to upgrade your Apple Watch to watchOS 6, first, you upgrade your iPhone to iOS 13. These are some interesting features new in watchOS 6.

New Apps

- The Find My app replaces the Find My Friends and Find my iPhone apps, and integrates with Siri. When you say, "Siri, where is Michael?" Siri displays a location map and additional info on your watch face.

- Cycle Tracking for women tracks symptoms, duration, and other metrics and predicts ovulation and more. The Cycle Tracking app also has a complication for your watch face.

- Your Apple Watch automatically syncs "Reading Now" and "Want to Read" Audiobook lists. The Audiobooks app also has a complication for your watch face.

- The new Noise app warns you with a vibration on your wrist when it detects loud environments. Imagine my surprise the first time I wore my Apple Watch to the gym and realized how loud the music was. The Health app Hearing metric shows sound levels and your 7-Day Exposure. The Health app displays Charts and records Headphone Audio Levels. The app also has a complication for your watch face.

- At last a Calculator app is native to your Apple Watch and includes a tip feature to divide the bill among several friends. The app also has a complication for your watch face.

- The Podcasts app is now available on your Apple Watch with the same screen layout as the updated Music app. The Podcasts app also has a complication for your watch face.

- The new Voice Memos app also includes a complication for your watch face.

Updated Apps

- The Maps "Smart Guidance" in the Show Navigation screen enables visual cues with stepping directions. The updated Maps app uses the Magnetometer to show the direction you're facing.

- The Alarms app was redesigned to make it easier to add an alarm.

- Your favorite Animoji and Memoji stickers are available in the Messages app.

- The Music app includes an AirPlay icon, and redesigned controls. The screen is similar to the new Podcasts app screen.

- The Now Playing screen has changed to the "Now Playing" app with AirPlay controls.

- Incoming phone calls have a new screen with a larger icon to answer the calls, which means it's not as easy to accidentally drop a call. The Phone app automatically detects calls from telemarketers and will send them straight to voicemail.

- The Clock app supports Taptic Time, and will now Chime the Hour or Speak the Time when you touch the screen with two fingers, as shown in 6.10.

- Siri Shortcuts support home automations in the Apple Home app and has a Siri integration, as shown in Chapter 6.

- The Weather app includes updates for the Air Quality Indicator (AQI) and UV Meters.

- Trends in the Activity app average the past 90-days of physical activity and then compare it to the past 365 days. The Trends app also offers personalized coaching based on your results.

- The Health app displays Highlights.

- International SOS Emergency Services is included with watchOS 6.

- Both the Health and Activity apps display Cycle Tracking data.

- Apple reorganized the Activity app, so it is easier to find and update data such as Body Measurements, Cycle Tracking, Hearing, Nutrition, Sleep, Vitals, Allergies, Conditions, Immunizations, Lab Results, Medications, or Procedures.

- The Reminders app on the Apple Watch includes a Today view with watchOS 6 and will flag overdue reminders. The redesigned Reminders app supports attachments and shared lists. New features include Smart Lists and a Quick Toolbar to add times, dates, and locations.

New Features

- Apple Watch finally has its own app store. Shop and download apps from your Apple Watch - no iPhone needed!

- There are Auto Hotspot Settings for your Wi-Fi Settings.

- The new watch faces include Modular Compact, Solar Dial, California, Gradient, Numerals Mono, and Numerals Duo. You can also reorder your watch faces on your Apple Watch.

- There are new complications for Audiobooks, Calculator, Cellular Strength, Decibel Level, Rain, and Voice Memos.

- A unique feature in iOS 13/watch OS 6 allows you to send unknown callers straight to voicemail.

- Siri now includes Shazam integration, and can also search the web and display full web page results in Reader View. You can also "handoff" the browser to your Apple Device, as shown in Chapter 3.

- The Taptic Engine for Apple Watch adds the ability to tap out the hour on your wrist with "Speak Time" and "Taptic Time," as shown in 6.10. The new swiftUI gives developers the ability to incorporate Digital Crown Haptics, and apps like Calculator and Alarms have an intuitive feel.

- The swiftUI development framework means watchOS 6 apps can operate without being tethered to an iPhone. swiftUI supports streaming audio directly to your Apple Watch, which means you don't have to "sync" audio from your iPhone. Listen to live music, podcasts, and sporting events at any time.

- The "List View" displaying apps curves slightly. The text is bold, and the app icons are larger.

- Review elevation and summary data on your Apple Watch during a workout and shuffle your workout playlist.

- watchOS 6 allows you to delete some built-in apps right on your Apple Watch screen using a "long press," and then tapping the "x."

- Accessibility options are now available in the Settings app on your Apple Watch.

- Respond to the login alert "Your Apple ID is being used to sign in to a device..." on your Apple Watch, and receive the Apple ID Verification Code.

1.4 What's Next?

At this point, are you thinking this all sounds a bit complicated? There's new jargon to learn (haptics, complications, watch faces, apps), and it can be both intimidating and frustrating. Don't despair - we'll take this one step at a time.

So now, are you wearing your Apple Watch with your iPhone nearby? You're ready to tackle this amazing gadget, so let us move on to Chapter 2.

Chapter 1

2. Setup & Getting Started

In this chapter we discuss

Force Touch

Human Interface Guidelines

A Quick Look at Watch Controls

Turn On or Wake

Charging the Watch

Turn Off

Pair Your Watch & iPhone

Rename Your Watch

Chapter 2

Setup Cellular Service

Passcode & Security Features

The Display

The Home Screen

The Side Button & Dock

Digital Crown

Control Center

Heart Sensors & Electrodes

Band Release Buttons

Display & Brightne

Sounds & Haptics

Change the Time Shown

iPhone Today View

iPhone App Switcher

iPhone Lock Screen

Apple Resources

What's Next?

Chapter 2 is meant to get you started quickly with your new Apple Watch. This chapter is laid out as a handy reference, so it should be easy to return and find what you're looking for at any time. You'll learn how to:

- Pair your watch with your iPhone.

- Setup cellular service.

- Complete basic setup steps.

- Manipulate basic controls.

While you can use your Apple Watch without your iPhone nearby, the Apple iPhone is an integral part of your day-to-day experience. In case you are new to Apple's smartphone and iOS mobile operating system, I've included several topics covering the iPhone setup, screens, and gestures. Those topic headings have an asterisk and special formatting, so you can quickly skip them if you aren't interested.

Settings are configured on your Apple Watch or in the Apple Watch app on your iPhone. On your watch, open the "Settings" app or swipe up to open "Control Center." On your iPhone, open the Apple Watch app and swipe to see various options.

- General

- Brightness & Text Size

- Sounds & Haptics

- Passcode

- Emergency SOS

- Privacy

- Change the Time Shown

2.1 Force Touch

Touch gestures may be a new world for some. I wanted to cover these terms before jumping into details. As a functioning adult, I have a pretty good handle on clicking buttons and turning knobs. I have even adapted to tapping or swiping on my smartphone, tablet screen, or Mac trackpad.

Apple introduced Force Touch Technology (FTT) in 2014 with its first Apple Watch. It is available today on several Apple products, including touchpads and the iPhone. The screen display, digital crown, and side button support FTT. The screen of the Apple Watch responds to taps, swipes, or firm presses. In the case of the side button on the Apple

Watch, it responds differently to a gentle press compared to when you press down and hold it.

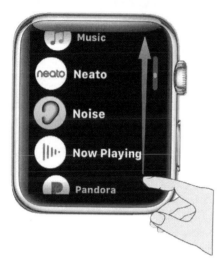

Figure 2.1   Swipe Up

- **Swipe** - Touch the screen with one finger and slide your finger in the direction indicated without lifting your finger: left, right, up or down.

- **Tap** - Quickly touch the screen with a light touch and release.

- **Firm Press** - Press down on the screen with a firm touch.

- **Drag** - Touch a selection on the screen with your finger and slide your finger across the screen without lifting.

- **Flick**- Touch a selection on the screen with your finger. Slide your finger quickly across the screen and lift your finger to "flick" the cursor in that direction.

- **Return to the top of a page** - In apps like "Settings" or "Mail" on your iPhone, touch the middle area at the top edge of the screen to scroll to the top of the page or list.

- **Preview Recent Files**- Touch an app on your iPhone Home Screen for a few seconds, and a preview screen opens listing recent files and other options.

iPhone Touch Gestures*

Some of these gestures you'll use every day, while others may not come up as often.

Swipe Left or Right on an Item to See Options*

On your iPhone, swipe left to delete or see more options on a message, file, contact, etc.

Swipe Down to See Search Options*

To search within Apps, touch the top area of the list and swipe down to open the "Search" dialog. This feature is available in apps like Contacts, the Mail inbox, and more.

Tip: The Search dialog in a list may not be shown until you scroll to the top of the list, and then swipe down.

Swipe to See a Text Entry Box on iPhone*

The first time I ran across this, I was really frustrated because I didn't know what to do. In case you run across a text box where the on-screen keyboard covers the area you need to type in, simply touch the screen area and swipe to see what's under the keyboard as shown below.

Figure 2.2   Swipe to See Under the Keyboard

Rotate with Two Fingers on iPhone*

Touch the screen with two fingers as shown in the next figure, and rotate your hand to reposition an object. In the following example, I'm rotating the ruler in the Notes app. Other apps like Maps also support the rotate gesture.

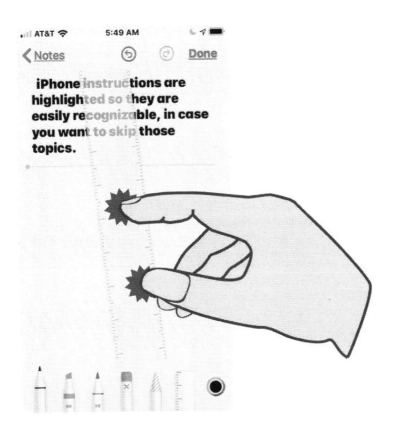

Figure 2.3   *Rotate with Two Fingers*

iPhone: Swipe to Go To the Next Step*

During setup, you'll probably run across screens where you have to "swipe" up or down through the material. It's pretty common to be forced to read through the material before you see a "Next" command. Simply swipe up on the screen until you get to the bottom of the material. Typically then you'll be presented with a button or link to continue.

Copy Between Apps on iPhone*

Select a photo or text. Tap the Home button or swipe up from the bottom of the screen to open the Dock. In Split View drag the photo from Safari to the Messages app. You can also just copy text, open a different app, then tap and hold to paste.

Two-handed Gestures on iPhone*

Sometimes you need to select and object with one hand and swipe across the screen with the other hand. For example, let's say you're moving files around in the Files app. You might have a long list of files and folders to navigate through, in order to find a destination folder.

1. Touch and hold the file you want to move.

2. With the other hand, touch the screen and swipe.

3. Drop the file at the new location.

2.2 Human Interface Guidelines

Apple developers, no doubt, cringe when they read instructions that use the wrong terminology for those switches, sliders, and tab bars. I made a serious effort to use the correct terms: toggle the switch, move the slider. The terminology is also important when you are using the Voice Control Accessibility feature, as outlined in Chapter 10.

- The **Switch** toggles a feature on or off. Green is on; white is off.

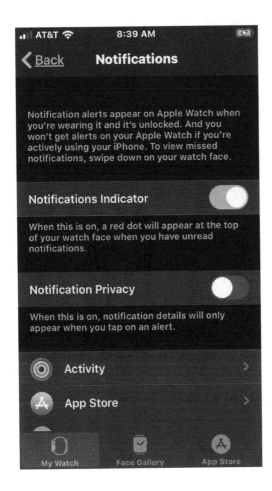

Figure 2.4   *Switch*

- **Slider** - touch the Slider Bar and slide it to move the bar.

Figure 2.5   *The Volume Slider*

- The **Add** icon looks like a plus **+** symbol.

- The **More** - icon looks like an ellipsis or three dots.

- The icon that looks like three horizontal bars is used to rearrange items in a list. Touch and item, hold and drag to rearrange items in a list.

Figure 2.6   Three Horizontal Bars and Tab Bar

- The **Tab Bar** is a group of icons in a row along the bottom of the screen. In the figure above, the Tab Bar includes Library, For You, Browse, Radio, and Search icons.

2.3 A Quick Look at Watch Controls

Three physical characteristics of your Apple Watch to which we will refer again and again are the Display, the Digital Crown, and the Side Button.

Figure 2.7   *The Watch Face Controls*

A - Display

B - Digital Crown

C - Microphone

D - Side Button

2.4 Turn On or Wake

There are several ways to turn on, or wake, your Apple Watch. These options are configurable as outlined in the Chapter 3 topic "Wake Screen on Wrist Raise" listed under "General Settings."

- Lift your wrist or tap the screen to wake your watch.

- Gradually turn the Digital Crown on your **Apple Watch** to slowly brighten the screen. This method is a discreet way to check the time.

- On the **Apple Watch**, press and hold the side button.

If the Apple logo does not appear after a few seconds, charge your Apple Watch.

2.5 Charging the Watch

A green lightning bolt symbol appears on the watch face when your Apple Watch is connected to a charging cable. The charging cable attaches to the back of your watch, as shown in Figure 2.2. The lightning bolt symbol is red when your watch needs charging. It may take a few minutes for the green lightning bolt symbol to appear if your battery level is low.

Figure 2.8   The Charging Cable

To troubleshoot charging try these suggestions.

1.   Completely remove any plastic wrap from both sides of the charger.

2.   Plug the charger into a different cable or power outlet.

3.   Reset your watch.

2.6 Turn Off

Place your palm over the watch face for a few seconds to turn off the screen. The "Cover to Mute" option is configurable along with Silent or Theater Mode, as shown in Settings, Sounds & Haptics. Follow these steps to turn off your watch.

1. On the **Apple Watch**, press and hold the side button until the menu appears.

2. Touch the "Power Off" slider and drag to the right to turn off your watch.

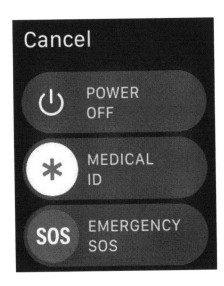

Figure 2.9   *Turn Off*

3. Press and hold the side button to turn your watch back on.

2.7 Pair Your Watch & iPhone

Pairing your Apple Watch with a companion iPhone unlocks the full potential of the Apple Watch. I recommend that you have a fully charged battery before starting the pairing process. In case you are new to Apple products and also new to setting up an iPhone, I included those setup steps in the next topics.

1. Turn on the **Apple Watch** and the iPhone.

2. Hold your Apple Watch near your iPhone and wait for the message, "Use this iPhone to set up your Apple Watch." If you don't see the message, open the Apple Watch app on your iPhone, and tap "start pairing."

3. Follow the prompts and wait for the devices to sync. The synchronization can take a while, so this might be a good time to get a cup of coffee or do your taxes. Don't be impatient, as I was, or you will interrupt the process and have to start over.

During setup, you'll probably run across screens where you have to "swipe" through the material. It's pretty common to be forced to read through the material before you see a "Next" command. Simply swipe up on the screen until you get to the bottom of the material. Typically then you'll be presented with a button or link to continue.

In case you replace or upgrade your iPhone, you needn't be concerned about your Health and Activity data. iCloud with the iPhone iOS version 11 stores "Health and Activity data" automatically. The only requirement is that you are signed in with the same Apple ID on all devices.

Your Apple ID

When you set up your iPhone, you are prompted to create or log in with your Apple ID. Your Apple ID is your account with Apple and is based on the e-mail address you enter when you create your Apple ID. Chapter 3 has additional information on your Apple ID and iCloud.

Figure 2.10   Apple ID in the Settings App

Sign in with Apple

The service "Sign in with Apple" was introduced as part of iOS 13, and is used to sign up for apps and services, while protecting your privacy. Apps and websites sometimes offer a third-party login with Google, Facebook, or Twitter, which saves you from having to enter your name, address, and other information. Sign in with Apple has an option to generate a random e-mail address, ensuring your privacy and protecting your e-mail address. Unlike some companies, Apple also promises it won't use your information to sell ads or track your activities.

iPhone Setup*

Charge your iPhone before starting the setup process. You will need your Apple ID and Wi-Fi network name and password to complete the setup. The previous section covered Apple IDs. The following is an example of the steps I used to set up my iPhone.

- Charge your iPhone before starting setup.

- It will simplify the setup process if you have an iPad or iPhone running iOS 11.0 or later nearby for Automatic Setup.

- Have your home Wi-Fi network name and password available. There is usually a label on the side or bottom of your router with this information.

- To complete Apple Pay setup have the CVC code available for credit cards you are adding to your Wallet. In Apple Pay, add your shipping information, e-mail, and phone.

- For third-party e-mail apps like Outlook, have your e-mail ID and password handy. Add those accounts in the Settings app on your iPhone, as outlined in the Passwords & Accounts section that follows.

1.   The Apple logo appears when you turn on your iPhone.

2.   Follow the prompts to create or enter your Apple ID, set up cellular service, log in to a Wi-Fi network, and other options. For additional information on network connections, see the next topic.

In addition to the basic Apple Setup, I perform a few additional tasks which may interest you, as outlined below.

1. Setup Mail for my AT&T e-mail account. In the Settings app, in the "Passwords & Accounts" section tap "Add Account."

2. In the App Store, I downloaded the Gboard app and added it as a keyboard. iOS13 includes a swipe keyboard called "QuickPath," but I like Gboard. I also turned dictation on in "Settings" app under "General," in the "**Keyboard**" section, as outlined in Chapter 3.

3. In the "Settings" app, in the section "**Bluetooth**," I paired my Yamaha amplifier.

4. Setup **iCloud** in the "Settings" app to access your files, passwords & accounts, or contacts, from any Apple device. In Settings, tap your "Apple ID" and then tap "iCloud."

5. On older iPhones, add additional **fingerprints** in the "Settings" app under "Touch ID & Passcode."

6. Configure "Display & Brightness" in the "Settings" app. Look for **Auto-Lock**, **Night Shift**, and **Text Size**.

7. Set a **Wallpaper** in the "Settings" app.

8. Add your phone, address, and related names in the **Contacts** app under "My Card." Siri uses this information to customize her responses.

Networks: Bluetooth and Wi-Fi

Today, mobile devices typically connect to networks over Wi-Fi or Bluetooth protocols. These networks can also include routers, repeaters, and switches. An ISP premises router connects a home network to the Internet. There are popular Wi-Fi protocols today that operate at 2.4Ghz and 5Ghz.

Chapter 2

iPhone Wi-Fi Setup*

During the initial setup of your iPhone, you probably connected to your home Wi-Fi network. Unless you choose to "Forget this Network," the network name and password are automatically saved once you've connected at least once to a Wi-Fi network. Occasionally you might want to connect to a different Wi-Fi network, and the steps to manage your Wi-Fi connections follow.

1.   Open the "Settings" app on your iPhone and tap "Wi-Fi." A green slider next to "Wi-Fi" indicates Wi-Fi is on. The line below that has a checkmark next to the Wi-Fi network you're currently connected to.

2.   In the section "Networks," a list of Wi-Fi networks in range of your iPhone is displayed. Tap to select a network, and enter the network password when prompted.

3.   At the bottom of the right panel, tap "Ask to Join Networks," if you want to be prompted any time your iPhone finds a Wi-Fi network.

Bluetooth

Bluetooth is a global standard celebrating 20 years of success. Bluetooth utilizes 2.4 GHz or 5.0 GHz radio frequencies. This wireless protocol is ideal for short distances and supports point-to-point, broadcast, or mesh network topologies. With Bluetooth, a router or switch is not required. For example, a smartphone connects to headphones.

Low Energy Bluetooth has speeds around 3 Mbps, and classic Bluetooth has speeds up to 2.1 Mbps. When selecting hearing aids and other devices, take into account that Bluetooth speed impacts direct streaming.

With iOS 13 and watchOS 6, your consent is required for apps to use Bluetooth-enabled beacons or tracking devices.

2.8 Rename Your Watch

To rename your watch, open the Apple Watch app on your iPhone.

1.   On the **iPhone,** open the Apple Watch app.

2.   Tap "My Watch," located in the left corner of the tab bar at the bottom of the screen.

3.   Scroll down to "General."

4.   Under "About," tap "Name."

2.9 Setup Cellular Service

You can activate a cellular network when you first set up your Apple Watch. During setup, look for the option to set up cellular, then follow the on-screen steps.

Although your Apple Watch will have a separate phone number from your carrier once you sign up for an airtime contract, your watch will use your companion iPhone number as well.

You can also set up cellular later from the Apple Watch app, as shown below.

1.   On the **iPhone**, open the Apple Watch app.

2.   Tap the My Watch tab, then tap "Cellular."

3.   Tap "Set Up Cellular."

4.   Follow the instructions for your carrier. You might need to contact your carrier for help.

There are two separate models for Apple Watch Series 4 and Series 5, optimized for the country of purchase to support LTE and UMTS bands used around the world.

To check cellular data usage on your iPhone, open the Apple Watch app. Usage is shown for the current period, as well as for each app.

1.   On the **iPhone**, open the Apple Watch app.

2.   Tap the My Watch tab, then tap "Cellular."

3.   Swipe to see cellular data usage for apps.

2.10 Passcode & Security Features

A 4-digit passcode secures your watch from unauthorized use. Although you can choose to turn passcode off, that option removes Apple Pay from your Apple Watch. You can enter the passcode with these passcode settings.

● Simple Passcode (4-Digit)
● Unlock with iPhone

If you want a passcode longer than four digits turn off simple passcode. The "Erase Data" option will protect your watch in case your watch is lost or stolen. It erases all data after ten failed attempts.

Change Apple Watch Passcode Options

1.   Open the **Apple Watch** app on your iPhone.

2.   Tap "My Watch," located in the left corner of the tab bar at the bottom of the screen.

3. Scroll down to "Passcode."

4. Touch the "Unlock with iPhone" switch to toggle the setting on or off.

Wrist Detection

Wrist Detection is a security measure to lock your watch when you're not wearing it. Follow these steps to turn on Wrist Detection.

1. Open the **Apple Watch** app on your iPhone.

2. Tap "My Watch," located in the left corner of the tab bar at the bottom of the screen.

3 Tap "Passcode."

4. Swipe up, then tap "Wrist Detection." A green slider bar indicates Wrist Detection is on.

Clear Website Data

Another security feature of the Apple Watch is the ability to delete browsing data from your watch.

1. On the **Apple Watch** press the side button.

2. Swipe and tap on "Settings."

3. Tap "General" and scroll to "Website Data."

4. Tap "Clear Website Data."

Turn on Find My Watch

By default, "Find My Watch" is turned on after pairing your watch to your companion iPhone.

1.   On the **iPhone** open "Settings."

2.   Tap "your name," and then scroll down and tap your Apple Watch.

3.   Ensure "Find My Watch" is turned on.

Find Your Apple Watch

In case you lose your watch, you can use the "Find My" app to locate it. If you have an Apple HomePod, you can say, "Hey Siri, find my watch." The app also has options to turn on "Lost Mode." Lost mode locks your watch and displays a custom message.

1.   On the **iPhone** open the "Find My" app and sign in.

2.   Tap your Apple Watch to locate your watch on a map.

3.   Tap "Actions" to play a sound, erase the watch, or turn on lost mode.

Two-Factor Authentication

To protect digital security, 2FA or two-factor authentication is becoming common. Instead of using only your normal account password, a second category is involved.

- Something you have. A smartphone, credit card, etc.

- Something you know. A PIN, password, answers to secret questions.

- Something you are. Your fingerprint or Face ID, for example.

One way to provide two-factor authentication is a text message or e-mail with a verification code displayed on one of your other Apple devices. When logging in to Apple on a new device, Apple sends an alert to your devices that "Your Apple ID is being used to sign in to a device..." Starting with watchOS 6, you can also respond to the alert on your Apple Watch. Tap "Allow" and the Apple ID Verification Code is displayed on your Apple Watch, iPhone, iPad, or Mac.

Figure 2.11   *Apple ID Verification Code*

Some apps add an additional level of passwords along with two-factor authentication. In that case, you generate a specific password for that app. For example, I don't share my Google password with Apple Calendar. Instead, at Google, I generate an "Apple app" password. I then enter that new special password and also enter my normal Apple password. You could think of this as a subordinate Google password that only works with my Apple app.

You enable two-factor authentication for your Apple ID in the Settings app on your iPad or iPhone. On your iPad, tap your Apple ID on the top left of the Settings screen, and then tap "Password & Security" on the right side of the screen. Toggle Two-Factor Authentication on.

Allow iPhone Access When Locked*

Open the "Settings" app on your iPhone and tap "Touch ID & Passcode" on older iPhone models. On iPhone X and later models tap "Face ID & Passcode." You can choose to allow access to the Today View, Notification Center, Control Center, Siri, Home Control, Return Missed Calls, and USB Accessories when the iPhone is locked.

Accounts & Passwords Settings on iPhone*

Apple introduced its "Passwords & Accounts" manager in iOS 12. All your accounts and passwords are stored in one place - your iCloud Keychain. Your security information is available on any Apple device when you authenticate with Face ID, Touch ID, or your passcode. The Password & Accounts app generates strong passwords for you, identifies weak passwords, and will autofill account information when you visit a login web page.

To add additional accounts like your Google, Yahoo, or Outlook.com account tap "Add Account." Open the "Settings" app on your iPhone and swipe up and tap "Passwords & Accounts."

Share an iPhone Password over AirDrop*

In the Settings app on your iPhone, tap "Passwords & Accounts." Tap "Website & App Passwords" to view and manage passwords, or share them over AirDrop. Select the account you want to share and then tap "Password." A menu opens with a choice to "Copy" or use "AirDrop."

iCloud Keychain on iPhone*

iCloud Keychain stores your passwords, credit card, Wi-Fi network configurations, and other accounts. An example of sharing Wi-Fi configurations is when your iPhone is nearby a family member's iPhone and you "share" a Wi-Fi password with their iPhone. Both devices must be logged in with the same Apple ID or family sharing account.

iCloud Keychain is set up in the Settings app on your iPhone, in the "Passwords & Accounts" section.

2.11 The Display

When you wake your Apple Watch, the watch face is displayed. Status icons in the middle along the top edge of the watch face indicate when you have a notification or an alert that your battery needs charging. Status icons are discussed in detail in Chapter 3. The Notification Center is covered in Chapter 5.

Press the watch face display firmly to change the watch face or see options in an app.

iPhone Display*

When you wake your iPhone, the Lock Screen is displayed. The Lock Screen suggests you press the Home button or enter your passcode, to continue. This wake behavior depends on what you were doing last on your iPhone, and how you configured passcode and lock settings.

On some models of the iPhone, the Home button is located under the screen area. Either touch the Home button or tap the screen on newer iPhone models, to wake your iPhone. Various screens and screen overlays are displayed as you navigate your iPhone.

- Lock Screen
- Home Screen

- Dock
- Today View
- Control Center
- App Switcher
- Spotlight Search
- Notification Center

Status icons in the top right of the Home Screen indicate the status of Wi-Fi connections, location services, battery usage, and more. The Dock along the bottom of the Home Screen, as discussed later in this chapter.

The Lock Button ⊕ in the Control Center turns off screen rotation. When the orientation lock is active, the button turns red, and the screen orientation will not change when you rotate your iPhone.

2.12 The Home Screen

The Home screen is a list of apps installed on your Watch, shown in grid or list view. In watchOS 6, the "List View" curves slightly, and the text is bolder, and the buttons are slightly larger. Press the Digital Crown to see the Home screen, or press the side button to see the "List View."

Apple Watch - Grid or List View

The Home screen on your Apple Watch has a grid or list view. The grid view resembles a honeycomb. I found getting comfortable in this view difficult and decided to switch from "Grid View" to "List View." Of course, then it drove me crazy that I couldn't remember how to go back to the honeycomb style grid view. Now I mostly hang out in List View, but at least I know how to change between the two.

To move around the Home Screen grid view, turn the Digital Crown to zoom in or zoom out. Continue zooming in to see a preview of the app, and keep turning the Digital Crown to open the app. To reposition the app icons, touch the screen and hold, and slide your finger on the screen to reposition the focus.

Switch Between Grid or List View

With the Home screen open, firmly press the screen and then tap either "Grid" or "List View."

Delete Apps From Your Apple Watch

watchOS 6 also allows you to delete some built-in apps like Breathe, Stopwatch, World Clock, Timer, Alarms, Walkie-Talkie, and Radio.

1. On your **Apple Watch** press the Digital Crown to open the Home Screen.

2. In Grid View, touch the app icon for a few seconds (also known as a long press) until the apps begin to wiggle. In the top right corner of the icon tap the small "x" to delete the app.

3. In List View, swipe right to left on the app you want to delete and tap the Trash Can icon.

Reset Apple Watch Home Screen Layout to Factory Default

1. On the **iPhone**, open the Apple Watch app.

2. Tap "My Watch," located in the left corner of the tab bar at the bottom of the screen.

3. Tap "General" and then tap "Reset Home Screen Layout."

iPhone Home Screen*

When you turn on your iPhone, the first page of the Home screen is displayed. Think of the Home screen as your starting place. On older iPhones press the Home button anytime you are unsure of your next step to return to the Home screen. You can always return to your running apps with the App Switcher, which we cover in just a bit. As you'll see in a moment when we look at the App Switcher, you may have several apps running at the same time.

The icons on the Home Screen represent apps installed on your iPhone. To open an app, tap the icon.

Apps are organized into folders, and we'll also show you how to work with folders. These apps run independently of each other but can exchange information through the clipboard. So, for example, you can easily copy text or photos from the Messages app into the Mail app.

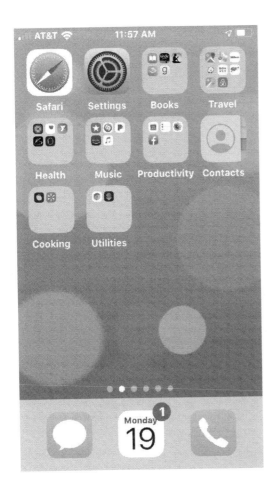

Figure 2.12   *The iPhone Home Screen*

There can be several pages of Home Screens. To move between pages, touch the left or right edge of the screen and swipe your finger across the screen towards the opposite side.

On older model iPhones, the Home button is located below the screen and activates the Home screen or Siri. On iPhone X and later models, glance at the screen and swipe up from the bottom edge of the screen. The Home button includes a fingerprint reader to support Touch ID. The newer iPhones replaced Touch ID with Face ID. In the Settings app on older iPhones, in the section "Touch ID & Passcode" toggle "Touch ID" on to enable Touch ID. You can also press and hold the Home button to activate Siri on older iPhones. With iPhone X and later models, press and hold the side button for 2-3 seconds to activate Siri.

When Siri is listening, a small Siri icon is displayed at the bottom of the screen.

Press the Home button from within an app to return to the Home Screen on older iPhones. Your app continues to run, and you can return to the same location in the app with the App Switcher. I have noticed this feature does not always work when I'm using Markup in Photo editing.

Swipe up from the bottom of the screen in any app to view the Dock. Continue swiping up, and the App Switcher is displayed. Next, and last, continue past App Switcher to the top of the screen, and the display returns to the Home Screen. Depending on your preferences, you could organize apps in the "Dock," instead of the Home Screen. The next section explains the Dock.

The dots above the Dock indicate additional Home Screen pages. Swipe left on the Home screen to see additional Home Screen pages. In the previous example, there are several dots indicating multiple pages. Swipe right on the first page of the Home screen to see the "Today View," which includes the "Search" feature. Swipe down on the Home screen or Today View to see notifications.

Tip: Tap the middle of the iPhone Home screen and swipe down to open the "Spotlight Search" dialog.

iPhone Home Screen Status Icons*

The top right corner of the Home Screen has several status icons, including location and battery levels. The middle area displays the date. The top left corner shows cellular and Wi-Fi connection strength.

The battery status icon displays your battery level.

Arrange Apps in Folders on your iPhone*

To organize apps in Folders on your iPhone, touch an app on the screen, and slide your finger across the screen to drag the app onto another app to create a new folder. A default name is suggested, but you can change the name. At any time you can move apps between folders, or back onto a Home Page.

1. Touch and hold the app icon on the Home Screen to select the app icon. When selected, the app icon is magnified slightly. If you touch the app icon for a few seconds, and a pop-up menu appears, just select "Rearrange Apps."

2. Without lifting your finger, slide the app icon across the screen. Lift your finger to drop the app onto another app icon, or into a folder. To move to another page of the Home Screen, drag the app icon to the middle area of the right screen edge and wait a few seconds until the next Home screen page is displayed. Lift your finger to drop the app on the new page.

3. To rename a folder, tap to open the folder. Touch the app icon for a few seconds until the pop-up menu appears. Select "Rearrange Apps," and all app icons will start to jiggle.

4. Tap the **folder name** at the top of the screen and enter a new name. Tap "Done" to save your changes. Press the "Home" button to exit edit mode.

Rename Folders on your iPhone Home Screen*

To rename the folder, open the folder and touch the app icon for a few seconds until the pop-up menu appears. Select "Rearrange Apps," and all app icons will start to jiggle. Tap on the folder name at the top of the screen to rename the folder.

Delete an App on your iPhone*

1. Touch and hold the app icon on the Home Screen until the pop-up menu appears. Select "Rearrange Apps." App icons begin to "jiggle," and a small "x" appears in the top left corner of the icons.

2. Tap the "x" to delete the app.

iPhone Home Screen Layout Factory Default*

1. Open the "Settings" app on your iPhone.

2. Tap "General" and scroll down to "Reset." Tap "Reset Home Screen Layout."

Add Web Pages to Your iPhone Home Screen*

Use the Share control to add a web page shortcut to your Home Screen. In the Share pop-up menu swipe up, and tap "Add to Home Screen."

2.13 Side Button & Dock

Press the Side Button to show the Dock. Double-click the Side Button to open Apple Pay. Press and hold the Side Button to turn your Apple Watch on or off or to call emergency services.

Figure 2.13   The Side Button

The Dock is a list of up to ten of your favorite apps. I change my Dock frequently, swapping apps in and out as needed. To see all apps available to the dock, tap the **side button** on your watch.

1.   On the **Apple Watch,** press the "Side Button."

2.   Swipe up to the end of the list and tap "All Apps."

Follow these steps to configure which apps appear in the Dock.

1.   On the **iPhone**, open the Apple Watch app.

2.   Tap "My Watch," located at the left corner of the tab bar at the bottom of the screen.

3.   Tap the "Dock."

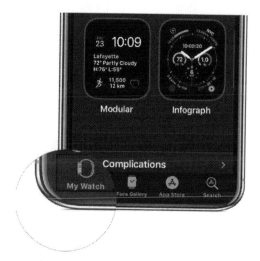

Figure 2.14   The Apple Watch App

4.   In the section "Dock Ordering," tap "Favorites" to choose which apps appear in the Dock.

5.   Scroll to find apps and tap more (the plus symbol) to add the app to favorites.

Add an App to the Apple Watch Dock

1.   On the **Apple Watch**, press the side button and tap on the app.

2.   Swipe and tap on "Add to Dock." This option is not available if you already have ten favorite apps.

Reorder the List of Apps in the Apple Wa Dock

1. On the **iPhone**, open the Apple Watch app.

2. Tap "My Watch," located in the left corner of the tab bar at the bottom of the screen.

3. Tap "Dock."

4. Tap "Edit."

On the right side of the app name, tap the three lines, and drag the app name to a different location in the list.

Remove an App from the Apple Watch Dock

To conserve battery power, remove apps you don't use from the Dock. To check battery levels, swipe up on the Apple Watch face to open Control Center, then swipe to see battery life.

- On the **Apple Watch**, open the Dock and tap an app.

- When the app is open, swipe left and tap the red X.

iPhone Dock*

The Dock shows your favorite apps, recently opened apps, and "suggested" apps. I change my Dock frequently, swapping apps in and out as needed. The Dock is displayed at the bottom of your Home screen. In the following example, the doc from left to right has the Messages, Calendar, and Phone apps.

Figure 2.15   The iPhone Dock

Favorite apps (if setup) appear on the left side of the dock. The right side of the dock displays recently used and suggested apps. To add an app as a "favorite" touch the app icon to select it, drag it onto the Dock, then lift your finger.

Suggested apps include "Handoff" apps running on nearby Apple devices. Apple's Continuity architecture enables you to handoff an app running on your Apple Watch to your iPhone. So for example, you start reading a book on your Watch, and your iPhone is close by. The Audiobooks app will show in your iPhone Dock at the bottom of your iPhone screen, on the right side of the Dock. Handoff is available on all Apple devices.

Swipe up from the bottom of the screen in any app to view the Dock. Continue swiping up, and the App Switcher is displayed. Next, and last, continue past App Switcher, and the Home Screen is displayed. The Dock is not the same as the App Switcher. The App Switcher displays apps actively running on your iPhone.

Delete Apps on the iPhone Home Screen*

Touch the app icon for a few seconds until the pop-up menu appears. Select "Rearrange Apps," and all app icons will start to jiggle. A small "x" is displayed in the top left corner of the app icon. Tap the "x" to delete the app. You can always reinstall the deleted app from the App Store. On older iPhone models when done making changes press the Home button. On iPhone X and later models, tap "Done." You will notice that some apps like "Settings" don't have an "x," because you can't delete core apps like Settings.

Move Apps on the iPhone Home Screen*

Touch the app icon to select the app as outlined above. The selected app icon will appear slightly larger on the screen. Slide your finger across the screen to move the icon. To move the app icon to another Home Page screen, drag the app icon to the middle area of the right screen edge. Hold the app icon for a few seconds, until the Home screen flips to the next page. Lift your finger to drop the app icon on the new page.

Add an App to the iPhone Dock*

1.   On the **iPhone**, go to the Home screen.

2.   Lightly touch an app icon to select it, and then drag the icon down onto the Dock.

Find an iPhone App*

When you've misplaced an app and can't find which folder the app is in, use the Search feature on the Today view as outlined later in this chapter. Search will tell you the app folder.

2.14 The Digital Crown

When I was learning to use my Apple Watch, I had no idea the Digital Crown was the gateway to hundreds of options. Although you can press it to wake your watch and go to your Home screen, that is just the tip of the iceberg. Press the Digital Crown to see the Home screen. Press and hold the Digital Crown to start Siri. Turn the Digital Crown to scroll or zoom.

Chapter 2

Turn the Digital Crown wheel to scroll through complications, lists, settings, and a myriad of other features - the Digital Crown zooms in and out of maps. Turning the Digital Crown creates a time-lapse effect as the sun moves across the Earth watch face, or the planets align in the Solar System watch face as the days scroll by.

Explore the Digital Crown

The following is a list of interesting things you can do with the Digital Crown.

1. On the **Apple Watch**, press the Digital Crown in the center to access the Home screen.

2. Press and hold for Siri.

3. Turn the Digital Crown to move through the days of the week in the Calendar app.

We can see another fun demonstration of the Digital Crown in action with weather apps. Let's say you added a weather app complication to your watch face. Tap to select the weather complication and turn the Digital Crown to see the hourly forecast, air quality, UV index, wind index, and the 7-day forecast. Cool, huh? When displaying the "hourly forecast," tap the screen, and it shows you the temperature; tap again, and it shows you rainfall.

The "Maps" app is another elegant example of the Digital Crown in action. On your Apple Watch, press the side button, swipe, and tap "Maps." Tap "Location," and then turn the Digital Crown to zoom in or out.

Switch Between Apps

To switch between the last two apps, double-click the Digital Crown.

Gradually Wake Your Watch

When your watch is asleep, gently turn the Digital Crown slowly to brighten the screen, and discreetly check the time.

2.15 Control Center

The Control Center has a series of icons. Swipe up on the **Apple Watch** face to open the Control Center. Tap to toggle the options on or off.

- Cellular
- Wi-Fi
- Airplane Mode
- Battery
- Find my (iPhone)
- Flashlight
- Do Not Disturb
- Mute
- Theater Mode
- Water Lock
- Audio Output

Tip: With watchOS 5 and later, you can open Control Center from any screen. Touch the bottom of the screen until a semi-transparent preview of the Control Center appears, then swipe up.

Rearrange Icons in the Apple Watch Control Center

To customize your Control Center apps, or set the app order, follow these steps.

1. Swipe up on the **Apple Watch** face to open the Control Center.

2. Swipe up and scroll to the end. Tap "Edit" to change items in the Control Center.

Apple Watch Control Center Icons

Cellular

When connected, the cellular status icon is green. When there is no connection, the status icon is grey.

Wi-Fi

When connected, the Wi-Fi status icon is blue. When there is no connection, the status icon is grey.

Airplane Mode

An orange airplane means Airplane Mode is active.

Battery

The battery status icon displays your battery level as a percentage. A red icon indicates your battery is low.

Tip: **The battery level of the paired AirPods is also shown on the status screen.**

Figure 2.16   Battery Level of Paired AirPods

Find My (iPhone)

Find My (iPhone) may be the handiest feature if you tend to misplace your iPhone as frequently as do I! Swipe up on your watch face and tap the icon to sound an alert on your companion iPhone instantly. The blue icon has an iPhone with signal bars. At night, touch and hold the icon to flash a light on your iPhone.

Flashlight

The flashlight setting has three modes: the basic light, a strobe light, or red light. Swipe to the left or right to choose your setting. When running at night, the strobe light is a nice safety feature. Press the Digital Crown to turn off the flashlight, or tap the icon in Control Center.

Do Not Disturb

Calls and alerts won't ring or light up the screen when "Do Not Disturb" is on. Alarms will still sound. The Do Not Disturb status icon on your watch face is a blue moon. You can continue a "Walkie-Talkie" conversation if you turn on "Do Not Disturb," but other calls are silenced.

Silent Mode

Silent Mode will mute your watch. If you turn on Silent Mode while using the "Walkie-Talkie" app, you can still hear chimes and your friend's voice.

Theater Mode

The picture of two masks is orange when Theater Mode is active. The screen stays, dark and silent mode is also active until you tap the screen or press a button. When Theater Mode is active, your Walkie-Talkie status is "unavailable."

Walkie-Talkie

The walkie-talkie icon is a stylized walkie-talkie radio. The icon appears after you create a connection with a contact. The icon is yellow when walkie-talkie is turned on and indicates your status in the Walkie-Talkie app is "available."

Water Lock

As I type this, I'm looking over my shoulder expecting someone to say, "No way; you can't do that!" But this is straight from the horse's mouth (Apple being the horse) - you **can** go for a swim with your Apple Watch. Not only that, the Workout app has an option for "Open Water Swim" or "Pool Swim." The "Water Lock" option is turned on automatically when you start one of these workouts and locks the screen to avoid accidental taps.

Turn on Water Lock

- On the **Apple Watch**, swipe up from the bottom of the screen to open Control Center.

- Tap the water lock icon. It looks like a drop of water.

Turn off Water Lock

When your workout ends, turn the Digital Crown to unlock the screen and clear water from the speaker. Turn the Digital Crown until you fill the "blue circle" on the screen. When complete, an alert sounds and the screen displays the message "Unlocked."

Audio Output

To stream music or videos to your favorite speakers, AirPods, or headsets, use the Audio Output in the Control Center.

1.   Swipe up on the **Apple Watch** face to open Control Center.

2.   Tap the Audio Output icon.

Tapping the audio output icon will also switch the audio output between paired Bluetooth devices.

Control Audio Volume

Tap the audio   status icon on your watch face, and turn the Digital Crown to adjust the volume. Control music, podcasts, or hearing aid volume.

The iPhone Control Center*

The Control Center has a series of controls in an overlay menu. Swipe up from the bottom of the screen to open the Control Center on older iPhones. On iPhone X and newer models, swipe down from the top right corner of the screen to open the Control Center. The controls are customizable and may include additional controls like Accessibility Shortcuts, the Apple TV Remote, Hearing, Calculator, Dark Mode, and more.

Figure 2.17   The iPhone Control Center

Connectivity controls appear in the top left panel. Use the music controls in the top right Audio Output panel to play, pause, or skip between songs. Tap the Audio Output control in the top right corner to display Bluetooth and AirPlay connections.

Tap to toggle the Control Center controls on or off, or touch and slide your finger to adjust brightness or volume.

- Airplane Mode
- Audio Output
- Wi-Fi
- Bluetooth
- Music Playback Controls

- Lock Screen Orientation
- Do Not Disturb
- Screen Mirroring
- Display & Brightness
- Volume
- Mute
- Timer
- Notes
- Camera
- Home Control (Smart Home)
- Hearing
- Guided Access
- Magnifier
- Camera (and Scan QR Code)
- Text Size
- Audio Output

The following topics briefly describe the normal iPhone controls and some of the additional controls, as well as how to add, remove, or rearrange controls. This list will probably change as Apple continues to update its iOS.

Change the Order of iPhone Controls*

To set the order of controls, follow these steps.

1. Open the Home Screen on your iPhone. Swipe up from the bottom of the screen on older iPhone models to open the Control

Center. On iPhone X or later models, swipe down from the top right corner of the screen to open the Control Center.

2. Swipe up and scroll to the end. Tap "Edit" to add or remove items from the Control Center. Touch and drag to reorder controls in the Control Center.

Add or Remove iPhone Controls*

To customize your Control Center apps, follow these steps.

1. Open the Home Screen on your iPhone, then tap to open the "Settings" app.

2. In the left panel tap "Control Center" and then tap "Customize Controls."

iPhone Control Center Icons*

Control Center icons on your iPhone also include these options.

Airplane Mode*

An orange airplane control means Airplane Mode is active. Wi-Fi and Bluetooth are turned off when Airplane mode is active.

Dark Mode*

Dark Mode was introduced with iOS 13 and works across the iPhone apps. I find the dark background with clear sharp text much easier to read.

Audio Output*

To stream music or videos to your favorite speakers, AirPods, or headsets, use the Audio Output in the Control Center. The top right quadrant of the Control Center shows music playback controls. Tap the controls to pause music, fast forward, or rewind songs. Audio Output is located in the top right quadrant of the Control Center.

1.   Swipe up from the bottom of the screen on older iPhone models to open the Control Center. On iPhone X or later models, swipe down from the top right corner of the screen to open the Control Center.

2.   Tap the Audio Output button.

Tap the audio output control in the music playback control quadrant to view or change the connected output device. Tapping the audio output button will also switch the audio output between paired Bluetooth or AirPlay devices.

Apple AirPlay mirrors audio from your Apple device, in this case, an iPhone, to a compatible AirPlay device. TVs, amplifiers, speakers, and the Apple HomePod are a few devices that support AirPlay. To mirror your screen, including videos, select an Apple TV.

Wi-Fi*

When connected, the Wi-Fi status button is blue. When there is no connection, the status button is grey.

Bluetooth*

Tap the Bluetooth control to disconnect paired Bluetooth devices. To turn off Bluetooth completely, use the Settings app.

QR Code Reader*

QR codes are small square icons that take you to a web page for more information about a specific topic. They are also used for "tickets" and other information, as discussed in the Apple Wallet topic.

Text Size*

The "Text Size" control is a slider that quickly changes the size of the text in menus. I find this handy when my eyes are tired at the end of the day, or when lighting conditions are poor.

Magnifier*

The magnifier is a handy way to read small print or magnify other items. Magnifier users your camera to magnify images in the camera view.

Lock the Screen (Orientation)*

To prevent screen orientation from changing when you rotate your iPhone toggle the Lock Screen on.

Chapter 2

Do Not Disturb*

Calls and alerts won't ring or light up the screen when "Do Not Disturb" is on. Temporarily silence calls, alerts, and notifications when Do Not Disturb is on. Alarms will still sound. Swipe down from the top right corner to open Control Center, then tap the Do Not Disturb button.

The Do Not Disturb status button looks like a blue moon. In Settings, in the "Do Not Disturb" section, there are several options to customize Do Not Disturb. For example, in the section "Phone" toggle "Allow Calls From" on to select a group of contacts. There is also an option in Settings to allow phone calls when "Do Not Disturb" is active.

Display Brightness*

The Control Panel adjusts screen brightness. The Camera app also has a "Display Brightness" button. Change display brightness depending on the time of day, or ambient lighting.

Volume*

The volume buttons on the top right area of your iPhone also control music, podcasts, iPods, or hearing aid volume. In addition, the Control Center has volume controls. Apps like Photos and iMovie also have volume control buttons.

Mute*

Mute will silence your iPhone. Slide the volume control to the bottom to mute.

Timer*

 Tap the Timer app to set a timer for cooking etc.

Notes*

 Tap the Note control to open the Notes app.

Camera*

 To take a picture, tap the Camera control.

Home Control (Smart Home)*

 To control smart home devices in the "Home" app tap the Home Control.

Hearing*

 To set hearing options, tap the Hearing control.

Accessibility Control*

The Accessibility control is active when the "Accessibility Shortcut" is enabled in the Settings app, in the "General" section.

Apple TV Remote*

The Apple TV Remote is an additional control for your Apple TV.

Screen Mirroring*

The Apple Screen Mirroring supports AirPlay devices like Apple TV or Vizio TVs. AirPlay mirrors audio or video from your Apple device, in this case, an iPhone, to a compatible AirPlay device. TVs, amplifiers, speakers, and the Apple HomePod are a few devices that support AirPlay.

Guided Access*

When enabled, the Guided Access control limits the iPhone to one app at a time. Enable the Guided Access control in the Settings app, in "Accessibility."

2.16 Heart Rate Sensors & Electrodes

The new ECG app provides heart rate monitoring similar to an electrocardiogram (EKG). The ECG app utilizes the electrical heart sensor, built-in electrodes, and the optical heart sensor.

2.17 Band Release Buttons

Changing watch bands seemed daunting to me at first, but after doing it one time, I realized how simple it is.

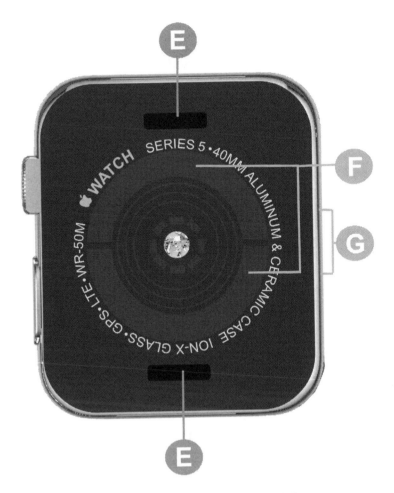

Figure 2.18   The Back of the Apple Watch

E - Band Release Buttons

F - Electrical Heart Sensor/Built-in Electrodes

G - Speaker/Air Vents

1.   Place your watch face down on a soft surface.

2.   Press the band release button on the back on the watch and slide the band left or right to remove it from the slot.

3.   Slide the new band into the slot until you feel and hear a click.

The end of the watch band that slides into the slot has a top and bottom. The top has three clips. The bottom has two clips on each end with a solid piece in the middle. If you reverse the top and bottom the band will not lock in place.

2.18 Display & Brightness

Configure brightness, text size, and bold text in the Apple Watch app in the "Settings" app. You can also turn the "Always On" watch display setting off or on, and "Hide Sensitive Complications."

1.   Open the "Settings" app on your Apple Watch.

2.   Tap "Display & Brightness."

3.   Tap "Always On" to toggle the setting on or off.

Configure brightness, text size, and bold text on your iPhone.

1.   Open the Apple Watch app on your **iPhone**.

2.   Tap "My Watch," located in the left corner of the tab bar at the bottom of the screen.

3.   Scroll down to "Brightness & Text Size."

2.19 Sounds & Haptics

The standard sound options are available under "Sounds & Haptics." I found two options to be very creative. The "Cover to Mute" option will silence alerts and mute your watch when you place your palm over the watch face for at least three seconds. Disney fans will appreciate the "Tap to Speak" option that pairs with the Mickey or Minnie Mouse watch face.

- Alert Volume

- Silent Mode

- Haptic Alerts

- Cover to Mute

- Tap to Speak (Mickey or Minnie Mouse)

Since it's related to sound, let me mention that I cover how to pair Bluetooth speakers in the next section, "Audio Output."

Haptics

Haptics is the science of applying tactile sensation (touch) and control when interacting with computer applications. Haptics encompasses both kinesthesia and cutaneous sensations. The kinesthesia sense involves location, motion, and force. Cutaneous sensations involve temperature, vibration, and texture. Chances are you're familiar with the role of Haptics in VR (virtual reality) games; but, are you aware that surgical simulators are also using Haptics to train the next generation of surgeons?

Apple introduced the Taptic Engine with the iPhone 6s. Chances are, you've found your muted iPhone at one time or another by following the vibrations. On the Apple Watch, the Digital Crown gently vibrates to indicate incremental clicks when you spin the Digital Crown. Digital Touch messages use Haptics to reach out and touch someone, literally.

In watchOS 6, the Taptic Engine for Apple Watch added the ability to tap out the hour on your wrist. The new swiftUI gives developers the ability to incorporate Digital Crown Haptics, and apps like Calculator and Alarms have an intuitive feel. The new Noise app warns you with a vibration on your wrist and alert when you are exposed to loud environments. The app also tracks your Headphone Audio Levels.

Haptics is also a useful accessibility feature for deaf or hard of hearing users, and drivers will appreciate the Map app that gently vibrates your Apple Watch to indicate an upcoming turn.

The options for haptic intensity are Default or Prominent. I haven't tried Prominent yet because I'm a little gun shy. There was an incident in which we purchased a dog collar deterrent. I said, "I'm not putting that on the dog unless I know what it feels like first." During the test, I seem to recall a knee-jerk reaction that involved throwing it across the room to get it as far away as possible from my body. I also recall several loud vocal outbursts. Okay, I may have cursed. Fortunately for our dog, the collar didn't work through his thick fur, so he never got to experience haptics first hand. But I did!

Adjust Volume

1.   Open the **Apple Watch** app on your iPhone.

2.   Tap "My Watch," located in the left corner of the tab bar at the bottom of the screen.

3.   Scroll down and tap "Sounds & Haptics."

4.   Touch the slider and drag it to adjust the **Alert Volume**.

Cover to Mute

The "Cover to Mute" setting means you can place your hand over the watch face to silence your Apple Watch and turn off the display.

Haptic Alerts

Haptics also play a role in alerts. For example, the Map app gently vibrates to indicate an upcoming turn. Haptic alerts are a useful accessibility feature for deaf or hard of hearing drivers.

1.   On the **iPhone** open the Apple Watch app.

2.   In the "Sounds & Haptics" section, tap the "Haptic Alerts" switch to toggle the switch on or off. The switch is green when on and white when off.

There is also an option to change the strength of the haptic alert to "Prominent."

Silent Mode

Silent mode is used to mute your Apple Watch. In comparison, "Do Not Disturb" keeps alerts and calls from lighting the screen. The options can be controlled on your Apple Watch in the Control Center or the Settings screen, or they can be set in the Apple Watch app on your iPhone. Silent mode will not silence alarms and timers when Apple Watch is charging.

Here we will look at three ways to control Silent Mode. There is also an option called "Cover to Mute" outlined earlier in the "Sounds & Haptics" discussion. When "Cover to Mute" is enabled, placing your hand over the screen for three seconds will silence your watch.

1. Open the Apple Watch app on your **iPhone**.

2. Tap "My Watch," located in the left corner of the tab bar at the bottom of the screen.

3. Scroll down to "Sounds & Haptics."

4. Tap the "Silent Mode" switch to toggle the switch on or off. The switch is green when on and white when off.

The sound icon (that looks like a bell) turns red to indicate silent mode is active. The sound icon turns green when sound is enabled. Silent Mode can also be controlled on your Apple Watch .

1. Press the side button on your **Apple Watch** to open "The Dock."

2. Scroll down and tap "Settings."

3. Scroll down and tap "Sounds & Haptics ."

4. Tap the "Silent Mode" switch to toggle it on or off.

The Control Center has a Silent Mode toggle that also mutes your Apple Watch.

1. Swipe up on the **Apple Watch** face to open Control Center.

2. Tap the "Silent Mode" icon.

Do Not Disturb

Obviously, the Apple engineers put a lot of thought into the "Do Not Disturb" option. It is configurable for 1 hour, till this evening, or until you leave the current geofencing location.

1.   Swipe up on the **Apple Watch** face to open Control Center.

2.   Tap the "Do Not Disturb" switch 🌙 (that looks like a moon). The switch is purple when on and grey when off. The Do Not Disturb status icon on your watch face is a blue moon.

When "Tap to Mirror iPhone" is also enabled, turning on "Do Not Disturb" on your Apple Watch also turns on "Do Not Disturb" on your iPhone, and vice versa.

1.   Open the Apple Watch app on your **iPhone**.

2.   Tap "My Watch," located in the left corner of the tab bar at the bottom of the screen.

3.   Scroll down to "Sounds & Haptics."

4.   Touch the "Do Not Disturb" switch to toggle it on or off. The switch is purple when on and grey when off.

2.20 Change the Time Shown

You can set the display time on the watch face ahead. The time does not change in any apps; the time displayed only changes on the watch face.

1. Press the side button on your Apple Watch to open the Dock.

2. Tap the gear icon to open "Settings." If you don't see the gear, touch the watch face and move your finger until you locate the gear icon.

3. Swipe and select "Clock" if you're using watchOS 6 or later. For watchOS 5, select "Time."

4. Tap to "Set Watch Face Display Time Ahead."

2.21 iPhone Today View*

From the first page of the iPhone Home screen swipe right to open the Today View with the Search feature. Swipe up or down to view widgets. At the bottom of the widget list, you can tap Edit to change widgets. Third-party apps like Kindle, CARROT Weather, and Drafts have widgets for the Today View.

Add a Widget to iPhone Today View*

Use the Add button (plus symbol) to add a widget. Remove a widget with the minus symbol. To change the order of widgets, use the three horizontal bars on the right, and drag the items up or down in the list.

1. From the first page of the **Home Screen** swipe right to open the Today View.

2. Swipe up to scroll to the bottom of the list and tap "Edit."

3. Swipe up and in the section "More Widgets" tap "Battery" or "Weather." The Battery widget will show you the battery level of your paired Apple Pencil.

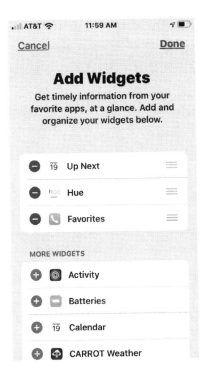

Figure 2.19   Widgets for Today View

2.22 iPhone App Switcher*

On older phones press the Home button twice to see all active running apps. Continue swiping up, and the App Switcher is displayed. On iPhone X and later models, swipe up from the bottom to the middle of the screen and hold to open the App Switcher.

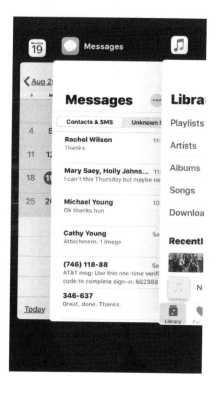

Figure 2.20   The App Switcher

The App Switcher displays running apps in small preview windows. Swipe left or right in the App Switcher to move between apps. Tap to select an app.

Close an Unresponsive iPhone App*

To close an unresponsive app follow the steps below. Keep in mind apps that are running in the background may still be using cellular and Wi-Fi if you enabled "background app refresh" in Settings for that app. Note, you can check the battery level in the top right corner of the Home Screen.

- On older phones press the Home button twice to see all active running apps. Continue swiping up, and the App Switcher is displayed. On iPhone X and later models, swipe up from the bottom to the middle of the screen and hold to open the App Switcher.

- Swipe left or right to flip through running apps. Swipe up on the app's preview window to close that app.

Switch Between iPhone Apps*

Open the App Switcher on your iPhone. When the preview windows of running apps are displayed, swipe left or right.

2.23 iPhone Lock Screen*

The iPhone lock screen does a lot more than lock your screen, as shown in the following topics.

Allow iPhone Access When Locked*

Open the "Settings" app on your iPhone and tap "Touch ID & Passcode" or "Face ID & Passcode." You can choose to allow access to the Today View, Notification Center, Control Center, Siri, Home Control, Return Missed Calls, and USB Accessories when the iPhone is locked.

iPhone Notifications*

Notification previews appear at the top of the iPhone screen. When you see the notification preview, swipe down from the top of the screen to open the Notification Center. The notification preview will turn off automatically after a few seconds.

2.24 Apple Resources

In addition to the online manual and copious articles, Apple goes above and beyond with these options to ensure you enjoy your Apple Watch.

- Apple Care

- A personal training session

- The Apple Support App

- The user guide "Apple Watch watchOS 5."

After two unfortunate incidents that involved water, now I always purchase Apple Care for my devices. I admit that I reacted in disbelief when my daughter explained how her phone slipped out of her back pocket into the water. However, the insurance representative said that is a common claim, and he wasn't at all surprised.

Shortly after my watch arrived at my house, I received an e-mail from Apple. The e-mail had a link to schedule a personal training session. A personal training class seems like a thoughtful and personal touch on Apple's part. Last but not least, you can download the user manual "Apple Watch watchOS 5" in the Books app for free. That's the next best thing to buying this book!

2.25 What's Next?

The next chapter on basic features continues the setup process, explaining the options so you can select the features that interest you.

3. Basics

In this chapter we discuss

Edit General Settings

Configure Medical ID in the Health App

Configure Emergency SOS

Automatic App Install

Watch Orientation (Wrist)

Wake Screen

Nightstand Mode

Language and Region

Siri

Privacy & Location Services

Screen Time: Content & Privacy Restrictions

Apple ID & iCloud

Accessibility

Continuity & Handoff

Enable Screenshots

iPhone Activity View

Chapter 3

Rename iPhone File or Folder

iPhone Keyboard

iPhone Text Editing

What's Next?

This chapter will explain the basics of using your Apple Watch and companion iPhone. Topics not covered in Chapter 2 will be in the following sections.

3.1 General Settings

General settings on your Apple Watch control much of the functionality of your Apple Watch. The settings do vary slightly between your Apple Watch and the Apple Watch app on your iPhone. The numbered, step-by-step instructions that follow highlight how to update General Settings.

- About
- Orientation
- Automatic App Install
- Wake Screen
- Nightstand Mode
- Location Services
- Accessibility
- Website Data
- Siri
- Workout

- Regulatory
- Reset

1. On your **Apple Watch**, press the Digital Crown.

2. Tap "Settings" and then tap "General" to configure these settings.

iPhone General Settings*

Your iPhone also has General Settings, as shown below.

- About
- Software Update
- AirDrop
- Handoff
- CarPlay
- Home Button
- iPhone Storage
- Background App Refresh
- Date & Time
- Keyboard
- Fonts
- Language & Region
- Dictionary

1.   On your **iPhone**, open the "Settings" app.

2.   Tap "General" to configure the settings shown below.

About*

The "About" section has your iPhone name, iOS version, model, and serial number. The iOS version is important because your iPhone must be a certain version of iOS before you can update your Apple WatchOS version. The capacity information includes available space, as well as the number of installed songs, videos, photos, and applications.

Tip: To manage and remove apps quickly see "iPhone Storage" in the following General section.

*Rename Your iPhone**

The name you assign to your iPhone is the network name for AirPlay, AirDrop, iCloud, or the personal hotspot. There is an option to create a personal hotspot, where you can share your Wi-Fi connection with other devices. Check with your cellular carrier to see if your plan includes personal hotspots.

To rename your iPhone, open the Settings app.

1.   Open the "Settings" app on your iPhone.

2.   Scroll down to "General."

4   Tap "About" and tap "Name."

iPhone AirDrop Settings*

AirDrop shares your data, website passwords and accounts, or Wi-Fi setup information with nearby devices over Bluetooth and Wi-Fi. To use AirDrop, you must sign in to your iCloud account and have iCloud Keychain set up. Configure AirDrop in the iPhone "Settings" app under "General" in the "AirDrop" section. The options include Receiving Off, Contacts Only, or Everyone.

iPhone Handoff Settings*

Handoff is the ability to switch an application from one Apple device to another. For example, if you're reading mail on your iPhone, you can continue reading the same message on your Mac or iPhone.

1. Open the "Settings" app on your iPhone.

2. Swipe to scroll to "Settings" and tap "General."

3. Scroll down and touch the "Enable Handoff" switch to toggle it on or off. The switch is green when on and white when off.

iPhone Language and Region Settings*

Change the language or region in the Settings app, in the "General" settings.

iPhone Storage*

The iPhone Storage screen provides a quick way to remove several apps. The "iPhone Storage" List View has all installed apps. The View includes the app size and last used date. I suspect it displays "Never

Used" when you download a new version of an app because I know I use my YMCA app all the time, but the app is usually marked "Never Used." I've learned to be careful when removing apps.

1.	Open the "Settings" app on your iPhone, and tap "General."

2.	Scroll down and tap "iPhone Storage."

3.	Tap the app you want to remove, then tap "Delete App."

Background App Refresh on iPhone*

When you are not actively using an app on your iPhone, after a short time, it changes to a suspended state and does not use system resources. When you turn on "Background App Refresh," suspended apps will check for updates or new content. For example, the Weather app can check if there's an advisory and send you a notification.

In the "Settings" app on your iPhone, tap "General" and then tap "Background App Refresh." Toggle the setting on, and then swipe to turn "Background App Refresh" on for particular apps.

iPhone Keyboard*

Initially, I debated whether to include a topic for the iPhone Keyboard, but with watchOS 6 you use the iPhone keyboard to enter your Apple ID password, so it seemed relevant. Go to Settings, General, Keyboard. Tap Keyboards, tap "Add New Keyboard," then choose a keyboard.

iPhone Text Replacement*

The option for "Text Replacement" is also found in the Keyboard settings under "General." On your iPhone, open the "Settings" app and tap "General." Text replacement settings allow you to customize your text replacement settings. For example, when I type "wed," I have a text replacement set up as "Wednesday." I discovered this handy feature the hard way after my daughter added a few text replacements to my phone as an April Fools joke. It took me a while to figure out why every time I typed "you," the phrase was changed to "they're."

Figure 3.1   Text Replacement

Reset iPhone*

You can reset all settings on your iPhone, erase content, remove subscriber services, or reset location & privacy.

Reset iPhone Home Screen Layout to Factory Default*

1. Open the "Settings" app on your iPhone.

2. Tap "General" in the left sidebar, and then tap "Reset Home Screen Layout."

3.2 Configure Medical ID in the Health App

1. On your **iPhone,** open the "Health" app.

2. In watchOS 6 or later, in the top right corner tap, the "Account" icon that looks like a person.

3. Tap "Medical ID" and enter your information.

3.3 Configure Emergency SOS

Emergency SOS is set up on your Apple Watch or your iPhone.

1. On your **iPhone,** open the Apple Watch App.

2. Tap "Emergency SOS."

3. Enter your information.

Enable Emergency SOS on your Watch

1. Open the **Apple Watch** app on your **iPhone**.

2. Tap "My Watch," located in the left corner of the tab bar at the bottom of the screen.

3. Scroll down to "Emergency SOS."

4. Touch the "Emergency SOS" slider. Continue holding the slider as you move it to enabled. The slider is green when enabled and white when disabled.

View Medical ID or Call Emergency Services

When anyone holds the side button on your watch for 3 seconds, your Apple Watch will call Emergency Services. The Apple Watch counts down with an alarm, and a slider prompts if you want to end the call. Also, this option automatically detects if you take a hard fall. If you don't respond, it will tap your wrist, sound an alarm, and then call emergency services.

1. On your **Apple Watch** press and hold the side button until the screen opens.

2. Tap Medical ID or Emergency SOS.

3.4 Automatic App Install

When "Automatic App Install" is on, iPhone apps that work with your Apple Watch will automatically appear on your Apple Watch Home screen.

1. On your **iPhone**, open the Apple Watch App.

2. Tap "My Watch," located in the left corner of the tab bar along the bottom of the screen.

3. Scroll down to "General."

4. Tap the "Automatic App Install" switch to toggle on or off. The switch is green when on and white when off.

3.5 Watch Orientation (Wrist)

Open the Apple Watch app on your iPhone to set the orientation. This feature accommodates both left-handed or right-handed individuals. It is also handy for yoga workouts, to avoid bumping the Digital Crown.

1. On your **iPhone**, open the Apple Watch App.

2. Tap "My Watch," located in the left corner of the tab bar along the bottom of the screen.

3. Scroll down to "General."

4. Under "Watch Orientation," select the left or right wrist.

If your Apple Watch doesn't wake when you raise your wrist, check the orientation of the digital crown and the "wake screen on wrist raise" settings.

3.6 Wake Screen

The "Wake Screen" options configure four parameters, as shown below.

1. Wake Screen on Wrist Raise.

2. Wake Screen on Crown Up.

3. Auto-launch Audio Apps.

4. On-Screen Wake Show Last App.

Gradually Wake Your Watch

When your watch is asleep, gently turn the Digital Crown to brighten the screen slowly and discreetly check the time.

Lift Your Wrist to Wake Your Watch

When "Wake Screen on Wrist Raise" is enabled, lift your wrist to wake your watch. This feature can be distracting if you sleep with your watch on so, on those occasions where I'm monitoring my sleep, I turn off "Wake Screen on Wrist Raise."

1. On your **Apple Watch**, press the Side Button.

2. Tap "Settings," and then tap "General."

3. Scroll down and tap "Wake."

4. Scroll down to the section "Wake Screen on Wrist Raise."

If your Apple Watch doesn't wake when you raise your wrist, check the orientation of the Digital Crown and the "Wake Screen on Wrist Raise" settings.

1. Open the **Apple Watch** app on your **iPhone**.

2. Tap "My Watch," located in the left corner of the tab bar along the bottom of the screen.

3. Scroll down to "General."

4. Under "Watch Orientation" select the left or right wrist.

Return to Last Activity on Screen Raise

When you wake your watch, it opens to the Home screen of the digital clock. On the General -> "Settings" screen, you can configure your Apple Watch to return to your last activity when you raise your wrist.

1. On your **Apple Watch**, press the Digital Crown.

2. Tap "Settings," and then tap "General."

3. Scroll down and tap "Wake Screen."

4. Scroll down to the section "On-Screen Raise Show Last App" and tap your selection.

Auto Launch the Now Playing App

When you listen to audio on our iPhone, the Now Playing app automatically opens on your Apple Watch. This feature can be disabled in the Settings app on your Apple Watch. watchOS 6 added the AirPlay control to the Now Playing app, and I find it convenient to connect to my Bose speakers or headsets using the app.

1. On your **Apple Watch**, press the Digital Crown.

2. Tap "Settings," and then tap "General."

3. Scroll down and tap "Wake Screen."

4. Scroll down to the section "On-Screen Raise Show Last App" and tap your selection.

3.7 Nightstand Mode

Use your Apple Watch as a nightstand clock while charging. If there is an alarm set, the screen will gently brighten before the alarm.

1. On your **iPhone**, open the Apple Watch app.

2. Swipe to scroll down to "Settings" and tap "General."

3. Touch the "Nightstand Mode" slider and continue holding the slider as you move it to enabled. The slider is green when enabled and white when disabled.

Set an Alarm

1. On your **Apple Watch**, press the side button to open the Dock.

2. Swipe to scroll and tap the "Alarms" app.

3. Tap "Add alarm."

4. Turn the Digital Crown to adjust the alarm time.

5. Tap "Set."

6. Tap the new alarm to set repeat options, or to change the alarm name.

3.8 Language and Region

Change the language or region in the **Apple Watch** app on your iPhone in the "General" settings. The region must be China for Apple Pay transit cards.

3.9 Siri

Siri is a personal digital assistant. With watchOS 5, Siri became an intelligent personal assistant. Siri monitors your schedule and calendar, suggesting relevant content throughout the day. Intelligent Siri will update you on your favorite team's score, display one of your photos from a year ago, or recommend a playlist for your commute Home.

If you don't use "Hey Siri" turn it off to save battery power.

1. On your **Apple Watch**, press the Side Button.

2. Tap "Settings," and then tap General.

3. Scroll down and tap "Siri."

4. Tap the "Hey Siri" switch to toggle on or off. The switch is green when on and white when off.

Some apps support "Siri Shortcuts" Siri also suggests shortcuts for tasks you frequently perform like visiting a favorite website or sending a text message to a friend. Chapter 6 has details on Siri and Siri Shortcuts.

Your Contact Card

Siri will customize your experience by using your Apple ID information in "Name, Phone Numbers, E-mail," as well as your Contact Card. When you open the Contacts app on your iPhone, your contact card is at the top of the list in the left sidebar.

View and Rerecord Shortcut Phrases on the iPhone*

Shortcuts are listed in the "Settings" app on your iPhone, in the "Siri & Search" section. At the top of the screen tap "My Shortcuts" to view and edit your shortcut phrases.

*iPhone Siri Spotlight Search**

The Spotlight Search feature is available at the top of the Today View on your iPhone, or when you touch the middle of the screen and swipe down. Siri searches the web, your contacts, apps, handwritten notes, and more.

You can also touch the middle of the screen or sidebar and swipe down to view the search bar.

3.10 Privacy & Location Services

Apple protects your privacy in Location Services and with Bluetooth access. Location services use GPS to track your current location. You choose to enable location services on an app-by-app basis. WatchOS 6 and iOS 13 introduced location notifications, so you know which apps are tracking your location in the background. There is also a choice to grant location services access one time. Your consent is required for apps to use Bluetooth-enabled beacons or tracking devices.

Some apps, like a weather app, will send notifications based on your location if you've enabled Location Services for that app. The following list shows a few apps that use location services.

- Weather Apps
- Geofencing apps
- Do Not Disturb
- Maps
- The Find People App
- Intelligent Siri

Apps and settings like Nightshift or "Home" use location services to determine sunrise and sunset.

1. Open the Settings app on your **Apple Watch** and tap "Privacy." Swipe and tap "Location Services."

2. In the list of apps, configure location services for each app. The options are "Never," "Always," or "While Using the App."

Enable location services for a more accurate reading of the distances you travel.

1. On your **iPhone**, go to Settings, Privacy, Location Services, and make sure Location Services is turned on.

2. Near the top of the list of apps, select Apple Watch Faces and Apple Watch Workout and choose the option "While Using the App."

If you don't see an app on your Apple Watch, check Content & Privacy Restrictions. These settings apply to Mail, Safari, FaceTime, Camera, Siri & Dictation, Wallet, AirDrop, and CarPlay.

3.11 Screen Time: Content & Privacy Restrictions

If you don't see an app on your Apple Watch, check Content & Privacy Restrictions. These settings apply to Mail, Safari, FaceTime, Camera, Siri & Dictation, Wallet, AirDrop, and CarPlay.

1. On the **iPhone**, open the Settings app.

2. Swipe up and tap "Screen Time."

3. Swipe up and tap "Content & Privacy Restrictions."

4. Tap "Allowed Apps" and enable "Camera."

3.12 Apple ID & iCloud

When you set up your Apple device for the first time, you are prompted to create or log in with your Apple ID using your e-mail address. Write down your Apple ID and password and keep it somewhere safe, you'll be using it again for many of the Apple apps and services like

Messages, Facetime, the App Store, Apple Wallet, iTunes, and iCloud, to name a few.

When creating a new Apple ID, keep in mind your Apple ID password will be unique to your Apple ID. It is not the same password you are already using for your e-mail. If you take advantage of the "Passwords & Accounts" feature introduced in iOS 12 to autofill account information, you'll have your Apple ID handy with a touch of your finger on the Home button, or with face recognition.

Because I have family sharing enabled, when I buy apps or songs in the App Store or iTunes, my husband and daughter can also download the same content.

Tap the gear button on your Home Screen on your iPhone to open the "Settings" app. When you tap your "Apple ID" you'll see options for your Name, Phone Numbers, E-mail; Password & Security; Payment & Shipping; Subscriptions; iCloud; iTunes & App Store; Find My; and Family Sharing. There is a list of your Apple devices shown at the bottom of the screen.

iCloud

In the Settings app, select your Apple ID name. Now tap "iCloud," swipe up, and then tap "iCloud." Tap each app if you want to store that app's data in iCloud Drive. The top of the screen displays Apple apps, and then the bottom of the screen has third-party apps like Amazon Drive, Drafts, Grocery, or ProCreate.

When Text Messaging Forwarding is active on your iPhone, it stores your entire message history in iCloud. When iCloud Drive is enabled, you'll have several folders available. Third-party apps like Drafts and Grocery add folders. Apple Apps, like Pages and Numbers, also add folders. You can also make additional folders. The next list is a few examples of folders.

- Documents
- Drafts
- Grocery
- Numbers
- Pages
- Shortcuts

Note the "Password & Accounts" system stores accounts and passwords in your iCloud Keychain. Your security information is available on any Apple device when you authenticate with Face ID, Touch ID, or your passcode. iOS 12 and later will generate strong passwords for you, identify weak passwords, and autofill account information.

Name, Phone Numbers, E-mail

Siri will customize your experience by using your Apple ID information in "Name, Phone Numbers, E-mail." The Mail app will use the e-mail addresses you add to "Name, Phone Numbers, E-mail."

There are also choices to receive announcements, new releases, news, and special offers for Apple subscriptions and services.

Password & Security

Change your password, enter a trusted phone number, or enable Two-Factor Authentication in the "Password & Security" section.

The Itunes & App Store settings allow you to configure automatic downloads and other settings for your Apple ID.

Subscriptions & Purchase History

Manage your subscriptions from the Settings app, your Apple TV, or iTunes. In the same location, you can see all your purchases.

While I have family sharing enabled, I can't see my daughter's subscriptions from my account. My daughter has to login to her account to cancel her app subscriptions. In-app purchases, especially in games, were a problem in our household. To avoid accidental purchases, I set up "Ask to Buy." Details about Ask to Buy for minors follow in the topic "Family Sharing."

1. Open the Settings app and tap "your name."

2. Tap "iTunes & App Store."

3. At the top of the screen, tap "your name" and in the pop-up tap "View Apple ID."

4. The "Account Settings" screen opens as an overlay. Touch the screen and swipe up. Tap "Subscriptions." Tap each subscription to manage settings. At the "Account Settings" screen, you can also select "Purchase History."

Family Sharing

With "Family Sharing," you can share your calendars, reminders, and more with up to six contacts. Family Sharing includes sharing purchases in the App Store, Apple Music, iCloud Storage, Location Sharing, and Screen Time. When you turn on family sharing a shared calendar is automatically created called "Family."

Third-party apps like the Grocery app also utilize shared reminder lists. The Grocery app outlined in Chapter 7 uses the iOS reminders lists to store your shopping list. With a combination of iOS "Family Sharing" and an IFTTT applet that automatically links my Alexa shopping list with my iOS reminder lists, I can easily add items to my grocery list with Alexa, Google Home, or Siri. Everyone in our family can access our family shopping list on their Apple device. I'm particularly fond of the Grocery app because while I may forget to bring my Smartphone to the grocery store, I will probably be wearing my Apple Watch with the Grocery app installed.

Enable Family Sharing

1. Open the Settings app and tap "your name."

2. Tap "Set up Family Sharing." Follow the prompts to invite contacts to join your family.

Ask to Buy

Ask to Buy is automatically active for children under 13. When enabled for a family member, the family organizer receives a request to approve all purchases.

1. Open the Settings app and tap "your name."

2. Disable or enable "Ask to Buy" for the 13 and under child.

Your Apple Watch Device Info

When configuring your Apple ID in the Settings app, scroll down to the bottom of the right page to see your Apple device. The screen also displays device information like Model, Version, Serial Number IMEI, or iOS version, along with these options.

- Find My Watch
- iCloud Backup
- Apple Pay Credit Cards

Turn on Find My Watch

"Find My" Watch is handy if you tend to misplace your Apple Device as frequently as do I! Whenever I'm not sure if I left my device at work or in the car, I use the "Find My" app to locate it.

By default, "Find My" is turned on after the initial setup with your Apple ID. In case you need to turn it back on, follow these steps.

1.   Open "Settings" and tap your name.

2.   Tap "Find My" and swipe up. Tap your Apple Watch name.

3.   Ensure "Find My Watch" is turned on.

iCloud Keychain

iCloud Keychain stores your passwords, credit card, Wi-Fi network configurations, and other accounts. An example of sharing Wi-Fi configurations is when your iPhone is nearby a family member's iPhone and you "share" a Wi-Fi password with their iPhone. Both devices must be logged in with the same Apple ID or family sharing account.

iCloud Keychain is set up in the Settings app, in the "Passwords & Accounts" section.

iCloud Backup

When iCloud Backup is off your iPhone is only backed up when you connect it to a computer running iTunes. To backup your iPhone to iCloud following these steps.

1.   Open "Settings" and tap "your name."

2.   Tap "iCloud."

3. Ensure "iCloud Backup" is turned on.

iCloud Photo Stream

When enabled iCloud Photo Stream copies your photos iCloud. Images are available from any of your Apple devices.

1. Open "Settings."

2. Tap "your name" at the top of the left sidebar. In the right panel, tap "iCloud."

3. Tap "Photos" and make sure the option "iCloud Photos" is toggled on. Also, tap "Upload to My Photo Stream."

Find People, Share My Location

The "Share My Location" option is used with family and friends in the "Messages," "Find People," and "Home" apps. Usually, I leave the "My Location" setting as my "This Device and Cellular Apple Watches," because when I leave the house, I might have either my iPhone or Apple Watch.

The other section on the screen is to Enable "Share My Location." Tap names to enable location sharing for each individual.

Share a Reminder List

Family sharing is active for my Apple ID. I share my "Family" reminder list with both my husband and daughter.

1.   Open the Reminders app and tap the "Family" list. Any list would work, but in this example, I happen to have a "Family" list.

2.   Tap "Edit" and then tap "sharing." Select a contact and click Add (the plus sign) to send an invitation to join the family.

Share Calendars

The bottom tab bar of the Calendar app has options for the Today view, Calendars, or Inbox. Tap Calendars to see all your calendars.

To add a new calendar tap "Add Calendar" in the bottom right corner of the pop-up menu. Tap the information symbol next to a calendar to see who the calendar is shared with, and set a color. Swipe to the bottom of the list to delete this calendar.

Apple Pay Setup on iPhone *

To complete Apple Pay setup have the CVC code available for credit cards you are adding to your Wallet, as outlined in Chapter 6 in the topic, "Apple Pay & the Wallet App." In the "Settings" app on your iPhone, you can also add credit and express transit cards, or set up your shipping address, e-mail, and phone. There is also an option to "Allow Payments on Mac."

1.   Open the "Settings" app on your **iPhone**.

2.   Swipe up and tap "Wallet & Apple Pay."

3.   Tap "Shipping Address."

In case you replace or upgrade your iPhone, your Apple Pay and Wallet information is stored in iCloud, but you will have to re-enter the credit card security codes. Chapter 6 has details of sending cash in a text message with Apple Pay.

3.13 Accessibility

The work Apple has done for accessibility is outstanding. In fact, in November 2018, Apple won the prestigious Eleanor Roosevelt Humanitarian Award from the Center for Hearing and Communication for its accessibility features.

I love large text and LED flashing alerts on my iPhone, so I thought I'd check out what settings are available on the Apple Watch. These accessibility settings are also discussed in Chapter 10 in detail, along with Vision, Hearing, and Physical & Motor Skills features unique to the Apple Watch.

- VoiceOver
- Zoom
- Grayscale
- Bold Text
- Reduce Motion
- Reduce Transparency
- On/Off Labels
- Side Button Click Speed

Apple designed its apps with accessibility in mind. Two wheelchair workouts introduced in watchOS 5 take into account different pushing conditions. Wheelchair mode in the Health app enables "Roll Goals" and "Time to Roll" notifications. The Activity app counts "pushes" instead of steps. The new Walkie-Talkie app instantly starts a conversation at a touch of your finger. Haptics (wrist taps) also play a role in alerts. For example, the Map app gently vibrates to indicate an upcoming turn.

Haptics is a useful accessibility feature for deaf or hard of hearing drivers. There are several ways to enable accessibility features.

- On your **Apple Watch**, go to Settings.

- Triple-click the Digital Crown.

- On your **iPhone,** in the Apple Watch app, go to the Accessibility screen.

watchOS 6 added Accessibility options to the Settings app on your Apple Watch, as shown below.

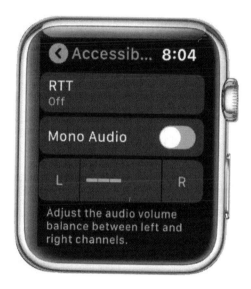

Figure 3.2   Accessibility Options in the Settings App

Accessibility Shortcut

The "Accessibility Shortcut" uses the Digital Crown to turn on "Zoom" or "VoiceOver" with a triple-click.

1. Open the Apple Watch app on your **iPhone**.

2. Tap My Watch, go to "General."

3. Tap Accessibility, then tap "Accessibility Shortcut."

4. Choose "VoiceOver" or "Zoom."

VoiceOver

Siri excels at toggling VoiceOver on or off. Press the Digital Crown to wake up Siri and say, "Turn on VoiceOver." Siri responds with "VoiceOver on." If you prefer, you can turn on VoiceOver in "Settings."

1. On your **Apple Watch,** press the Side Button.

2. Tap "Settings," and then tap General.

3. Swipe to select Accessibility.

4. Tap "VoiceOver" to toggle on or off.

Zoom

The "Zoom" feature will magnify the Apple Watch display. Press the Digital Crown to wake up Siri and say, "Turn on Zoom." There is a setting for the Digital Crown to turn either VoiceOver or Zoom on with a triple-click.

1. On your **iPhone,** open the Apple Watch app.

2. Tap My Watch, go to "General."

3. Tap "Accessibility," then tap the "Zoom" switch to toggle it on or off and set the zoom level.

*Accessibility Settings on iPhone**

Now that I am of a certain age, accessibility features take on a whole new meaning. Since I love large text and LED flashing alerts on my iPhone, I thought I'd check out what other settings are available on the iPhone. These accessibility settings are also discussed in Chapter 10, along with Vision, Hearing, Physical & Motor Skills, and other accessibility settings unique to the iPhone.

- VoiceOver

- Zoom

- Grayscale

- Bold Text

- Reduce Motion

- Reduce Transparency

- On/Off Labels

Apple apps are designed with accessibility in mind. There are several ways to enable accessibility features.

- Triple-click the Home Button on your iPhone.

- Open the "Settings" app and tap "General." Swipe to see the Accessibility screen.

*Accessibility Shortcut on iPhone**

The "Accessibility Shortcut" uses the iPhone Home Button to turn on "Zoom," "VoiceOver," or other accessibility options with a triple-click. You can choose one of the following options for your accessibility shortcut.

- Assistive Touch
- Classic Invert Colors
- Color Filters
- Reduce White Point
- Smart Invert Colors
- Switch Control
- VoiceOver
- Zoom

1. Open the "Settings" app on your iPhone.

2. Tap My iPhone, go to "General."

3. Tap Accessibility, scroll down to the bottom, and tap "Accessibility Shortcut."

4. Choose "Classic Invert Colors" or another option.

Read Screen Contents Out Loud on iPhone*

The "Speak Screen" choice in the section "Speech" is one of my favorites. Swipe down from the top of the screen with two fingers to hear the content of the screen. This feature works in the Books, and most iPhone apps. In apps like Safari, you can say, "Hey Siri, turn on Speak Screen."

1. Open the "Settings" app on your iPhone.

2. Tap My iPhone, go to "General."

3. Tap Accessibility.

4. Tap "Speech" and toggle on "Speak Screen".

Chapter 3

VoiceOver on iPhone*

Siri excels at toggling VoiceOver on or off. Wake Siri and say, "Turn on VoiceOver." Siri responds with "VoiceOver on." If you prefer, you can turn on VoiceOver in "Settings."

1.   Open the Home Screen on your iPhone.

2.   Tap "Settings," and then tap General.

3.   Swipe to select Accessibility.

4.   Tap "VoiceOver" to toggle on or off.

Zoom on iPhone*

The "Zoom" feature will magnify the iPhone display. Wake Siri and say, "Turn on Zoom." There is a setting for the Home Button to turn either VoiceOver or Zoom on with a triple-click.

1.   Open the "Settings" app on your iPhone.

2.   Tap My iPhone, go to "General."

3.   Tap "Accessibility," then tap the "Zoom" switch to toggle it on or off and set the zoom level.

Subtitles on iPhone*

The "**Audio & Subtitles**" control is available in the TV app when watching videos on your iPhone. Tap the screen to see the playback controls. On the right side tap the "**Audio & Subtitles**" control. You can also turn subtitles on in the Settings app. Tap "General" and tap "Accessibility." Swipe to scroll down to the "Media" section and tap "Subtitles & Captioning."

3.14 Continuity & Handoff

The Apple Continuity platform encompasses Cellular Calls, Auto Unlock, and Handoff. Handoff is a way to seamlessly switch tasks between your Apple Watch, iPad, Mac, or iPhone. To use Continuity features, the devices must be signed in with the same Apple ID, and Bluetooth and Wi-Fi must be active.

Requirements

Apple devices must have these settings.

- Bluetooth is enabled.

- Wi-Fi is enabled.

- Both devices are signed in with the same Apple ID.

- Handoff is turned on. Handoff is the ability to switch an application from one Apple device to another. For example, if you're reading mail on your Apple Watch, you can continue reading the same message on your Mac or iPhone. Chapter 8 has details on Handoff.

1. On your **iPhone,** open the Apple Watch app.

2. Swipe to scroll to "Settings" and tap "General."

3. Scroll down and touch the "Enable Handoff" switch to toggle it on or off. The switch is green when on and white when off.

Handoff is especially useful when you answer a phone call on your Apple Watch and want to switch to your iPhone. With watchOS 6, I like to handoff my web browsing to my iPhone or iPad, because the browser on my Apple Watch displays web pages in Reader View. On your iPhone, when you press the home button to switch apps, the handoff banner is displayed at the bottom of your iPhone, as shown below.

Figure 3.3   Handoff Web Browser to iPhone

3.15 Enable Screenshots

When enabled, you can take a screenshot on your Apple Watch. View screenshots in the camera roll on your iPhone. To enable screenshots, follow these steps.

1. On your **iPhone**, open the Apple Watch app.

2. Swipe to scroll down to "Settings" and tap "General."

3. Scroll down and tap "Enable Screenshots." The slider will turn green when enabled.

Take a Screenshot

Press the side button and hold, and then tap the Digital Crown. The screen flashes to indicate a screenshot was successful. View screenshots on your iPhone in the Photos app.

3.16 iPhone Share Sheet*

The Action or Share button [⬆️] opens the Activity View on your iPhone. This control displays in the top right corner of an app on your iPhone. The Activity View displays relevant activities for the current task. So depending on the app, and what you are doing, the choices in the Activity View will change.

There are two tab bar rows in the Share Sheet, as shown below. The first row is "AirDrop" contacts. The second row has "Share Extensions." Swipe up to see a list of the available "Action Extensions" at the bottom. To see the sharing in action, open the Photos app and tap the "Share" button in the top right corner of the screen.

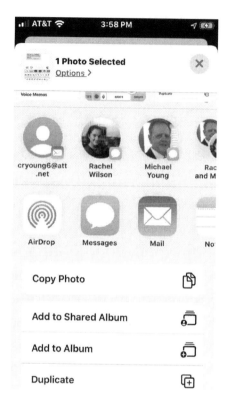

Figure 3.4   Share and Action Extensions

The second row below AirDrop contacts has Share extensions such as:

- Share with Messages

- Share with Mail

- Shared Notes

The bottom area has Action Extensions which include Copy, Slideshow, Airplay, Add to Album, Use as Wallpaper, Save to Files, Assign to Contact, Print, and more.

Tip: When the Activity View is open, swipe left and right in the tab rows to view more buttons.

Reorder Extensions*

To control the order of Share Extensions on your iPhone swipe left and tap any "App button" and drag it to the new location. You can also swipe left and tap the "More" button. Touch the three horizontal lines to reorder the items.

Add or Remove Extensions*

To toggle Share Extensions on or off on your iPhone, swipe left and tap the "More" control that looks like three dots or an ellipsis. To turn a Share Extension off, toggle the switch on or off. Tap "Done" to confirm changes.

To add or remove Action Extensions, swipe up and tap "Edit Actions." iOS 13 has the action "Create Watch Face" in the section "Other Actions."

3.17 Rename iPhone File or Folder*

To rename a file or folder on your iPhone, touch and hold the file or folder name. Whenever you see a file name, whether it's a directory view or while editing a file, you can rename it. Renaming works on the Home screen, the Pages app, or in the Files app. For example, open the Files app and navigate to the file or folder you want to rename. Tap the filename and then type the new name.

3.18 iPhone Keyboard*

Your iPhone has an on-screen keyboard with options for entering numbers, special characters, other language keyboards, and more. Entering and editing text, dictation, and special characters are covered in the next section, "Text Editing."

Numbers*

Tap the on-screen number key 123 on your iPhone to use the numeric and symbol keyboard. Tap "ABC" to return to the alphabetic keyboard.

Emoji*

Tap the smiley face ☺ icon to open the Emoji keyboard. To return to the alphabetic keyboard, tap the "ABC" key in the lower-left corner of the screen.

Install Other Keyboards*

In addition to Apple keyboards, you can add third-party keyboards. To configure keyboards for your iPhone, open the "Settings" app, and tap "General," then "Keyboard." Tap "Add New Keyboard," then choose a keyboard.

To add a third-party keyboard, download the keyboard app in the App Store. For example, download the "Gboard" app for the Google keyboard. Gboard includes Themes and Stickers, and Gboard supports "Swiping" across the screen with your finger to type a word. iOS 13 and later includes the QuickPath swipe keyboard, as shown below.

Figure 3.5   iPhone Keyboard

The figure above illustrates swiping across the iPhone keyboard to type the word "nail."

Tap the Globe button ⊕ to switch keyboards. The Globe button appears in the lower-left corner of the keyboard.

Next, tap the Google logo Ⓖ to change to the Google keyboard. Slide your finger across the keyboard to select the keys and Gboard suggests a word or phrase.

*Switch iPhone Keyboards**

Tap the Globe button located in the lower-left corner of the screen to switch between keyboards. This icon is visible when you have more than one keyboard installed on your iPhone. Tap again to move to the next installed keyboard, including other language keyboards.

Press the Shift and Control keys at the same time, and tap the "space bar" to switch between keyboards.

*3.19 iPhone Text Editing**

Text editing is a bit different on an iPhone. There is an on-screen keyboard, but you can also edit the text using gestures like tapping, swiping, and sliding your finger across the screen. The next sections cover pop-up menus that add additional functionality.

- Entering Text
- Predictive Text
- Text Replacement

*Entering Text**

To type text in any app on your iPhone, tap within the text box. The on-screen keyboard is displayed. There are a few keyboard shortcuts for text entry, as shown below.

- **Uppercase letters:** Touch the "Shift" key, or tap the shift key, and then tap a letter. You can also tap the shift key and swipe across the keyboard to tap a letter. For number keys, touch the edge of the key to see other characters, then lift your finger. For example, the letter "E" includes accented characters for "E." To change several keys at once, you can also touch the "Shift" key with your left hand, and tap letter keys with your right.

- **Numbers:** Select the "number" 123 key to view the number keyboard.

- **Symbols:** Tap the symbol key "#+=" to the left of the period to see the symbol keyboard. Depending on the keyboard you are using, you may have to view the numbers keyboard first, then tap the symbols key.

- **Emoji:** Tap the Emoji ☺ or ⊕ world button to see the Emoji keyboard.

- **Period and space:** Double-tap the space bar to add a period and space.

- **Turn on Caps Lock:** Tap the shift key twice to turn on Caps Lock. The Arrow key is underlined when Caps Lock is active.

- **Switch keyboards** ⊕ **(or change settings):** To view Settings or change to another keyboard, touch and hold the globe key for several seconds

- **Accented letters:** Touch a key for a few seconds, until a pop-up menu of accented letters and options appears, then tap your selection.

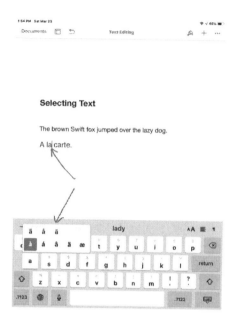

Figure 3.6   Text Accents

For information on keyboards, in general, see the next section. We'll look at Swipe keyboards and Predictive Text later in this chapter, which may mean spelling errors are a thing of the past.

Selecting Text*

When editing text on your iPhone, tap the text on the screen to select the text. Pointers on the screen indicate the location you tapped within the text. Once you select the text, pop-up menus and gestures are used to edit the text. Tapping the screen displays a vertical bar that extends slightly above and below the line of text. This "pointer" or "vertical bar" is the insertion point. With iOS 13 and later, touch the bar to drag it to a new location. Tap twice to select a word. Tap three times to select the paragraph.

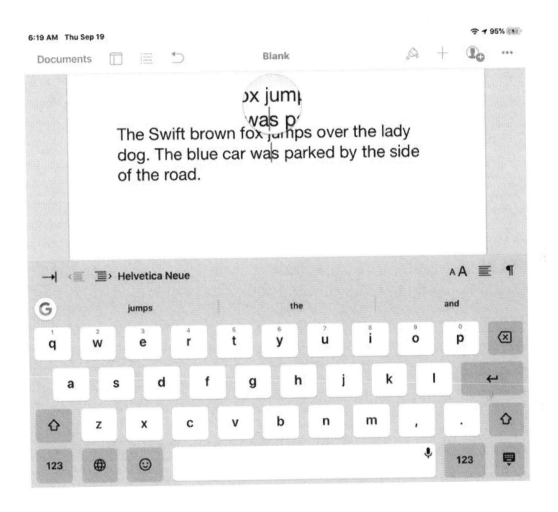

Figure 3.7   The Insertion Point

A second type of "pointer" appears when working with the "Select" and "Select All" menus, as outlined in the following section.

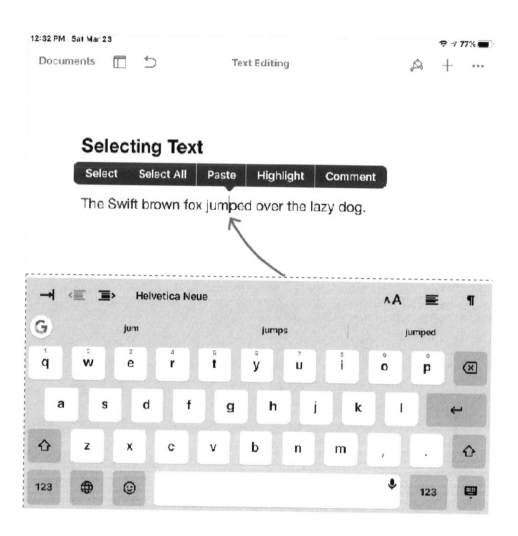

Figure 3.8   Select Pop-up Menu

When you touch the iPhone screen for a few seconds and then lift your finger, a pop-up menu appears with these options.

- Select

- Select All

- Paste

- Highlight

- Comment

When you choose "Select" or "Select All" from the first menu, another pop-up menu opens with these additional options.

- Cut
- Copy
- Delete
- Replace
- Define
- Link
- Bookmark
- Comment
- Highlight
- Style

In the following example, there is a highlighted selection box around the selected word.

Chapter 3

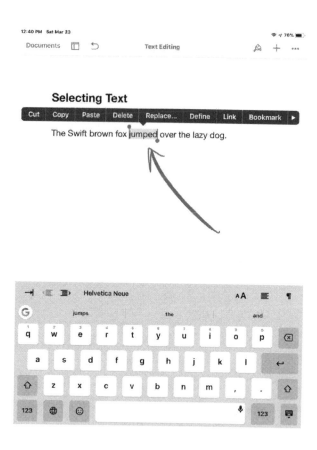

Figure 3.9   Selecting a Word

On your iPhone screen, there are two small blue circles, called drag points, at each end of the highlighted selection box, located at the top left corner and the bottom right corner. I think of this blue highlighted area as a bounding box.

When you drag the small blue drag points over text, the blue highlighted selection box changes size. You can select word(s), sentence(s), or paragraph(s).

The Swift brown fox|jumped|over the lazy dog.

Figure 3.10   Selection Box

I found using the blue drag points to select text areas frustrating at first because I didn't understand how to use them. I'd encourage you to take a moment to practice these steps, and you'll master the process in no time.

In this example, we are going to select the text using the pop-up menu. We aren't going to change anything at this point. We're only practicing selecting text.

1.   Type a sentence with a few words. Touch the text on the screen for a few seconds, then lift your finger. For this example, touch in the middle of your text, so you can practice sliding the small blue circles (the drag points) left and right to select the text.

2.   Tap "Select" in the first pop-up menu. The word is highlighted with a blue box, and the second pop-up menu is displayed.

3.   Touch the top left blue drag point. Do not move your finger to the left until the pop-up menu disappears, to ensure you grabbed the blue drag point. Slide your finger, dragging the small blue drag point to the left. Repeat with the right drag point, dragging the circle to the right.

4.   The selected area has a blue highlighted box, and should now include several words (or lines.)

5.   To end the example, tap in a blank area at the edge of the screen. The text is no longer selected or highlighted.

In the previous example, we selected text using the pop-up menu command "Select." Now we'll repeat the same scenario by Double-tapping a word.

1.   **Double-tap** a word in the middle of your sentence. The word is highlighted, as shown in Step 2 in the previous example.

Moving Text*

To move a word or text when typing on your iPhone keyboard, you select the text and then drag it to a new location, as outlined in the following example.

Figure 3.11   Moving Text

1. Double-tap a word in the middle of your sentence. The selected word is highlighted in a blue box.

2. Touch the word until the blue highlight disappears, and a small white pop-up displays with your selected text. Drag the white box to the new location. A vertical blue line is displayed indicating the insertion point.

3. Lift your finger to move the text to the new location.

With iOS 13, undo text editing by swiping left with a three-finger swipe. Redo text editing with a three-finger swipe to the right. Copy with a three-finger pinch.

Predictive Text*

When you type on your iPhone, Siri will suggest words based on the current context, as well as your recent activity. It took me a while to adjust to using predictive text, but eventually, I realized it was useful for more than editing spelling errors. Suggestions for unusual words (or names) appear in quotes, and this is a simple way to bypass autocorrect.

The predictive text example in the online manual is to type "I'm at…" and Siri asks if you want to send your current location. No doubt, Intelligent Siri will have all kinds of suggestions for us in the future.

The predictive text option is configured in the Settings app, in the General setting, under the Keyboard settings. Swipe to the "English" section and toggle the "Predictive" switch on or off.

iPhone Shortcut Bar*

The top row of the iPhone keyboard displays the "Shortcut Bar." The items shown vary depending on the app. For example, in Notes, on the left side, there is a button to create a table.

*Text Replacement**

Similar to predictive text, "Text Replacement" settings allow you to customize your text replacement settings. For example, when I type "wed," I have a text replacement set up as "Wednesday." I discovered this handy feature the hard way after my daughter added a few text replacements to my phone as an April Fools joke. It took me a while to figure out why every time I typed "you," the phrase changed to "they're."

This option is also found in the Settings app on your iPhone, in the General setting, under the "Keyboard" settings. Chapter 2 has an example of Text Replacement.

*Dictation**

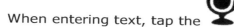

Touch the microphone button   on the iPhone keyboard to dictate. Because Apple servers in the Cloud transcribe your dictation into text, you must have an Internet connection for dictation to work. Make sure Enable Dictation is turned on in the Settings app, as outlined below.

1.   Open the "Settings" app on your iPhone. Swipe down and tap "General," then tap "Keyboard." Turn on, "Enable Dictation."

Tip: If dictation doesn't work, check you have a connection to the Internet.

When entering text, tap the   microphone to dictate text.

When done typing tap the keyboard   button.

Dictation Commands*

Certain phrases will add punctuation, as shown below. If you search the Internet for Apple Dictation commands for the Mac, there is an extensive list of punctuation and formatting commands.

- All Caps
- Apostrophe `
- Caps On
- Caret ^
- Colon :
- Comma,
- Dash -
- Dollar Sign $
- Exclamation Mark !
- Hashtag or Pound Sign #
- Minus Sign -
- New Line
- New paragraph
- Numeral
- Percent Sign %
- Period
- Plus Sign +
- Quote ... end quote "
- Question Mark?

- Tab Key

- Underscore _

- Vertical Bar |

3.20 What's Next?

The next chapter on watch faces and complications completes the process of customizing your Apple Watch. The chapter wraps up with ideas for sample combinations. For example, for Disney, I use the Mickey Mouse watch face and add the complications for Find People, Calendar, and Magic Guide to Disney World.

4. Watch Faces

In this chapter we discuss

Update Your Watch Face

Exploring Interactive Watch Faces

Changing the Watch Face Style

Customizing a Watch Face

The 'My Faces' Screen

Complications

Customized Samples

What's Next?

The beauty of the Apple Watch is that you control which features, apps, or app complications appear on your Watch face. In this chapter, we will look at how to harness all that power and provide samples of how you can use it in particular situations.

Folks who own high-end timepieces probably recognize the term "complications" when discussing a watch. Any jeweler will tell you that a watch complication is any dial or sub-dial other than the primary display of time on a mechanical watch. Apple Watches are no different from an elegant Swiss watch in that they also use the term complications. Speaking of a Swiss watch, did you know sales of the Apple Watch beat Rolex in 2017?

In this Apple Watch World, individual features of apps are available as complications. I think of complications as little snippets of information. A fitness app might display the number of steps you've taken today in a complication. The Apple Calendar app uses your World Clock time zones as separate complications. For example, once you create a World Clock location for Mumbai and another for New York, you can add both complications to your Watch face. As of this writing, 41 complications from Apple are available for the Apple Watch. Not all third-party Apple Watch apps provide complications, but the list of third-party apps with Apple Watch complications is growing daily.

Apple Watch faces have "**template areas**" for complications. Where you position a complication on your Watch face affects what information is displayed. If the "template area" is relatively small, an icon might be displayed. A larger template area at the bottom of the Watch face can display a description of your calendar event. To get you started, I will show you several real-world examples.

The "Utilitarian template" is ideal for displaying data - think stock market, steps, or calories. The Utilitarian template occupies a rectangular area in the top left and right corners of the Utility, Motion, Mickey Mouse and Minnie Mouse Watch faces. Utilitarian templates also occupy three corners of the Chronograph Watch face and all four corners of the Simple Watch face.

The style of the particular Watch face may allow you to customize the color, markings, or complications in the template areas. You decide which app complications you want in the various template areas. A few Apple app complications are Mail, Messages, or Activity. The addition of third-party app complications like Hotwire or ESPN expands the possibilities for your Watch face.

You can choose from 26 basic styles of Watch faces that you customize and save in as many combinations as you like. The "My Faces" screen displays your favorite Watch faces. Make changes to the "My Faces" selections directly on your watch or within the Apple Watch app on your iPhone.

The "Faces Gallery" displays all the standard Apple Watch Faces. If you delete a Watch face from your "My Faces" list, you can always find the Watch face again in the "Faces Gallery." The iPhone Apple app also includes a preview option and is generally easier to navigate.

With the release of major watchOS versions, Apple usually adds new Watch faces. For example, watchOS 6 introduced the Watch faces shown below. Note that some Watch faces are limited to newer Apple Watch models.

Figure 4.1   Modular Compact Watch Face

The Modular Compact Watch face includes choices for an analog or digital clock. There is a wide complication template area that is ideal for complications that show data over time like Stocks, Wind, Weather, Rain, UV Index, Noise, or Heart Rate.

Figure 4.2   The Solar Dial Watch Face

The Solar Dial is a striking display of the sun as it moves around the dial and is the best illustration of the sunrise and sunset I've ever seen. The inset Digital Clock highlights each second-hand bar as it marks sixty seconds in a minute.

The Meridian watch face is showcased on the cover of this book and includes four complications.

Figure 4.3   The Meridian

California is a mix of standard numbers and Roman numerals. In the following example, the California Watch face is using Red Arabic Indic and the Pandora complication.

Figure 4.4   California Watch Face

The colors on the Gradient Watch face shift as the hour and second hands move.

Figure 4.5   Gradient Watch Face

The Numerals Mono and Numerals Duo Watch faces have very large numbers.

Figure 4.6   Numerals Uno Watch Face

4.1 Update Your Watch Face

1. On your **Apple Watch** press the Digital Crown to display the Watch Face.

2. Swipe left or right from edge to edge.

3. Stop when you find the Watch face you want.

4.2 Exploring Interactive Watch Faces

Depending on the Watch face, interactions or animations might be available when you double-tap or turn the Digital

Crown. These "Easter Eggs" are an unexpected fun surprise. For example, when you double-tap the screen, Mickey Mouse announces the time. A few of these Easter Eggs are highlighted in the following section "Customized Samples." For a complete list of Watch faces and their respective complications check out the Apple User Guide.

Astronomy

The Astronomy category includes three Watch faces: Earth, Moon, and Solar System. Double-tap the Solar System Watch face to align the planets, or turn the Digital Crown to see the planets move throughout the year. Turning the Digital Crown with the Earth Watch face shows the sun moving across the sky, and in the evening hours, the lights in metropolitan areas are visible.

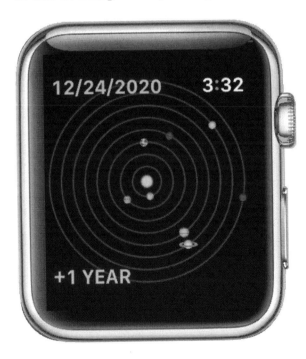

Figure 4.7   The Solar System Watch Face

4.3 Changing the Watch Face Style

You can make multiple versions of any Watch face, as shown below.

Figure 4.8   Customize the Watch Face

1. On your **Apple Watch**, press the Digital Crown to go to the Watch Face.

2. Firmly press the display.

3. Swipe all the way to the right, then tap Add (the plus symbol.)

4. Turn the Digital Crown and tap your selected Watch face.

1. On your **iPhone**, open the Apple Watch app.

2. Along the bottom of the screen, tap "Face Gallery."

3. Scroll and tap the Watch face you want, then tap "Add."

Delete a Watch Face

It is possible to remove Watch faces you do not want to show on your Apple Watch. I found all the Watch face choices a bit overwhelming, so I decided to remove the ones that didn't grab my attention. You can easily add them back if you change your mind. Follow these steps to remove Watch faces.

1. On your **Apple Watch**, press the Digital Crown to go to the Watch Face.

2. Swipe left or right from edge to edge to scroll through Watch faces and select the Watch face you want to remove.

3. Firmly press the screen and swipe up to remove the Watch face.

4.4 Customizing a Watch Face

While editing a Watch face, you can customize a highlighted feature. For example, the color of the second hand, or the markings on the face.

1. Press the Digital Crown on your **Apple Watch** to go to the Watch Face.

2. Firmly press the display and then tap "Customize."

3. Swipe to select the desired feature, for example, the date style.

4. Turn the Digital Crown to change the highlighted feature, for example, the numbers on the dial.

Figure 4.9   Change the Color of the Second Hand

To change your Watch Face on your iPhone, follow these steps.

1.   On your **iPhone**, open the Apple Watch app.

2.   In the "My Faces" section, tap the Watch Face.

3.   Tap the options for color or style.

4.   In "Complications," choose the apps for each option.

5.   Scroll down and tap "Set as current Watch Face."

4.5 The 'My Faces' Screen

Think of "My Faces" as your personal, customized Watch faces. This is not the same as the "Face Gallery" which is all possible Watch faces.

1. On your **iPhone**, open the Apple Watch app.

2. In the section "My Faces," tap "Edit."

3. Scroll through the gallery to select a Watch face.

4. To reorder the list of Watch faces, touch the drag icon that looks like three horizontal bars on the right. Drag the icon up or down to move the Watch face.

5. To remove a Watch face from the list, tap the delete button.

Organize Your Watch Faces

1. On your **iPhone**, open the Apple Watch app.

2. In the "My Faces" section, tap "Edit."

3. Touch and hold the drag icon on the right side of a Watch face. The drag icon is three horizontal bars.

4. Drag the Watch face up or down to change the list order.

Reorder Watch Faces

With watchOS 6 you can reorder your Watch faces on your Apple Watch.

1. Press the Digital Crown on your **Apple Watch** to go to the Watch Face.

2. Firmly press the display. Your "My Faces" gallery is shown, and a "Customize" button appears at the bottom of the screen.

3. Swipe to select the desired Watch face.

4. Touch and hold the Watch face to open an overlay displaying the Watch face location in the My Faces list. A small green box is displayed at the top of the screen with a number, for example, "2 of 3."

5. Drag the Watch face to the new location.

4.6 Complications

Complications on your Watch Face mean your apps are now part of your Apple Watch face. Tapping complications on your Watch face opens the app. For example, tap the Calendar complication (date) on your Watch face to open the Calendar app.

Apple does a good job of encouraging you to move and exercise all on its own, but adding apps like AllTrails, Big Year Birding, Scavenger, or Pokémon introduces a bit of fun into the equation. For example, the "LoseIt!" app reminds me of how many calories I should have for lunch. "Notice I didn't say will have but should have." The Pedometer app displays my step counter. Apple has 41 possible complications.

- Activity
- Air Quality Index (AQI)
- Alarm
- Audiobooks
- Battery
- Breathe
- Calculator
- Calendar
- Cellular Strength
- Date
- Decibel Level
- Digital Time

- Earth
- Favorite Contacts
- Find My Friends
- Heart Rate
- Home
- Mail
- Maps
- Messages
- Monogram
- Moon
- Moon Phase
- Music
- News
- Now Playing
- Phone
- Podcasts
- Radio
- Rain
- Reminders
- Remote
- Siri
- Solar
- Solar System
- Stocks
- Stopwatch
- Sunrise/Sunset
- Timer
- UV Index
- Voice Memos

- Walkie-Talkie
- Weather
- Weather Conditions
- Wind
- Workout
- World Clock

First, we will look at the basic steps to add and customize these apps for your watch. Next, we will explore tons of app complications available today and how to find new apps at any time. For a complete list of the Apple Watch faces and their supported Apple complications check out the Apple User Guide.

Select complications for your Watch faces using the "Customize" option. Keep in mind that not all apps have complications, and not all Watch faces allow you to add complications.

Add a Complication to Your Watch Face

To change a complication on a Watch face, follow these steps.

1. On your **Apple Watch**, press the Digital Crown to go to the Watch Face.

2. Firmly press the display and then tap "Customize."

3. Swipe to display the highlighted area to customize.

4. Turn the Digital Crown to change the highlighted feature or select an app "Complication."

The Favorite Complication

The Infograph and Infographic Modular Watch faces support adding your "favorite contacts" as a complication.

Add or Remove a Favorite Contact

A favorite contact complication is shown as a letter or photo on your Watch face. In this example, the Favorites complication for Michael is shown along the bottom of the screen.

Figure 4.10   The Favorite Complication

1. On your **iPhone**, open the "Phone" app.

2. Tap "Favorites," located in the left corner of the tab bar at the bottom of the screen.

3. Tap the plus symbol in the top left corner to add a contact.

Remove Complications

Depending on the apps installed on your iPhone, you could have a lot of available complications. That may not be a good thing. For example, I am never going to use the CVS complication on my Apple Watch. Follow the instructions below to remove a complication from your Apple Watch. You can always add it back in the future.

1. On your **iPhone**, open the Apple Watch app.

2. Scroll down and tap "Complications."

3. Swipe to delete a complication. Notice the complication is moved to the bottom in the section "Do Not Include."

Complication Not Showing on iPhone

Occasionally I've noticed that a complication won't show as available in the Apple Watch app on the iPhone. However, it is still possible to add the complication on the Apple Watch itself.

1. On your **Apple Watch**, press the Digital Crown to go to the Watch Face.

2. Firmly press the display and then tap "Customize."

3. Swipe to display the highlighted area to customize.

4. Turn the Digital Crown to change the highlighted feature or select an app "Complication."

Strangely, the complication will then show in the Apple Watch app on your iPhone, but only for that particular Watch face.

Edit Complications

Many app complications work the moment the app is installed, but others do require further setup. For example, Pedometer++ is a third-party app with a "complication" to add steps to your Watch face. Before using the complication, you must add Pedometer as a source in the "Health" app.

1. Open the "Health" app on your **iPhone**.

2. Tap the "Sources" tab, located in the left corner of the tab bar at the bottom of the screen.

3. Scroll down to Pedometer. If you don't see Pedometer in the list of apps, install it on your iPhone and launch the app at least once.

4. Tap "Turn All Categories On."

Navigating Complications

In the following example, I have the calendar complication on my Watch face.

1. On your **Apple Watch**, press the Digital Crown to open your Watch face.

2. Tap the calendar complication.

3. Turn the Digital Crown to move through days.

Another fun option is the Weather complication. Tap to select the weather complication, and turn the Digital Crown to see the hourly forecast, air quality, UV index, wind index, and the 7-day forecast. How cool is that!

4.7 Customized Samples

The following is a gallery showcasing some of the Apple Watch faces. These are organized by interest and include relevant customizations.

Astronomy

The Astronomy Watch face category is custom made for astronomy fans. The Astronomy category includes three Watch faces.

- Earth
- Moon
- Solar System

Double-tap the "Solar System" Watch face to align the planets, or turn the Digital Crown to see the planets move throughout the year. In an amazing piece of programming, you can spin the Digital Crown to watch the sun rays move across the "Earth" Watch face, and in the evening hours, the lights in metropolitan areas are visible. Apps like "SkyGuide" are also designed for Astronomy fans.

Breathe Watch Face

The Breathe app is available as a Watch face in three styles: Focus, Calm, and Classic. When you raise your wrist the Watch face guides you through a deep breath. Recent research into the neuroscience of mindfulness shows deep breathing reduces stress and has long-term health benefits.

Color

The simplistic view of the color Watch face appeals to me for some reason. With this Watch face, it's also easy to scroll through the colors using the Digital Crown.

Figure 4.11   The Color Watch Face

1.   On your **Apple Watch**, press the "Digital Crown" to go to the Watch face.

2.   Firmly press the display and tap "Customize."

3.   Turn the Digital Crown to select a color.

Cooking and Kitchen

When cooking, I prefer to tap and swipe on my watch, rather than on my iPhone.

Ideas for Complications:

1. Timer

2. Kitchen Stories

3. Smart Grocery

4. Reminder List (shopping list)

5. Music

6. Siri

Disney

How fun is it to be on vacation at Disney World, and have your own personalized Watch face! The Mickey Mouse Watch face and Toy Story Watch face are perfect for this adventure. It's also super cool to tap the Watch face and have Mickey Mouse announce the time.

1. Open the **Apple Watch** app on your iPhone.

2. Tap "My Watch," located in the left corner of the tab bar at the bottom of the screen.

3. Scroll down and tap "Sounds & Haptics."

4. Touch the "Tap to Speak" switch to turn this feature on.

The "**Magic Guide to Disney World**" app has a complication for the Apple Watch that works with the Mickey Mouse Watch face. This app has Disney World wait times, park maps, dining menus, park hours, photos, and more.

Figure 4.12   The Mickey Mouse Watch Face

On my Mickey Mouse Watch face, I added **Reminders** to track my "Disney Fast Pass" selections, as well as **Pedometer**.

1. Install the Magic Guide to Disney World app on your **iPhone**.

2. Open the Apple Watch app on your **iPhone**.

3. Tap "My Watch," located in the left corner of the tab bar at the bottom of the screen.

4. Scroll down and tap "Complications." Make sure "Magic Guide" appears on the list. When done, tap "Back."

5. In the "My Faces" section, tap the Mickey Mouse Watch face.

6. Scroll down to "Complications" and select the "Magic Guide."

Another complication to consider for Disney is the "**Find Friends**" app. The "**Walkie-Talkie**" app is also handy when you're trying to coordinate rides or meals.

Kaleidoscope

The Kaleidoscope Watch face has infinite possibilities. You select a stock or custom image and choose a style. Turn the Digital Crown to see the kaleidoscope you created.

Figure 4.13   The Kaleidoscope Watch Face

Motion

The motion Watch face has been around a while, but it is one of those things you just have to try out because it's so fun. There are three collections: butterflies, flowers, and jellyfish. When you firmly press the screen, the display cycles through the animations.

Figure 4.14   The Motion Watch Face

Fire, Water, Liquid Metal, and Vapor

The Vapor, Liquid Metal, Fire and Water motion faces are included with Apple Watch Series 4 and later. On the Apple Watch Series 4 and later, you can set the footage to cover the screen from edge-to-edge completely. These backgrounds are not computer-generated digital effects. The CoolHunting YouTube video, "Apple Watch Series 4 Making of Fire Water and Vapor Faces" is an exclusive behind-the-scenes look into how the videos were created. A high-speed camera captured high-resolution recordings of a real fire, water splashing, smoke vapor, and liquid metal.

Siri

With watchOS 5, Siri became an intelligent personal assistant. In watchOS 6, Siri includes Shazam integration, and can also search the web and display full web page results. The Siri Watch face monitors your schedule and calendar, suggesting relevant content throughout the day. Intelligent Siri will update you on your favorite team's score, display a photo from a year ago, or recommend a playlist for your commute home. There is also an option to change the Siri Watch face to grey.

Figure 4.15   The Siri Watch Face

1.   On your **Apple Watch**, press the "Digital Crown" to go to the Watch face.

2.   Firmly press the display and tap "Customize."

3.   Turn the Digital Crown to select "Grey" or "Siri Color."

Stocks

The Apple app "Stocks" can display up to 20 stocks and has four complications, as shown below. Configure the list of stocks in the iPhone app.

- Current Price
- Points Change
- Percentage Change
- Market Cap

Figure 4.16   Stocks - Market Closed

Timelapse

Displaying location photos throughout the day is an elegant and natural way to indicate the time. The scenes dynamically adjust throughout the day based on time and include these locations.

Figure 4.17   The time-lapse Watch Face

- Mack Lake
- New York
- Hong Kong
- London
- Paris
- Shanghai

World Traveler

Global travelers will appreciate the idea of a world traveler Watch face. You customize a Watch face to keep track of flight times, hotel reservations, train schedules, car rental, and Uber ride information. The modular Watch face is well suited to this task. If you're visiting one of the locations in the Timelapse collection, you may want to use that Watch face.

Leverage these apps when traveling:

- App in the Air
- Babble
- Calendar
- Carrot Weather or Dark Sky
- Citymapper
- ELK (currency converter)
- ETA
- Glympse
- HotWire
- iTranslate
- Weather
- World Clock

To add various world clock complications to your Watch face configure them in the clock app.

Configure the World Clock Time Zones

1.   On your **iPhone**, open the "Clock" app.

2.   In the bottom left corner of the screen tap "World Clock.

3.   Add Mumbai and New York locations.

Add World Clock Complication

1.   On your **iPhone**, open the "Watch" app.

2.   Tap a Watch face, and then swipe to view complications.

3.   Select a time zone.

Figure 4.18   The Activity Digital Watch Face and the World Clock Complication

Your Photo

Each time you raise your wrist, a different photo from your album is displayed on the Photo Watch face. First, sync a photo album from your iPhone with your watch.

Create a Photo Album on your iPhone

1. On your **iPhone**, open the Apple Watch app.

2. Scroll down to "Photos" and select "Synced Album" to select your album.

3. On the main screen, scroll back up to the "My Faces."

4.   Tap "Edit" to open the Watch face gallery.

4.8 What's Next?

Now that you've configured your Apple Watch exactly the way you want it, it's nice to know your Apple Watch settings are automatically backed up to your iPhone. This is one less task for me to remember. Thank you, Apple!

There is a lot going on at any time on your watch. At times, I feel like I'm bombarded with too much information. The next chapter covers how to customize messages and alert notifications. I will also explain the various app and status icons.

Chapter 4

5. Notifications

In this chapter we discuss

Status Icons

Open the Notification Center

Turn App Notifications Off

Change Notification Delivery

Enable Haptic Notifications

Enable the Notification Indicator

Customize App Notifications

Adjust Alert Volume

High or Low Heart Rate Alerts

Troubleshooting Notifications

What's Next?

Once I started gathering all my notes on alerts, status icons, and notifications I realized there are so many they deserve their own chapter. The "Notification Center" is like an inbox for your Apple Watch. The Apple

S and various apps are continuously sending messages and alerts ...ie Notification Center. First, we will look at status icons.

5.1 Status Icons

Status icons communicate information about connections and app activity. Status icons appear in the center section of your watch face along the top edge of the screen. Notifications go to your Apple Watch or your iPhone, but not both. If your iPhone is locked or asleep, you'll get notifications on your Apple Watch.

A blue lock means your watch is locked.

A red dot displayed in the center of your watch face at the top of the screen indicates you have unread notifications. The status icon is configurable as outlined in the following section "Enable the Notification Indicator."

 A red X indicates the Apple Watch has lost connection to the cellular network.

Your Apple Watch isn't connected to your iPhone as indicated by a red iPhone symbol with a slash.

Green dots indicate a connection to a cellular network. The number of dots indicates signal strength.

A green lightning bolt indicates your watch is charging. A red lightning bolt means the battery level is low.

Water lock is active when a blue water drop icon is displayed, indicating your screen is locked. Turn the Digital Crown to turn off water lock.

A purple half-moon symbol means Do Not Disturb is active. The Do Not Disturb status icon on your watch face is a blue moon.

An orange airplane means Airplane Mode is active.

 The map symbol is displayed while using the Maps app.

 Orange masks indicate Theater Mode is active. Silent Mode is also on. The screen stays dark until you tap the screen or press a button.

 A green phone icon indicates a phone call is active.

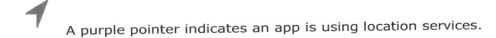 A purple pointer indicates an app is using location services.

 White bars on a red background indicate music is playing.

The icon with concentric circles with an arrow at the bottom represents AirPlay. AirPlay connects to Bluetooth devices like speakers or headsets.

 Tap the yellow walkie-talkie icon to talk to friends instantly.

The runner on a green background indicates a workout is in progress.

5.2 Open the Notification Center

Thanks to watchOS 5 and later you can open the Control or Notification Center from any screen.

1. On the **Apple Watch**, touch the top of the screen until a semi-transparent preview of the Notification Center appears, then swipe down.

2. Swipe to the right to confirm or delete the notification.

3. To remove all notifications at once, firmly press the screen and tap "Clear All."

5.3 Turn App Notifications Off

1. On the **Apple Watch**, touch the top of the watch face until you see the Notification Center, then swipe down.

2. Tap the notification, and swipe to the left.

3. Tap the more icon that looks like an ellipsis or 3 dots.

4. Select "Deliver Quietly" or "Turn off on Apple Watch."

To delete all notifications at once, firmly press the screen and tap "Clear All."

5.4 Change Notification Delivery

You decide how notifications are displayed. The options are "Deliver Quietly" or "Turn off on Apple Watch." Delivery Quietly sends notifications to the "Notification Center" without showing you the alert or delivering a sound or haptic touch. Quiet notifications from the Breathe app immediately go to the Notification Center.

WatchOS 5 introduced "grouping" settings for notifications. For example, you can group all "message" notifications or all "e-mail" notifications. Simply tap on the "Messages" stack to see all message notifications. This setting is found in the Watch app on your iPhone.

1. On the **iPhone**, open the Apple Watch app.

2. Tap "Notifications."

3. Swipe up and tap an app. Swipe up and tap "Notification Grouping," and then tap "By App".

In addition to changing app notification settings in the watch app on your iPhone, you can also change alerts for individual apps on your watch.

1. On the **Apple Watch**, touch the top of the watch face, then swipe down.

2. Swipe left on a notification, then tap "More" (the ellipsis icon).

3. Tap "Deliver Quietly" or "Turn off on Apple Watch."

4. To see or hear notifications again tap "Deliver Prominently."

Tip: When an annoying group chat is constantly sending notifications to your watch, turning on "Deliver Quietly" for that app is a simple way to quietly deliver only those alerts to notification center. Your other notifications will continue to alert you. Reverse the process to receive notifications from that app again.

5.5 Enable Haptic Notifications

Haptics also play a role in alerts. For example, the Map app gently vibrates to indicate an upcoming turn. This is a useful accessibility feature for deaf or hard of hearing drivers.

1. On your **iPhone**, open the Apple Watch app.

2. In the "Sounds & Haptics" section, tap the "Haptic Alerts" to toggle on or off. The switch is green when on and white when off.

Change the haptic alert strength to "Prominent" in this section.

5.6 Enable the Notification Indicator

A red dot displayed in the center of your watch face at the top of the screen indicates you have unread notifications.

1.   On the **iPhone**, open the Apple Watch app.

2.   Tap "Notifications."

3.   Enable "Notifications Indicator." When enabled a red dot at the top of your watch face indicates you have unread notifications.

5.7 Customize App Notifications

Some apps allow you to customize notification options. There is also a choice to "Mirror my iPhone" to use the same notification settings on your iPhone and Apple Watch. There are three settings for notifications.

● Allow Notifications
● Send to Notification Center
● Notifications Off

To set app notification options follow these steps.

1.   On the **iPhone**, open the Apple Watch app.

2.   Tap "Notifications."

3.   Swipe up and tap an app, and then select the option.

Mail Notifications

In addition to notifications for each of your e-mail accounts, you can set preview and other options in the Mail settings. For example, if you tap the "VIP" option, you will only get an alert when you receive an e-mail from someone you've marked as important.

1. Open the Apple Watch app on your **iPhone**.

2. Tap "My Watch," located in the left corner of the tab bar at the bottom of the screen.

3. Scroll down and tap "Mail."

4. Tap "Allow Notifications."

Set Mail VIPs

1. On your **iPhone**, open the **Mail** app.

2. In the section mailboxes, tap VIP.

3. Select a contact, then tap VIP Alerts, and toggle "Allow Notifications" on.

4. Open the Apple Watch app on your **iPhone**.

5. Tap "My Watch," located in the left corner of the tab bar at the bottom of the screen.

6. Swipe and tap Notifications.

7. Scroll and tap "Mail."

8. Tap "VIPs" and choose Sound or Haptic alerts.

Map Notifications

The gentle haptic (wrist tap) notifications are invaluable when navigating with Maps. Navigation "Turn Alerts" are configurable in the Apple Watch app. If you'd also like haptic alerts, enable those under Sounds & Haptics as shown earlier.

1. On your **iPhone**, open the Apple Watch app.

2. Tap "Notifications."

3. Swipe up and tap "Maps."

4. Tap the toggle switch for "Driving," "Driving with CarPlay," or "Walking." The switch is green when on and white when off.

Message Notifications

Message notifications are configurable for individual contacts. If you don't want to receive message notifications on your watch enable "Hide Alerts" for that contact.

1. On your **iPhone**, open a message from John.

2. At the top of the screen tap "Info."

3. Swipe up and tap "Hide Alerts" to enable hide alerts.

A "Do Not Disturb" icon will appear on the left side of the message indicating notifications are off. Repeat steps 1-3 to disable "Hide Alerts."

Troubleshooting Message Notifications

There are a few things to check when you are not receiving message notifications.

1. In the Apple Watch app on your **iPhone** check if the setting "Mirror My iPhone" is enabled. In the Watch app open "Notifications" and then tap "Messages."

2. On your **iPhone** disable "Allow Notifications" and force restart your iPhone. Enable "Allow Notifications." Try turning on "Badge App Icon" and "Show on Lock Screen."

3. Check if "Mute" or "Do Not Disturb" is enabled.

4. Unlock your watch screen.

5. Force restart your watch. Press the side button and Digital Crown for three seconds until the Apple logo appears.

6. Check connectivity. Swipe up on your **watch face** to open the Control Panel.

7. Check your settings for iMessage. iMessage allows you to send to an e-mail address if that contact has an Apple device. On your **iPhone** in "Settings" open "Messages." In the section "Send & Receive" verify your Apple ID and SMS phone number.

8. A basic test involves sending a test SMS message by typing in a phone number in the "To" section of the message.

Workout Reminders

The Apple Watch will automatically detect certain types of workouts like running or walking. To enable this feature use the Apple Watch app on your iPhone.

1. On your **iPhone**, open the Apple Watch app.

2. Tap "My Watch," located in the left corner of the tab bar along the bottom of the screen.

3. Tap the toggle switch for "Start Workout Reminder" and "End Workout Reminder." The switch is green when on and white when off.

Calendar Notifications

Calendar notifications are customizable, depending on the type of event and notification method. Notification methods are either "sound" or "haptic."

1. On your **iPhone**, open the Apple Watch app.

2. Swipe up and tap on "Calendar."

3. Scroll down and tap one of the options: Upcoming Events, Invitations, Invitee Responses, Shared Calendar Alerts.

5.8 Adjust Alert Volume

1. On your **Apple Watch**, press the Side Button.

2. Swipe and tap "Settings."

3. Scroll down and tap "Sounds & Haptics."

4. Move the slider bar to adjust volume.

5.9 High or Low Heart Rate Alerts

The Apple Watch has a new set of features that warn you if your heart rate is higher or lower than usual. Your watch compares data with your average heart rate to identify temporary changes. Check out the "Heart Rate" app in Chapter 6 for instructions on how to view your "Heart Rate Recovery."

1. On your **iPhone**, open the Apple Watch app.

2. Tap "Notifications."

3. Tap "High Heart Rate" or "Low Heart Rate" and set the threshold.

5.10 Troubleshooting Notifications

If you don't see notifications, check your paired iPhone is connected and the Apple Watch is not locked.

1. On your **Apple Watch**, press the Digital Crown to open the Home screen.

2. Swipe up from the bottom of the screen to open the Control Center.

3. In the top left corner, verify the companion iPhone status icon is green.

4. Ensure Wi-Fi is enabled.

5. Make sure "Do Not Disturb" is disabled.

5.11 What's Next?

Chapters 2 through 5 covered the logistics and configuration of the Apple Watch. Now it's time to look at the apps, and explore what the Apple Watch can do on a daily basis.

6. Watch Apps

In this chapter we discuss

Installing Apps on your Apple Watch
Alarms
Apple Pay & the Wallet App
Audiobooks
Books
Breathe
Calculator
Calendar
Camera Remote
Clock
Compass
Contacts
Cycle Tracing
Emergency SOS, Fall Detection, & Medical ID
Find People
The Heart Rate App
The Home App
Keynote
Mail

Chapter 6

Maps
Messages, Digital Touch, & Apple Pay
Music and the Now Playing App
The Noise App
Phone
Photos
Podcasts
Reminders
Remote Control
Siri
Siri Shortcuts
Stocks
Stopwatch
Timer
Voice Memos
Walkie-Talkie
Weather
Web Browser
What's Next?

There are two kinds of apps, Apple apps, and third-party apps. Not all iPhone apps will work on your Apple Watch. While you can install apps through the regular iPhone App Store, when browsing for new apps, it's a good idea to use the Apple Watch App Store to ensure compatibility.

If you've been searching for a watch app to no avail, chances are there is already an IFTTT applet that does what you need, as outlined in Chapter 7.

6.1 Install & Delete Apps on your Apple Watch

After watchOS 6, compatible iPhone apps are listed in the "App Store" in the Apple Watch app, or on your Apple Watch. watchOS 6 includes the Apple Watch app store. Shop and download apps from your Apple Watch - no iPhone needed!

The Apple Watch App Store

1. With watchOS 6 or later, open the **App Store** on your Apple Watch. Browse to select an app to download or purchase.

Figure 6.1   App Store on Apple Watch

2.   Your Apple Watch will prompt you to enter your Apple ID password.

Figure 6.2   Finish entering Text on iOS Device

3.   Enter your password using your iOS device, as shown below.

Figure 6.3   Apple Watch Keyboard

Search for Apps to Install

To find a new app in the "App Store" tap "Search." Use Dictation or Scribble to search. Chapter 3 has examples of common phrases for Dictating.

Remove Apps

I like to have a firm handle on what apps are on my Apple Watch or iPhone. Unused apps waste valuable storage space. Chapter 11 includes instructions to check storage space.

1. Open the **Apple Watch** app on your iPhone.

2. In the section "Installed on Apple Watch," tap the app you want to remove.

3. Ensure "Show App on Apple Watch" is not enabled. The slide bar should be white.

Tip: Apps are automatically removed from your Apple Watch when you delete the app from your iPhone.

Remove Apps from the Home Screen

watchOS 6 also allows you to delete some built-in apps like Breathe, Stopwatch, World Clock, Timer, Alarms, Walkie-Talkie, and Radio.

1. On your **Apple Watch** press the Digital Crown to open the Home Screen.

2. In Grid View, touch the app icon for a few seconds (also known as a long press) until the apps begin to wiggle. In List View,

swipe right to left on the app you want to delete and tap the Trash Can icon.

3.   In the top left corner of the icon tap the small "x" to delete the app.

Remove Apps Using iPhone Storage

The iPhone Storage screen provides a quick way to remove several apps. The "iPhone storage" list view lists all installed apps. The view includes the app size and the "last used date." I suspect it displays "Never Used" when you download a new version of an app because I know I use my YMCA app all the time, but it's usually marked "Never Used." I've learned to be careful when removing apps.

1.   On your **iPhone,** open Settings and tap "General."

2.   Scroll down and tap "iPhone Storage."

3.   Tap the app you want to remove, then tap "Delete App."

6.2 Alarms

It's pretty easy to add or delete an alarm on your Apple Watch. You can add the complication for Alarms to your watch face, or use the Alarms app. The Alarms app was redesigned with watchOS 6 to make it easier to create an alarm. An animated indicator circle spins around the watch face as you adjust the alarm time. As you spin the Digital Crown, haptics gently vibrates the Digital Crown to indicate changes in hours or minutes.

Add an Alarm

1. On your **Apple Watch** press the side button to open the Dock.

2. Swipe to scroll and tap the "Alarms" app.

3. Tap "Add alarm."

4. Turn the Digital Crown to adjust the alarm time.

5. Tap "Set."

6. Tap the new alarm to set options for repeat or to change the alarm name.

Turn Alarm Off or Snooze

On your **Apple Watch**, when the alarm sounds tap the side button to turn it off. If you press the Digital Crown, the alarm will snooze for 9 minutes.

Delete an Alarm

1. On your **Apple Watch**, tap the alarm.

2. Swipe to scroll down.

3. Tap Delete.

6.3 Apple Pay & the Wallet App

Apple Pay integrates with the Apple Wallet App. I probably went overboard with examples in this section, but it's not my fault you can use Apple Pay in so many ways!

First, we'll look at what's in your wallet. Next, I explain how to use your watch with Apple Pay and Siri in messages, at a store, or how to confirm a transaction in Safari on your Mac. There are five examples of adding third-party app cards and reservations (Fandango, Hilton, Marriott, Sephora, and Starbucks.) Next, we'll look at how to add any card, ticket, or pass that has a bar code to your wallet using the "Pass2U" app.

Funds for Apple Pay come from credit cards or Apple Pay Cash stored in the Apple "Wallet" app. The "Wallet" app houses this information:

- Hotel Reservations

- Credit Cards

- Membership Cards

- Airline Boarding Passes

- Movie Tickets

- Coupons

- Transit Cards

- Student IDs

- Tickets

Figure 6.4   The Apple Wallet App

There are several ways to use Apple Pay with your Apple Watch, as outlined in the detailed examples that follow.

- Ask Siri to send cash in a message.

- Confirm a Safari transaction with your watch.

- Pay a store merchant using your watch.

For example, at Subway, you click the side button on your watch twice to pay the merchant.

Ask Siri to Send Cash in a Message

Apple Pay integrates with SiriKit. On your Apple Watch ask Siri to "Pay Michael one dollar," and Siri does the rest.

Figure 6.5   Sending Cash in a Message with Apple Pay

Safari Apple Pay and Apple Watch

On Apple devices, you can also use Apple Pay in Safari. Start the transaction in the Safari web browser, and when prompted "confirm" the payment on your Apple Watch.

Figure 6.6   Confirm Safari Apple Pay Transaction

Pay a Merchant on Your Watch

To initiate an Apple Pay transaction, the merchant activates Apple Pay on their payment terminal. Next, you press the side button on your Apple Watch twice.

Tip: Apple Pay is unavailable if you turn off passcode.

1. Open the **Apple Watch** app on your iPhone.

2. Tap "My Watch," located in the left corner of the tab bar along the bottom of the screen.

3. Scroll down to "Passcode."

Add Cards and Passes to Apple Wallet

Third-party apps that support the Apple Wallet PassKit framework include a button to "Add to Apple Wallet," as shown below.

Figure 6.7   Add to Apple Wallet Logo

The instructions for adding third-party cards to the Wallet app vary depending on the particular third-party app, so I've provided a few examples below. The Marriott example includes adding both the Marriott Rewards card, as well as a particular hotel reservation.

- Fandango

- Hilton

- Marriott

- Sephora
- Starbucks

When you install a third-party app on your iPhone or Apple Watch, look for an option to add the app's "membership card" or "pass" to Apple Wallet. The following examples demonstrate the steps, although they vary slightly.

Starbucks: Launch the Starbucks app, select Manage, Details, and click "Add to Apple Wallet."

Hilton Honors: Launch the Hilton app, select Stays, Upcoming, and click "Add to Apple Wallet."

Marriott: Launch the Marriott app and select "My Account." Swipe up and tap "Add to Apple Wallet." To add a reservation, tap the menu icon. Your reservations are displayed. Tap the **confirmation number**, and then click "Add to Apple Wallet."

Sephora: Open the Sephora app and click on Beauty Insider. Click "Add to Apple Wallet."

Fandango: Open the Fandango app and go to "Account." Select "Purchases," swipe up and tap "Purchase Details." Click "Add to Apple Wallet."

Another option to add cards to your Wallet is to scan a QR code to add a card.

1. Open the "Wallet" app on your iPhone.

2. Tap the plus symbol to add a card, or swipe up and tap "Edit Passes."

3. Follow the on-screen instructions to add credit cards. For passes, tap "Find Apps for Wallet" or "Scan code."

Alternatively, with iOS 13 and later, use the Settings app on your iPhone.

1. Open the "Settings" app on your iPhone and tap "Wallet & Apple Pay."

2. Swipe up and tap "Add Card" or "Express Transit Card."

3. Follow the on-screen instructions to complete setup.

When scanning codes, the Apple Wallet app launches the camera and displays a square finder marquee to select a "QR code." The Apple PassKit framework supports 128 QR Codes. You can also add bar code tickets or passes with a third-party app like "Pass2U."

Add Bar Code Tickets with Pass2U

There are probably several third-party apps that create QR codes for your Apple Wallet, but I use "Pass2U." In the figure below, you can see a ticket for the Atlanta Symphony in my Apple Wallet. I scanned the bar code on the original ticket into the "Pass2U" app, added a logo photo, location, time, and seat.

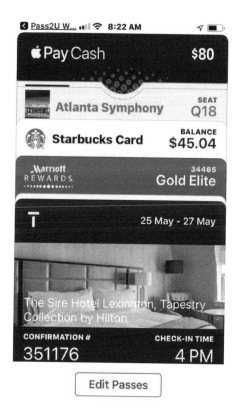

Figure 6.8   Symphony Ticket in Apple Wallet

After clicking "Add," the new ticket is shown in my Apple Wallet.

Figure 6.9   The Wallet App on Your Watch

Activate Credit Cards on Your Watch

Although you may have credit cards set up in Apple Pay, you must activate the card on your Apple Watch. Enter the corresponding card security code in your Apple Watch app on your iPhone to activate the card. Student IDs require the eAccounts and Duo Mobile apps.

Reorder Cards in the Wallet

To reorder cards touch the card in the Wallet app and drag it up or down to change the order. Drag a card to the top of the list to make it your default card.

Transit Cards

In Japan, the Tokyo transit Suica card works with Apple Pay. First, add Suica as your Express Transit Card. Next, hold your watch close to the ticket gate scanner. There is no need to wake or unlock your watch.

In Beijing and Shanghai, you can also use transit cards; however, ensure your region is China in "Settings" on your watch and iPhone, as outlined in Chapter 3.

Alternatively, with iOS 13 and later, use the Settings app on your iPhone.

1. Open the "Settings" app on your **iPhone**.

2. Swipe up and tap "Add Card" or "Express Transit Card."

3. Follow the on-screen instructions to complete setup.

Status of the Apple Pay System

Occasionally the Apple Pay system is down for maintenance. You can check the Apple Pay system status at https://www.apple.com/support/systemstatus/.

6.4 Audiobooks

watchOS 6 introduced the Audiobooks app to the Apple Watch. You can choose to have titles in your "Reading Now" or "Want to Read" list automatically synced with your Apple Watch, as shown below.

1. On your **iPhone**, open the Apple Watch app.

2. Swipe up and tap "Audiobooks."

3. Select synchronization options or add an Audiobook from your library.

You can purchase books on your iPhone in either the Apple Watch app or the Books app in the Audiobooks store. When you switch between your Apple Watch and the Books app on your Mac, iPhone, or iPad, the app remembers where you left off and picks up reading at that location. The next topic discusses the Books app.

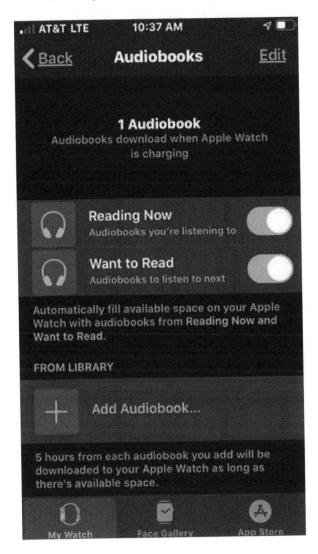

Figure 6.10   Audiobooks App Settings

6.5 Books

The Book app was the first app I learned to use on my iPhone and remains one of my favorite apps to this day. Within the app, you can purchase books and audiobooks from the Apple Book Store, or read PDFs or unlocked ePUBs. I wanted to include some basic information on the Books app here, in case you're using it in combination with your Audiobooks app on your Apple Watch.

Buy Books

When you open the Books app on your iPhone or iPad, the tab bar along the bottom has options for Reading Now, Library, the Book Store, Audiobooks, or Search. Tap Search or Audiobooks to buy Audiobooks. Tap Search or Book Store to purchase eBooks.

Organize Books in Collections

A collection is like a bookcase. Open your Library and in the top right corner, tap "New Collection." Move books to your collection. Rearrange books in your collection by selecting them and dragging them to a new location.

6.6 Breathe

Intellectually, I understand the concept of Mindfulness and that it reduces stress. In real life, I struggle to practice Mindfulness. I often ignore alerts from my Breathe app, but honestly, it's not that hard to take seven slow breaths. I hate to admit it, but I find I do feel better at the end of the day, so maybe the medical experts are right. I like the app tapping my wrist as I breathe in.

6.7 Calculator

With watchOS 6, the Apple Watch finally has a native Calculator app. Not to be outdone by competitors, the new Calculator app includes a Tip button with a "People" setting so you can easily split the bill with friends. As you spin the Digital Crown, haptics gently vibrates the Digital Crown to indicate incremental changes.

Figure 6.11   The Calculator App

6.8 Calendar

The Apple Calendar app is the simplest way to display your schedule on your Apple device. Tap the Calendar complication (date) on your watch face to open the Calendar app at any time, or open the Calendar app with the side button. If you enable Family Sharing for iCloud, it creates a shared family calendar. In this section, we'll look at these topics.

1.   On your **Apple Watch** open the calendar app.

2.   Firmly press the screen to see the options "Up Next," "List," or "Today" to change the calendar view.

3.   Tap to select an event, firmly press the screen to see the option for "Directions."

Display Calendar Month View

1.   On your **Apple Watch** open the calendar app.

2.   Tap the top left corner of the screen to change views. Swipe to scroll through days.

Add a Calendar Event

Use the calendar app on your iPhone to add an event to your calendar.

If you've enabled "handoff," you can quickly switch to the calendar app on your iPhone. Unlock your iPhone and tap the banner, along the bottom of the screen, to open the calendar app on your iPhone. Enable handoff in the Apple Watch app in the "General" settings screen, as shown in Chapter 3.

Customize Calendar Notifications

Calendar notifications are customizable depending on the type of event, as well as the notification method: "sound" or "haptic." Chapter 5 has details on calendar notifications.

1. On your **iPhone,** open the Apple Watch app.

2. Swipe up and tap on Calendar.

3. Scroll down and tap one of the notification options: Upcoming Events, Invitations, Invitee Responses, or Shared Calendar Alerts.

Integration with Third-Party Calendar Apps

There are several integration options for third-party calendar accounts.

- Use a third-party app like Tiny Calendar.

- Add your other calendar account to your iPhone calendar app, as shown below.

- Setup the other calendar app to send alerts to your iPhone. Every time you create an appointment set a reminder.

Add Accounts to Apple Calendar on Your iPhone

1. On your **iPhone**, go to "Settings."

2. Scroll down to "Passwords & Accounts."

3. In the "Accounts" section, tap "Add Account."

4. Select Google and follow the login prompts. If you have trouble connecting your Google account, log in to your Google account from a web browser, and follow the prompts to set up an App password.

Add Accounts to Apple Calendar on Your Mac

You can also add a Google calendar to your Mac calendar, and then it will be available to your Apple Watch.

1.   On your **Mac**, launch your calendar.

2.   On the "Calendar" menu, select "Preferences."

3.   On the "Accounts" tab, click the plus symbol in the bottom left corner of the window to add your Google account.

Calendar Sync Issues

When your contacts or calendar are not properly syncing, try a reset.

1.   On the **iPhone**, open the Apple Watch app.

2.   Tap "My Watch," located in the left corner of the tab bar at the bottom of the screen.

3.   Tap "General" and then tap "Reset."

4.   Tap "Reset Sync Data."

6.9 Camera Remote

You're probably thinking, "the Apple Watch doesn't have a camera," and that's true. However, the Apple Watch makes a great remote control. In addition to Apple's "Camera Remote" app, third-party apps like ProCamera, Hydra, and Camera Plus enhance camera remote control features.

If you don't see the Camera Remote app on your Apple Watch, check Content & Privacy Restrictions, as shown below.

Screen Time: Content & Privacy Restrictions

1.   On the **iPhone**, open the Settings app.

2.   Swipe up and tap "Screen Time."

3.   Swipe up and tap "Content & Privacy Restrictions."

4.   Tap "Allowed Apps" and enable "Camera."

Camera Remote and Timer

Position your iPhone to take a photo, then use the "Camera Remote" app on your Apple Watch to view a preview and take a photo. Note that your Apple Watch must be within 33 feet or 10 meters of your iPhone.

1.   On your **Apple Watch** open the "Camera Remote" app.

2.   Position your iPhone to frame the shot, using your Apple Watch as a viewfinder.

3.   Tap the "Shutter" button.

6.10 Clock

The Clock app on your iPhone has an option for "World Clock," where you create "time zones." Each time zone you create is available as a separate complication for your watch face.

watchOS 6 introduced "Speak Time" and "Taptic Time." Taptic Time taps your wrist at the hour or half-hour. Taptic Time and Speak Time options are configured in the Settings app on your Apple Watch, in Sounds & Haptics. When Speak Time is enabled, Siri will announce the time when you tap the screen with two fingers.

Figure 6.12   Taptic Time

The Apple Watch app on your iPhone also has the watchOS 6 Taptic Time and Speak Time settings. Open the Apple Watch app on your iPhone and swipe up. Tap "Clock." In the following example, the Taptic Time settings have choices for Digits, Terse, or Morse code.

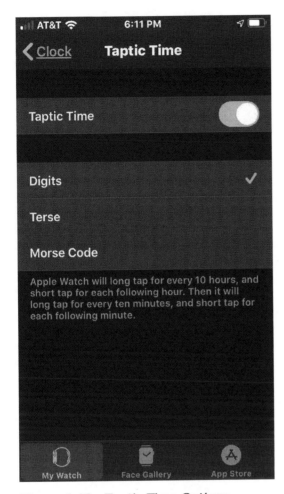

Figure 6.13   Taptic Time Options

With watchOS 6, your Apple Watch also has settings to Chime the Hour or Speak the Time, as shown below.

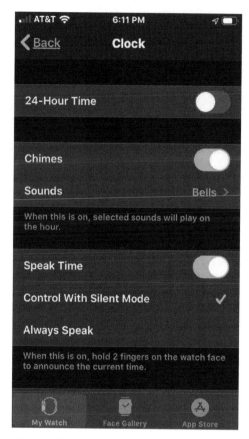

Figure 6.14   Clock Options

Configure the World Clock Time Zones

1. On your **iPhone**, open the "Clock" app.

2. Tap "World Clock" located in the left corner of the tab bar at the bottom of the screen.

3. Add Mumbai and New York locations.

Figure 6.15   World Clock

Add the World Clock Complication

1.   On your **iPhone**, open the "Watch" app.

2.   Tap a watch face, and then swipe to view complications.

3.   Select a World Clock complication.

Figure 6.16   Time Zones

Monogram

The clock monogram is up to 5 characters. The monogram displays in the center of your watch face.

1.   On your **iPhone,** open the Apple Watch app.

2.   Scroll down and tap "Clock."

3.   Tap "Monogram" and choose up to 5 letters.

6.11 The Compass App

The Series 5 Magnetometer relies on a magnetoresistive permalloy sensor to detect magnetic north. Apple Warns the Milanese Loop, Modern Buckle, and Leather Loop watch bands with magnetic clasps may cause magnetic interference. The updated Maps app can now show the direction you're facing. Swipe up to see additional options, or use a Firm Press on the screen to set your bearing. The new Compass app displays elevation, latitude, longitude, and incline.

Figure 6.17   The Compass App

6.12 The iPhone Contacts App*

The Contacts  app on your iPhone does more than store your contact information. It is the central hub for communication. When you select a contact, you can initiate a message, FaceTime call, or FaceTime chat. You can also send mail, or send money with Apple Pay, or share your location.

Tip: The Search dialog in a list may not be displayed until you scroll to the top of the list, and then swipe down.

Your Contact Card

Siri will customize your experience by using your Contact Card, as well as related Contact names, as shown below. iOS 13 added new relationship types. When you open the Contacts app on your iPhone, your contact card is at the top of the list in the left sidebar.

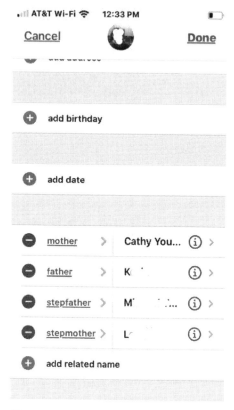

Figure 6.18   Add Related Name

Animoji

With Apple's Animoji app, on some iPhone models with iOS 13, you can create Animoji. After you send Animoji's on your iPhone in the

Messages app, they are then available in the Messages app on your Apple Watch in "Recents."

Open the Contacts app on your iPhone and tap the "Animoji" app icon in the **App Drawer**. The App Drawer is below the text area in the Messages app.

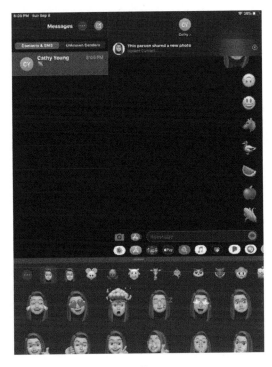

Figure 6.19   Animoji

Tap the "More" icon in the top left corner of the tray to create an Animoji. To edit an existing Animoji, tap the Animoji, and tap More, and then tap "Edit." You can also create Animoji for yourself or others in the Contacts app on your iPhone by editing the photo.

Enable Emergency Bypass

To allow emergency messages for a particular contact, open the Contact in the Contacts app on your iPad or iPhone. Tap "Edit" and then tap "Ring Tone" or "Text Tone." Tap "Turn on Emergency Bypass."

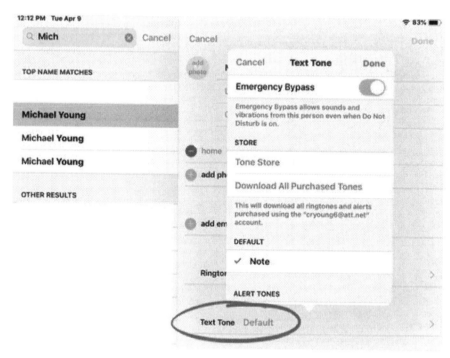

Figure 6.20   Contact Emergency Bypass

6.13 Cycle Tracking

Apple added a new Cycle Tracking app in watchOS 6, and also included an Apple Watch complication. Before using the app for the first time on you watch, you have to setup Cycle Tracking in the Health App on your iPhone.

1. Open the Health app on your iPhone.

2. In the bottom right corner, tap "Search."

3. Swipe up and tap "Cycle Tracking" and tap the "Getting Started" button.

Women can log information and symptoms related to their menstrual cycles such as nausea, mood, hot flashes, fatigue, trouble sleeping, spotting, and more. The app also identifies irregularities and is an aid in fertility tracking.

Log Data

1. On your iPhone, open the Health app.

2. In the bottom right corner of the screen, tap "Search" and swipe up, then tap "Cycle Tracking."

3. In the top right corner of the screen, tap "Add Period." To log other data, tap the metric in the "Cycle Log" section.

4. To enable predictions and choose what to include in the "Cycle Log," tap "Options."

6.14 Emergency SOS, Fall Detection, & Medical ID

Medical ID and SOS information are displayed on your Apple Watch screen when someone presses the side button for three seconds. watchOS 6 includes International SOS Emergency Services.

Apple Watch Series 5 uses the accelerometer and gyroscope to detect a significant, hard fall. When your watch detects a hard fall, it taps you on the wrist, sounds an alarm, and displays an alert. You can choose to contact emergency services or dismiss the alert by tapping, "I fell, but I'm OK," or by scrolling down and tapping, "I did not fall."

Figure 6.21   The Hard Fall Alert

Dr. Sumbul Desai says falls are one of the most common reasons to go to the ER across all age groups, which means we all can benefit from fall detection.

Configure Medical ID in the Health App

1. On your **iPhone,** open the "Health" app.

2. In watchOS 6 or later, in the top right corner, tap the "Account" icon that looks like a person.

3. Tap "Medical ID" and enter your information.

Configure Emergency SOS

1. On your **iPhone,** open the Apple Watch App.

2. Tap "Emergency SOS."

3. Enter your information.

View Medical ID or Call Emergency Services

When anyone holds the side button on your watch for 3 seconds, your Apple Watch will call Emergency Services. The Apple Watch counts down with an alarm, and a slider prompts if you want to end the call. Also, this option automatically detects if you take a hard fall. If you don't respond, it will tap your wrist, sound an alarm, and then call emergency services.

1. On your **Apple Watch** press and hold the side button until the screen opens.

2. Tap Medical ID or Emergency SOS.

Enable Emergency SOS

1. Open the **Apple Watch** app on your **iPhone**.

2. Tap "My Watch," located in the left corner of the tab bar at the bottom of the screen.

3. Scroll down to "Emergency SOS."

4. Touch the "Emergency SOS" slider. Continue holding the slider as you move it to enabled. The slider is green when enabled and white when disabled.

6.15 Find People

Introduced with watchOS 6, the "Find People" app is similar to the new "Find My" app released with iOS 13. The apps locate people based on their Apple device location using Bluetooth, even when cellular and Wi-Fi is off. With iOS 13, Macs occasionally send a Bluetooth signal and create a mesh network of Apple devices. The app also integrates with Siri. In the following example, after Siri locates a friend, you can swipe up to see Directions and other Info.

Figure 6.22   Find People

The app complication is one of the more advanced in terms of features. It shows where your friends are with a timestamp. A great security feature for teenagers, it's also handy when you're at a theme park, trying to coordinate rides or meals.

Say, "Hey Siri. Find Michael."

Share Your Location with a Friend

To add friends to the list, add them to the "Find My" app on your iPhone.

1. Open the "Find My" app on your iPhone.

2. Tap "Share My Location" to invite friends.

3. Tap "Send."

Find a Friend

To find a friend on your Apple Watch use the "Find People" app. If you don't see the name of your friend, follow the steps above to share your location.

1. On your **Apple Watch** press the "Digital Crown" to open the Dock. If you don't see the "Find People" app, follow the instructions for adding apps to the Dock in Chapter 2.

2. Tap the "Find People" app.

3. Tap the name of your friend. The Display shows the time, location, and map of your friend's last known location.

Notifications When a Friend Arrives or Leaves

Open the "Find My" app on your iPhone. Select a friend then swipe up on "Notifications" and tap "Add." Tap "Notify Me" and follow the prompts. To receive a notification when your friend is close to your Current Location, drag the circle to expand the radius. To add a new location on a map, tap "Add Location." Touch and swipe on the map to find your location, then **tap and hold** to drop a pin and set that location.

Which Device Determines Your Location?

Usually, we have our iPhones with us when we travel, but there are occasions when you only have your Apple Watch. Your location information will switch to your Apple Watch automatically if you "send" your location to a friend in Messages. Another option is to change which device is used to determine your current location. You can also use Find My Friends on iCloud.com to set the default device used to identify your location for friends.

6.16 The Heart Rate App

The Heart Rate app displays your current, resting, and walking average heart rate. When you open the Heart Rate app on your watch, it measures your heart rate every five seconds. To measure your heart rate every second, touch your finger to the Digital Crown. When you lift your finger, the Heart Rate app goes back to measuring your heart rate every five seconds.

1. On your **Apple Watch**, press the Side Button.

2. Scroll and tap the "Heart Rate" app.

3. Swipe or turn the Digital Crown to see your "Resting Rate" and your "Walking Average" heart rate.

Heart Rate Recovery

The Heart Rate app also records your Heart Rate Recovery after a workout. Heart Rate Recovery in watchOS 4 and later measures your heart rate when you end a workout and compares it to your heart rate two minutes later. So for instance, depending on your age, a heart rate recovery over 60 would be considered very good. Search the internet for the latest information on heart rate recovery and see where you stand. There is scientific evidence that suggests a low heart rate recovery indicates heart problems.

1.   After a workout, on your **Apple Watch** press the side button.

2.   Swipe and tap "Heart Rate" to open the Heart Rate app.

3.   Swipe up to view your "Recovery Rate."

View Heart Rate Data

The Health Data tab is also where you can view data from the "Heart Rate" app.

1.   On your **iPhone**, open the "Health" app.

2.   In the bottom tab bar tap "Health Data."

3.   Swipe up and tap "Heart."

4.   Tap the arrows at the top of the screen to move between days. Tap again to change to the hour, day, week, month, or year view. Tap anywhere on the graph to view the day, time, minimum, and maximum information.

6.17 The Home App

The Apple "Home" app is a convenient way to control your smart home devices. With iOS 13, Siri Shortcuts are available for the Home app. Rooms and devices set as "Favorites" automatically appear in the Apple Watch "Home" app. In this section, we'll look at these topics.

- Home Automation

- Apple HomeKit Automation Platform

- Configure your iPad as a Home Hub

- Invite People to Join Your Home

- Configure Rooms and Devices

Because I think home automation is wonderful, I wanted to include a few examples of what home automation can do. Some of these examples use IFTTT and other third-party apps in addition to the Home app. At this point, I wanted to mention some possibilities. If you're interested in learning more, Chapter 7 includes additional information on setting up IFTTT and smart home apps.

- Alert When Doors or Cabinets are Opened

- Arrive Home

- Calendars

- Combine Motion, Lights, and Sound

- Deliveries & Visitors

- Adjust Shades When Temperature Changes

- Close the Garage Door When Severe Weather is Forecast

- Fire Alarm

- Leave Home (or Sleep)

- Refrigerator or Freezer Temperature Change

- Reminder to Buy a Birthday Gift

- Schedule Appliances for Off-Peak Times

- Shopping List

- Setup Siri Shortcuts for Home Automations in the Apple Home app. Siri Shortcuts are available in the Home app with iOS 13 and later.

- Sports

- Surveillance

- Timer

- Traffic Commute

- Travel

- Turn on Christmas Lights

- Wake

- Weather

Configure Rooms and Devices for Apple Watch

1. Open the "Home" app on your **tablet**, **smartphone**, or **MAC**.

2. Double click, or firmly press, on a room. Click on "Settings."

3. Ensure the toggle "Include in Favorites" is turned on.

4.   Open the "Home" app on your **Apple Watch** and swipe to control rooms and devices.

Home Automation

Smart home automation is composed of connected devices, skills, and cloud services. This automation involves more than mere devices in your home since smart home devices interact with the IoT world beyond your home. There are services available today that require only e-mail or text messaging to provide you the exact information you request when you request it.

This is an illustration of this technology: You step off the plane and receive an e-mail with a map of your location because you set up an IFTTT applet to send an e-mail with a map, when you entered the location of Maui, Hawaii. This illustration uses Geofencing and your Apple device.

Combining smart devices has the most potential to add value to your smart automation lineup. The ability to combine multiple connected things is starting to appear in virtual assistants and mobile apps.

A few smart home categories include these topics:

- Lighting, Electrical, HVAC and Plumbing
- Security
- Outdoor: Garage, Lawn and Garden
- Home Entertainment
- Smart Speakers and Virtual assistants
- Window Coverings
- Smart Vacuums
- Cooking
- Printing

Apple HomeKit Automation Platform

Apple's HomeKit automation platform works with Philips Hue, Honeywell, August, First Alert, Lutron, Logitech, and others. Look for this logo to find HomeKit compatible devices.

Figure 6.23   Works with Apple HomeKit

Invite People to Join Your Home

Apple can identify when everyone in the family has left home if you add members to your home in the mobile app.

1. Start the Apple Home app.

2. Select your home.

3. Invite people to join your home account.

Automation

To create a new Apple HomeKit automation for when people leave, choose the action **everyone leaves**.

Configure Rooms and Devices

1.   Open the "Home" app on your **tablet**, **smartphone**, or **Mac**.

2.   Double-click a room. Click on "Settings."

3.   Ensure the toggle "Include in Favorites" is turned on.

4.   Open the "Home" app on your **Apple Device**, and swipe to control rooms and devices.

6.18 Keynote

Keynote presentations are easily controlled with your Apple Watch, although there are a few settings that will ensure things work smoothly.

1.   On your **Apple Watch**, press the side button to open the Dock.

2.   Tap "Settings."

3.   Tap "General," then tap "Wake Screen."

4.   Turn on "Wake Screen on Wrist Raise."

5.   Under "Resume To," select "Previous Activity."

6.19 Mail

In addition to reading mail, you can reply, delete, flag, or mark a message unread on your Apple Watch. iOS 13 has the ability to block a sender, and also added a Format Bar.

Read and Reply to an e-mail

1. On your **Apple Watch** press the Digital Crown.

2. Swipe and tap "Mail."

3. Swipe to scroll, or turn the Digital Crown.

4. Tap to read the message.

5. Swipe up and tap "Reply."

To see additional options like delete, **firmly press** the screen while the message is displayed.

Delete an E-mail

To delete an e-mail in your inbox on your Apple Watch, tap and swipe left.

Set Mail Options

In addition to notifications for each of your e-mail accounts, you can set preview and other options in the mail settings. For example, the "VIP" option ensures you are alerted only when you receive an e-mail from someone you've marked as important.

1. Open the **Apple Watch** app on your iPhone.

2. Tap "My Watch," located in the left corner of the tab bar at the bottom of the screen.

3. Scroll down and tap "Mail."

4.   Tap "Allow Notifications."

Search the iPhone Mail Inbox

The Search dialog in the list of messages may not be displayed until you scroll to the top of the list, and then swipe down.

Mail Settings - Inboxes on your iPhone*

1.   On your **iPhone,** open the "Apple Watch" app.

2.   Swipe and tap "Mail."

3.   In the section "Mail Settings," tap "Include Mail."

4.   Tap the accounts you want to include.

Figure 6.24   Select Mail Accounts

*Mute an e-mail Conversation on your iPhone**

Occasionally you may want to "Mute" an e-mail conversation on your iPhone. This setting is especially useful to avoid unnecessary e-mails popping up on your Apple Watch.

1. On your **iPhone**, open the **Mail** app.

2. In your Inbox, touch and hold the e-Mail.

3. In the pop-up menu, swipe up and tap "Mute."

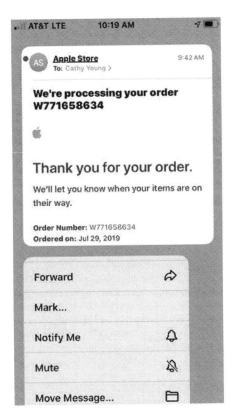

Figure 6.25   Mute an e-mail Conversation

*Format Bar on iPhone**

With iOS 13 there are new format options available in the Mail app on your iPhone. The Format Bar appears along the top of the keyboard, as shown in the next figure. The format options include:

- Font Style

- Size

- Color

- Alignment

- Indenting/Outdenting

- Numbered and Bulleted Lists

- Scan

- Insert Photo/Video

- Attachments

*Flag Style on iPhone**

Use the Apple Watch app to set the style for mail flags.

1. Open the Apple Watch app on your **iPhone**.

2. Tap "My Watch," located in the left corner of the tab bar at the bottom of the screen.

3. Scroll down and tap "Mail."

4. Tap "Custom."

5. Swipe down and select the "Flag Style" color or shape.

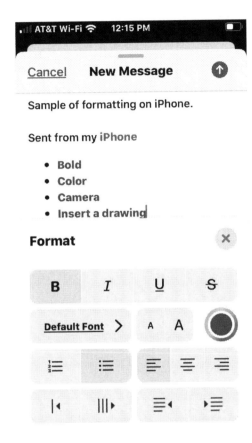

Figure 6.26   Format Bar

Forward, Mark, Notify Me, Move, or Delete an e-Mail on your iPhone*

The are several other mail actions available from the pop-up menu.

1. On your **iPhone**, open the **Mail** app.

2. In your Inbox, touch and hold the e-Mail.

3. In the pop-up menu, swipe up and tap Forward, Mark, Notify Me, Move, or Trash.

Set VIPs on your iPhone*

1. On your **iPhone**, open the **Mail** app.

2. In the section "mailboxes," tap VIP.

3. Select a contact, then tap "VIP Alerts." Toggle "Allow Notifications" on.

4. Open the **Apple Watch** app on your **iPhone**.

5. Tap "My Watch," located in the left corner of the tab bar at the bottom of the screen.

6. Swipe and tap "Notifications."

7. Scroll and tap "Mail."

8. Tap "VIPs" and choose Sound or Haptic alerts.

6.20 Maps

Have you wondered what the Map application can do? If you're not familiar with the Maps app, you're in for a surprise. The Apple

Maps app links to many of the other Apple iOS apps, and I use this cross-platform app every day. A few of my favorite features follow.

- Show your location on the map.

- Search for a business, then tap to create or update a contact card.

- Search for a business and see the location on a map.

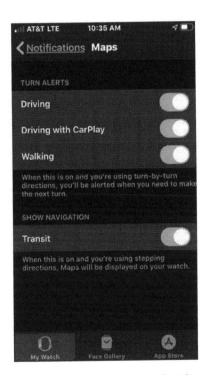

Figure 6.27   Show Navigation in Maps

Siri will also prompt you with step by step directions when navigating. Your Apple Watch can display maps, the location of friends in the "Find Friends" app, and provide navigation directions. For example, the app indicates an upcoming turn by gently vibrating your watch. With iOS 13 and watchOS 6, "Smart Guidance" in the Show Navigation screen enables visual queues with stepping directions. The updated Maps app uses the Magnetometer to show the direction you're facing.

Tip: Recent locations are shown when you swipe up on your watch face.

Navigation

On your **Apple Watch**, press the side button, swipe, and tap "Maps." Tap "Location" and then turn the Digital Crown to zoom in and out.

Map Notifications

Navigation "Turn Alerts" are configurable in the Apple Watch app.

1. On your **iPhone**, open the Apple Watch app.

2. Tap "Notifications."

3. Swipe up and tap "Maps."

4. Tap the toggle switch for "Driving," "Driving with CarPlay," or "Walking." A switch is green when on and white when off.

Search

When searching on your Apple Watch, you can dictate, scribble, search contacts, or use one of the "Nearby" choices.

- Restaurants

- Fast Food

- Gas Stations

- Coffee

- Groceries

- Hotels

- Bars

- Centers

watchOS 6 introduced detailed 3D imagery with "Look Around," as well as Siri Suggestions and "Favorites & Collections."

Figure 6.28   Maps App ETA

Collections

Create a new Collection in the Maps app on your iPhone or iPad. Swipe up from the middle of the screen and open the Collection. In the bottom right corner of the screen, tap the plus symbol to add a location. While searching for a location, you can tap the "Add" plus symbol to add the location to a collection.

Tap the send icon to share your collection with a friend.

To remove a location from a collection, open the Collection and swipe up. Tap "Edit" and select the locations to delete.

Find an Address for a Contact

To find a contact address, open a map on your Apple Watch, firmly press the display, tap "Search Here," tap Contacts, turn the Digital Crown to scroll, then tap the contact. If the contact information includes an address, you can select walking or driving directions.

'Search Here' and 'Transit Map'

1. On your **Apple Watch**, press the Side Button to open the Dock.

2. Tap the 'Maps' app.

3. Select a map location.

4. Firmly press the screen.

5. Select "Transmit Map" or "Search Here." The search options include dictation, scribble, and contacts.

6. When searching, swipe up to select nearby options such as food, drinks, shopping, travel, services, fun, health, or transport.

7. For directions to a particular location, tap the location, then scroll down and choose walking, driving, or bus.

8. Turn the Digital Crown to pan or zoom on the map. To add a pin, tap the map and hold till you see a pin, then release. **Tap the pin to see the address information.**

Parked Car

Rather than dig my iPhone out of my purse to find my parked car, I prefer to use my Apple Watch.

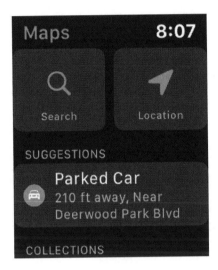

Figure 6.29   Suggestions, Parked Car

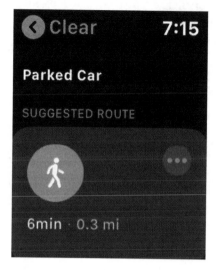

Figure 6.30   Suggested Route to Parked Car

Maps on iPhone*

In case you handoff the Maps app from your Apple Watch to your iPhone, I wanted to mention a few of the new iOS 13 features available in the Maps app. The high-resolution navigation screen in Maps is now more realistic, and when navigating to a destination, there is an option to "Share ETA."

When using the Messages app and you receive a message with an Airline Flight Number, tapping the message bubble will open an option to "Preview Flight" information, as shown below.

Figure 6.31   Flight Status

6.21 Messages, Digital Touch, & Apple Pay

The Apple messaging app supports dictating traditional text messages, audio clips, tap backs (handy phrases), sending money with Apple pay, scribble, sharing a map of your location, and emoticons. WatchOS 6 also added Animoji and Memoji stickers.

Digital Touch is a fun way to include animation or sketches in your messages. Digital touch is only available if the recipient also has an Apple device.

Create a Message

1. Press the Side Button on your **Apple Watch** to open the Dock.

2. Swipe the screen with your finger, or turn the Digital Crown.

3. Tap on the "Messages" app.

4. Firmly press the screen and tap "New Message."

5. Choose a contact, enter a phone number, or dictate a phone number.

6. Touch anywhere on the screen to send the message.

Read a Message

Turn the Digital Crown to scroll through a message. To quickly return to the first message, tap your friend's name at the top of the screen. Turn the Digital Crown to see previous messages from that contact. Firmly press the screen to see options.

- Reply
- Details
- Send Location
- Choose Language

To delete a message, select the message in your inbox and swipe left. Click on the trash can symbol.

Tip: The Search dialog in the list of messages may not be displayed until you scroll to the top of the list, and then swipe down.

Reply to a Message

Turn the Digital Crown to scroll to the bottom of the message, then tap one of the icons to reply. Tap the microphone to dictate your response. Chapter 3 has examples of common phrases for Dictating.

Scroll past the icons to the end to respond with a "Tap Back." Touch "Tap Back" and choose one of the responses.

Emojis are tiny symbols. In addition to emojis, you can reply with a sticker. Stickers include handwritten responses. Tap the emoji icon, swipe, and tap "Stickers."

Animoji

On some iPhone models with iOS 13, you can create Animoji. After you send Animoji's on your iPhone in the Messages app, they are then available in the Messages app on your Apple Watch in "Recents."

Open the Messages app on your iPhone and tap the "Animoji" app icon in the **App Drawer**. The App Drawer is below the text area in the Messages app. In the example below, the Animoji app is to the right of the App Store.

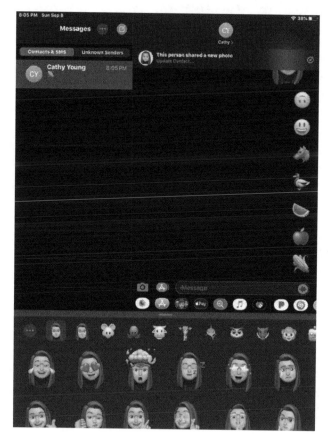

Figure 6.32   Animoji

Tap the "More" ⬤⬤⬤ icon in the top left corner of the tray to create an Animoji. To edit an existing Animoji, tap the Animoji, and tap More, and then tap "Edit." You can also create Animoji for yourself or others in the Contacts app on your iPhone by editing the photo.

Scribble

Scribble a quick note if the built-in responses aren't appropriate. For example, if you're in a meeting, and your daughter asks you to meet for lunch; you can reply "OK," and then scribble a time like "12." Tap "Scribble" and then write your message. As you write, turn the Digital Crown to see predictive text options, then tap one to choose it. Tap "Send" to send the message.

Dictate

Tap the microphone icon , dictate your message, then tap "Done." You can also verbally add punctuation. For example, "Did it arrive question mark." Chapter 3 has examples of common phrases for Dictating.

Create an Audio Clip

To change a text message to an audio clip, follow these steps.

1.   Open the Apple Watch app on your **iPhone** and tap "My Watch."

2.   Swipe and tap on "Messages."

3.   Tap "Dictated Messages," then tap Transcript or Audio.

The Default Type of Audio Response

1. Open the **Apple Watch** app on your iPhone. Tap "My Watch," located in the left corner of the tab bar at the bottom of the screen.

2. Tap "Messages," and then tap "Dictated Messages Transcript."

3. Choose from "Transcript," "Audio," or "Transcript or Audio."

View a Message Timestamp

To view the message timestamp swipe left on the message.

Options

Force touch the screen to view the message options. The "Details" option displays contact information. The "Details" has choices to phone, text, or e-mail the contact.

- Reply
- Details
- Send Location
- Choose Language

Smart Replies

Apple provides a customizable list of handy phrases, sometimes referred to as "tap backs."

1. Open the Apple Watch app on your **iPhone** and tap My Watch.

2. Swipe up, tap "Messages," then tap "Default Replies." Tap "Add Reply."

3. To reorder the default replies, tap "Edit." To reorder replies, drag the icon on the right that looks like three horizontal bars.

4. To delete a smart reply, touch, and swipe to the left. You can also tap the red minus symbol.

Message Alerts

Message alerts can be set to repeat never, once, twice, three times, five times, or even ten times.

Use Apple Pay to Send & Receive $

With Apple Pay, you can send or receive money. Apple Pay is available on your Apple Watch if you've enabled "Apple Pay Cash" in your Apple Wallet app on your iPhone. If you've added "cash" to your account, you can send cash to friends or family in a message.

1. On your **Apple Watch**, press the Digital Crown.

2. Swipe and tap "Messages."

3. Start a new conversation or continue an existing conversation.

4. Tap the icon for Apple Pay.

5. Select an amount to send using the plus or minus symbol, or turn the Digital Crown.

6. Tap "Pay."

7. Double-click the side button to send.

Digital Touch

When you send friends a digital touch message, they also receive a haptic (wrist tap) response. Digital Touch messages are a new take on the idea of reaching out and touching someone.

1. On your **Apple Watch**, press the Digital Crown.

2. Swipe and then tap "Messages."

3. Start a new conversation or continue an existing conversation.

4. Tap the icon for Digital Touch.

To Show Emotion Try These Digital Touch Options.

Send a Kiss: Tap two fingers on the screen.

Send your Heartbeat: Touch two fingers to the screen until you see and feel your heartbeat.

Break a Heart: Touch two fingers to the screen until you see and feel your heartbeat, then drag down.

Show anger: Touch and hold one finger on the display till you see a flame.

Sketch: Draw on the screen.

6.22 Music and the Now Playing App

With the Apple Music app, you can listen to songs, albums, playlists, or artists. The Music app is redesigned with iOS 13 and watchOS 6. There are two options for playing music: either stream music over a cellular network or download music to your watch.

When you listen to audio on our iPhone, the Now Playing app automatically opens on your Apple Watch. This feature can be disabled in the Settings app on your Apple Watch under the General category. Tap "Wake Screen" and then tap the toggle to disable "Auto-Launch Audio Apps."

In watchOS 6, the Play/Pause button includes a progress circle, and the AirPlay button connects to headphones or speakers quickly. The controls for the Music app are similar to the Podcast controls.

Play Music

Both the "Music" app and the "Now Playing" apps allow you to control music from your Apple Watch. In the "Now Playing" app, you can control music on your Apple Watch, as well as music playing on your iPhone.

1. On your **Apple Watch**, press the Digital Crown.

2. Swipe and tap "Music."

3. Swipe up, or turn the Digital Crown.

4. Tap "On iPhone," "Now Playing," or "Library."

5. Swipe and tap to select Playlists, Artists, Albums, or Songs.

6. Tap the song to play.

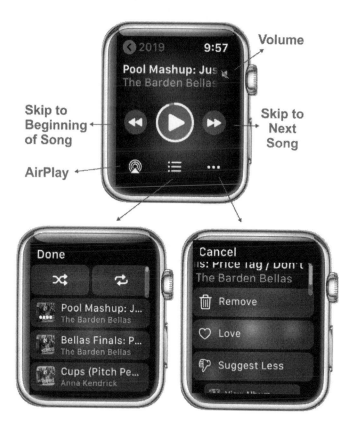

Figure 6.33   Music App

Add a Workout Playlist

Whenever you start a workout, you can automatically play music from a workout playlist. With watchOS 6, you can shuffle your workout playlist. Configure the playlist in the Apple Watch app on your iPhone.

1.   On your **iPhone**, open the Apple Watch app.

2.   Swipe to scroll down and tap "Workout."

3. Swipe up and tap the option "Workout playlist" to select a playlist for your workouts.

Use Audio Output With Apple Watch

To stream music or videos to your favorite speakers, AirPods, or headsets, use the Control Center.

1. Swipe up on the **Apple Watch** face to open Control Center.

2. Tap the "Audio Output" icon.

Tapping the audio output icon will also switch the audio output between paired Bluetooth devices.

Shuffle, Repeat, Source and Output

When playing music, firmly press the screen to view these options.

- Shuffle
- Repeat
- Source
- Output

Change Volume With the Digital Crown

Tap the audio status icon on your watch face and turn the Digital Crown to adjust the volume. Control music, podcasts, or hearing aid volume. If you have Bluetooth speakers or a headset connected to your Apple Watch, this is a simple way to adjust the volume.

Download Music to Your Apple Watch

To listen to music on the go when you don't have your iPhone with you, download albums or playlists to your Apple Watch. If you subscribe to Apple Music, the "Favorites Mix" and "New Music Mix" are automatically added.

1. On your **iPhone**, open the Apple Watch app.

2. Tap "My Watch," located in the left corner of the tab bar at the bottom of the screen.

3. Swipe to scroll down and tap "Music."

4. Tap "Add Music" and then tap the playlist or album you want to add. This is also where you could delete a playlist.

5. To download music, connect your watch to Power and place it near your iPhone.

Check Available Space

Music files can use up a lot of storage space. In case you're wondering how much space is used, on your iPhone open the Apple Watch app to see detailed information.

- The count of songs on your watch.

- The count of photos on your watch.

- The number of applications on your watch.

- The total capacity.

- The available capacity.

1.   On your **iPhone**, open the Apple Watch app.

2.   Tap "My Watch," located in the left corner of the tab bar at the bottom of the screen.

3.   Swipe to scroll down and tap "General."

4.   Tap "About" to see available capacity.

6.23 The Noise App

The Noise app was introduced in watchOS 6 along with a Decibel Level complication, and updates to the Health app. The app taps your wrist to warn you when your environment noise level is greater than 90 decibels over three minutes. The Noise Threshold and other options are configurable in the Apple Watch app on your iPhone.

Figure 6.34   Warning Loud Environment on Apple Watch

The Health app has a Hearing metric that displays sound levels and your 7-Day Exposure. The Health app also displays Charts and information about the risks of high noise levels over time. I think the Headphone Audio Level metric is particularly interesting.

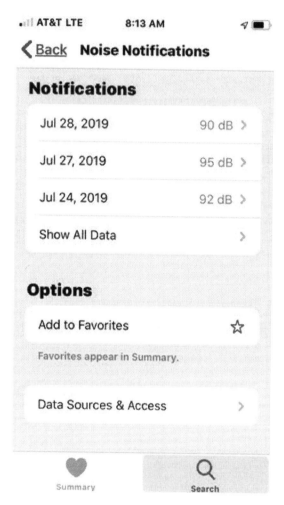

Figure 6.35   Health App Noise Notifications

6.24 Phone

The "Phone" app on your Apple Watch controls phone calls. With the cellular option on your Apple Watch, you don't need your companion iPhone nearby. I love the feature in iOS 13/watchOS 6 that allows me to send unknown callers straight to voicemail. This feature catches anyone who's not in your contacts list which is considered an unknown caller. In watchOS 6, incoming phone calls are displayed on a new screen with a larger icon to answer the calls, which means it's not as easy to drop a call accidentally. The Phone app includes these features.

- Favorites
- Recents
- Contacts
- Keypad
- Voice mail

Make a Call

1. Press the Side Button on your **Apple Watch** to open the Dock.

2. Swipe the screen with your finger, or turn the Digital Crown.

3. Tap on the "Phone" app.

4. Firmly press the screen and tap "New Call."

5. Tap "keypad," enter the number, then tap the phone symbol. Tap the More symbol (three dots) and select Keypad to enter an extension.

Emergency Phone Call

Press and hold the Side Button on your Apple Watch to make an emergency phone call. Enable Emergency Services, set your Medical ID, and configure SOS settings on your iPhone as outlined earlier.

Answer a Call

To answer a call, tap the green "Phone" icon. To see additional options, turn the Digital Crown or swipe up on the screen.

- Answer on iPhone
- Send a Message

During a call swipe up to see options or activate the keypad.

- Mute
- Volume
- Keypad

Decline a Call

To decline an incoming call, double-tap the Digital Crown. Another option is to tap the red phone icon. The call is sent to voice mail.

Transfer a Call to Your iPhone

Thanks to Apple's "Continuity" platform, you can easily handoff a call from your Apple Watch to your iPhone.

1.   On your **Apple Watch**, swipe up on the screen when receiving an incoming call.

2.   Tap "Answer on iPhone" to place the call on hold.

3.   On your **iPhone**, swipe up on the phone symbol located in the bottom left corner of the iPhone lock screen.

After answering a call on your watch, at any time you can tap the banner on your iPhone, to switch the call to your iPhone.

Call a Favorite Contact

There are two ways to call a favorite contact, as outlined below.

● Add the "favorite" contact complication to your watch face, and tap your contact's photo or initial.

● Use the "Phone" app on your Apple Watch to browse "Favorites."

Both the Infograph and Infographic Modular watch faces support adding your "favorite contacts" as a complication. The "Favorite complication" is discussed in Chapter 4.

1.   On your **Apple Watch**, open the Phone app.

2.   Tap "Favorites."

3.   Turn the Digital Crown to locate your favorite contact.

Add or Remove a Favorite Contact

1.   On your **iPhone**, open the "Phone" app.

2.   Tap "Favorites," tap the name of a contact, and swipe left to remove the contact from the favorites list.

3.   Tap the plus symbol in the top left corner to add a contact.

For the complication to display a photo of your favorite contact, add a photo for your contact on your iPhone in the "Contacts" app.

6.25 Photos

To browse photos using the Apple Watch app "Photos," turn the Digital Crown. To add a photo library to your Apple Watch, follow the steps below.

1.   Open the **Apple Watch** app on your iPhone.

2.   Tap "My Watch," located in the left corner of the tab bar at the bottom of the screen.

3.   Swipe to scroll down and tap "Photos."

4.   In the section "Photo Syncing" select photo albums.

The setting "Photos Limit" controls the number of photos on your watch. Only recent photos sync when the album size exceeds the limit. Chapter 11 includes instructions to check the number of photos on your watch.

6.26 Podcasts

The Podcast app was redesigned in watchOS 6, as shown below. You can view Shows, Episodes, Stations, or Groups of your favorite Podcasts. Podcasts are usually original audio or video recordings. Podcasts include recorded broadcasts of a television or radio program, a lecture, a performance, or other events. NPR, the New York Times, MSNBC, ESPN, and iHeartRadio are a few of the Podcast providers.

Figure 6.36   The Podcast App

Open the app on your **iPhone** and tap "Browse" to subscribe to a playlist or create Groups of your favorite playlists. Top Charts and Featured Providers are a great starting point. Once you download episodes on your iPhone, you can listen to them in the Podcasts app on your Apple Watch.

6.27 Reminders

The Reminders app was redesigned in iOS 13, and the iPhone app supports attachments and shared lists. New features include Smart Lists and a Quick Toolbar to add times, dates, and locations. Location suggestions like "Getting in Car" or "Cathy Young's Work" are available in the app on your iPhone, or you can add your own location. The app will also flag overdue reminders.

The Reminders app on the Apple Watch includes a Today view with watchOS 6. While you can only create a basic reminder directly on your Apple Watch. The time, date, and location information for reminders you create on your iPhone are displayed on your Apple Watch.

Tip: The Search dialog in the Reminders app on your iPhone may not be displayed until you scroll to the top of the screen, and then swipe down.

Initially, I didn't use the Apple Reminders app often. However, when I realized I could use family sharing with reminders to sync my grocery list, I fell in love with the app.

Figure 6.37   The Reminders App

The Grocery app outlined in the next chapter uses the iOS reminders lists to store your shopping list. With a combination of iOS "Family Sharing," and an IFTTT applet that automatically links my Grocery shopping list with my iOS reminder lists, I can easily add items to my grocery list with Alexa, Google Home, or Siri. Everyone in our family can access our family shopping list on their Apple device. I'm particularly fond of the Grocery app because while I may forget to bring my iPhone to the grocery store, I will probably be wearing my Apple Watch with the Grocery app installed.

Add a Reminder or Show Completed Reminders

1. Open the Reminders app on your **Apple Watch** and firmly press the screen.

2. Tap "Show Completed" to view completed reminders.

3. Tap ➕ "Add" to create a reminder.

Enable Family Sharing

1. On your iPad or iPhone, open the Settings app, and tap your name in the Apple ID banner in the left sidebar.

2. Swipe and tap "Set up Family Sharing." Follow the prompts to invite contacts to join your family.

Share a Reminder List

Family sharing is active on my iPhone. My "Family" reminder list is shared with both my husband and daughter.

1. Open the Reminders app on your iPhone or iPad and tap the "Family" list. Any list would work, but in this example, I happen to have a "Family" list.

2. In watchOS 6, tap More, the ellipsis, and tap "Share With."

3. Select a contact and click ✚ "Add" to send an invitation.

6.28 Remote Control

The Remote app is a remote control for your Apple TV or iTunes library. Once you pair your Apple Watch to your Apple TV, you tap or swipe your watch face to control the TV. **Make sure your Apple Watch, iPhone and computer are all on the same Wi-Fi network.**

At home, I play my iTunes music on my Yamaha amplifier that is connected to my surround sound system. After pairing the Apple Watch remote app to my iTunes computer, I can control everything from my watch.

Add Apple TV

1. On your **Apple Watch** press the side button to open the Dock.

2. Swipe and tap "Remote."

3. Swipe up and tap "Add Device." A passcode is displayed on the screen.

4. Switch to your **Apple TV** and go to Settings -> General -> Remote.

5. Select Apple Watch and type the passcode displayed on your watch screen.

6. Switch to **iTunes** on your **computer**, and click on the black play icon.

7. Enter the passcode displayed on your watch screen.

6.29 Siri

Siri isn't an app you download, but rather is a core part of the iOS or watchOS operating system. Siri is a personal digital assistant. With watchOS 5, Siri became an intelligent personal assistant with a custom Siri watch face. In watchOS 6, Siri includes Shazam integration, and can also search the web and display full web page results.

Siri monitors your schedule and calendar, suggesting relevant content throughout the day. Intelligent Siri will update you on your favorite team's score, display one of your photos from a year ago, or recommend a playlist for your commute home.

Siri is also perfect for controlling your Apple Watch. You can ask Siri to start a specific workout, send messages, place a call, or turn on a setting such as "Do Not Disturb."

Note: Siri requires an Internet connection. Occasionally Apple's Siri servers are unavailable, so wait a few minutes and try again.

Personal virtual assistants are found in smartphones, tablets, smart speakers, and more. Amazon Echo, Google Home, Apple HomeKit, and Microsoft Invoke are examples of smart speakers that have virtual assistants.

Using virtual assistants requires a fundamental change in the way we interact with the world around us. Adopting a mindful approach can make the transition easier. Each week I set aside a few minutes and ask myself, "Can Siri do this task for me?" Then I spend a few minutes exploring what's possible today. I say "today" because the list of what these virtual assistants can do is changing daily. In this section, we'll look at these topics.

- What can Siri do?

- Enable Siri on Your iPhone or Watch

- Ask Siri a Question

- Teach Siri About You

- Shortcuts

- Siri Doesn't Respond

What Can Siri Do?

Siri can answer questions, surf the web, and control devices through smart home apps like Apple Home. For example, with watchOS 6, you can say, "Siri, where is Michael?" and Siri will display a map of your friend's location on your Apple Watch.

The topic "Web Browser" that follows illustrates using Siri to search the web, and there is an example of handing off the browser from your Apple Watch to your iPad or iPhone in Chapter 3.

In addition to voice commands and app integrations, the Siri "Shortcuts" app combines several devices or apps into one command, as shown in the next topic.

Enable Siri on Your Watch

1. On your **Apple Watch**, go into "Settings."

2. Scroll down and tap "Siri."

3. In the ASK SIRI section tap the "Listen for Hey Siri" switch to toggle on or off. The switch is green when on and white when off.

Enable Siri on Your Apple Watch

1. On your **Apple Watch** press the Side Button.

2. Tap "Settings," and then tap General.

3. Scroll down and tap "Siri."

4. Tap the "Hey Siri" switch to toggle on or off. The switch is green when on and white when off.

Enable Raise to Speak

Raise to Speak is a new way to engage Siri. After you ask Siri a question, you can lower your wrist. Siri will gently tap your wrist when she has a response.

1. On your **Apple Watch** press the Side Button.

2. Tap "Settings," and then tap General.

3. Scroll down and tap "Siri."

4. Tap the "Raise to Speak" switch to toggle on or off. The switch is green when on and white when off.

Ask Siri a Question

There are two other ways to ask Siri a question.

- On your **Apple Watch** press and hold the Digital Crown.

- Raise your wrist and say, "Hey Siri, start my walk workout."

Siri Shortcuts

Some apps support "Siri shortcuts." Siri also suggests shortcuts for tasks you frequently perform like visiting a favorite website or sending a text message to a friend. A few of my favorite apps are:

- Carrot Weather
- Google Calendar
- Kindle

- The Apple Home app
- Pandora
- Amazon Prime Video
- Waze

To demonstrate how powerful Siri Shortcuts are, I'd like to give you a few examples.

- Start your favorite Pandora station.

- Open the Waze app with your route Home.

- Setup Siri Shortcuts for Home Automations in the Apple Home app. Siri Shortcuts are available in the Home app with iOS 13 and later.

- Open Kindle and continue reading your book from your last location.

- Open Safari and navigate to your favorite web page. With Apple's Accounts & Passwords, you're automatically logged in to saved locations.

For example, to set up a Siri Shortcut open the Waze app and search for a location like "Home." Tap the "more" button that looks like an ellipsis or three dots. Tap "Add Shortcut" and record a personal phrase for Siri to launch Waze.

Suggested Shortcuts

In the Settings app on your iPad or iPhone, tap "Siri & Search." To customize the Siri phrase, use the original app, or your iPad. On your iPad, in the "Suggested Shortcuts" section in the right panel, tap "All Shortcuts." The default shortcuts for iOS are displayed, as well as suggested shortcuts for third-party apps. This list of shortcuts is not all possible shortcuts, just the ones Siri is suggesting based on your history. Tap any of these shortcuts to record your shortcut phrase.

Teach Siri about You

The more Siri learns about you, as you interact with her on your Apple device, the better her responses will be. Siri learns about you as you use apps like Safari, Photos, Contacts, or Mail. iOS 13 added new relationship types, which Siri uses to identify relevant contacts. When you use "Hey Siri," she'll get better at recognizing your voice. Before long Siri will be like an old friend, who knows your likes and dislikes.

Your Contact Card

Siri will customize your experience by using your Apple ID information in "Name, Phone Numbers, E-mail." Siri also uses information from your Contact Card. When you open the Contacts app on your iPhone or iPad, your contact card is at the top of the list, in the left sidebar.

Siri Phrases

- Text Michael.

- Show me directions to Walmart.

- How far away is Atlanta?

- Call Michael on speaker.

- Read my last text message from Michael.

- Open the Waze app.

- Show me my timers.

- Show me the weather.

- Play music.

- Play "The Greatest Showman."

Siri Doesn't Respond

When Siri doesn't respond, check your internet connection. Wi-Fi and Bluetooth should both be active on your iPhone. To check connectivity on your Apple Watch, press the Digital Crown to go to your watch face. Swipe up to see Control Center and the status of connectivity.

1   On your **iPhone**, turn Siri off and back on.

2   On your **Apple Watch** open "Settings," and in the "General" section, turn Siri off and back on.

3   Turn off your Apple Watch and turn it back on. Press and hold the side button and tap "Power Off."

6.30 Siri Shortcuts

With the Apple "Shortcuts" app introduced with iOS 12, you can build shortcuts to perform many routine tasks. Think of shortcuts as macros or quick commands. You'll configure Shortcuts on your iPad or iPhone, and then you can access them with your Apple Watch using Siri. Although Shortcuts for Apple Watch may not be available in the first watchOS 6 release, because Apple plans to include Shortcuts eventually I decided to include information on Shortcuts. Shortcut suggestions on the Siri watch face are more relevant with watchOS 6.

With Siri Shortcuts, you record a personal phrase in your app for a particular task. For example, say "Siri, open travel plans." The Siri Shortcut opens the Hotels.com app and displays your hotel photo, address, and check-in time. In this scenario, you recorded a Siri Shortcut in the Hotels.com app named "travel plans." To really understand how powerful Siri Shortcuts are, I'd like to give you a few examples.

- Start your favorite Pandora station.

- Open the Waze app with your route Home.

- Open Kindle and continue reading your book from your last location.

- Open Safari and navigate to your favorite web page. With Apple's Accounts & Passwords, you're automatically logged in to saved locations.

Figure 6.38   Siri Shortcuts

The list below shows a few apps that have announced plans to support Siri Shortcuts or have them available today.

- AirBnB

- Amazon Prime Video

- American Airlines

- App in the Air

- Bonvoy (Marriott/SPG)

- Booking.com

- British Airways

- Carrot Weather

- Caviar (Food Delivery)

- Dark Sky Weather

- Dexcom (Blood Glucose Monitor)

- ETA

- Grocery

- Hotels.com

- HotelTonight

- Kayak

- Lufthansa

- Open Table

- Trello

- VRBO

- Waze

You can add your shortcuts to your Apple device "Today View," or ask Siri to run a shortcut. Third-party apps are starting to appear with the "Add to Siri" button to create custom shortcuts. The next section, "Add to Siri," has a few examples.

Shortcuts are listed in the "Settings" app on your iPhone, in the "Siri & Search" section. The next topic, "Create a Shortcut," explains these settings.

Download the new Shortcut App from the App Store. The scripting features of the Shortcuts app pass text, URLs, clipboard contents, and other actions between applications. The following is a brief list of tasks to inspire you.

- Send E-mails

- Make Phone Calls

- Search Local Businesses

- Find Music

- Record Audio

- Ask for Scripting Input

- Get Current Weather

Create a Shortcut

Open the "Shortcuts" app on your iPhone, and tap "Create Shortcut." Swipe up. In the Music section, tap "Get Playlist." Enter your options and tap "Done." To rename the shortcut, in the Library tap the shortcut, and then tap the Settings button in the top right. In the pop-up menu, you can set the button, name, Siri phrase, and more. Swipe up and tap "Add to Home Screen."

Suggested Shortcuts

In the Settings app on your iPad, tap "Siri & Search." To customize the Siri phrase use the original app, or your iPad. On your iPad, in the "Suggested Shortcuts" section in the right panel, tap "All Shortcuts." The default shortcuts for iOS are displayed, as well as suggested shortcuts for third-party apps. This list of shortcuts is not all possible shortcuts, just the ones Siri is suggesting based on your history. Tap any of these shortcuts to record your personal shortcut phrase.

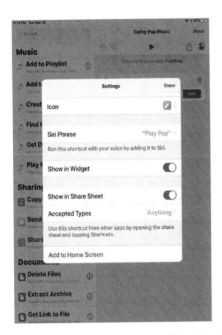

Figure 6.39   Creating a Shortcut

Chapter 6

Favorite Shortcuts

In Shortcut Editor, tap the name of the action you want to mark as a favorite.

Waze

When Waze introduced a Siri Shortcut in February 2019, I was very excited. To set up a Siri Shortcut, open the Waze app, and search for a location like "Home." Tap the "more" button that looks like an ellipsis or three dots. Tap "Add Shortcut" and record a personal phrase for Siri to launch Waze.

Earlier, we discussed the "Shortcuts" app for creating your multi-step shortcuts, or third-party apps that support these "Siri Shortcuts." There is a third choice for shortcuts, found in the "Suggested Shortcuts" screen discussed in the next section.

Suggested Shortcuts

In the Settings app, in the left sidebar, tap "Siri & Search." In the "Suggested Shortcuts" section, in the right panel, tap "All Shortcuts." The default shortcuts for iOS are displayed. Tap any of these shortcuts to record your shortcut phrase.

View and Rerecord Shortcut Phrases

Shortcuts are listed in the Settings app, in the "Siri & Search" section. At the top of the screen, tap "My Shortcuts" to view and edit your shortcut phrases.

6.31 Stocks

The "Stocks" app can display up to 20 stocks and has four complications, as shown below. Configure the list of stocks in the iPhone app.

- Current Price
- Points Change
- Percentage Change
- Market Cap

Figure 6.40   The Stock App

6.32 Stopwatch

On your Apple Watch touch the side button to open the Dock. Swipe to open the "Stopwatch" app. You can add the Stopwatch complication to your watch face as outlined in Chapter 4.

1.   On your **Apple Watch** touch the side button.

2.   Swipe to scroll and tap the "Stopwatch" app.

3.   To start the Stopwatch, tap the green switch in the bottom right corner of the screen. This switch turns red to indicate the stopwatch is running.

4.   To switch between analog, digital, graph, or hybrid modes, firmly press the Stopwatch screen.

Laps

The white switch in the bottom left corner of the screen is used to record laps.

1.   While using the "Stopwatch" app on your **watch**, tap the white switch. In the analog view tap the green button to start the stopwatch.

2.   Double-tap the white button in the bottom left corner of the screen. The tab bar shows "Lap" and "Start."

3.   Tap "Start."

4.   While the stopwatch is running, tap "Lap" to record a new lap. The screen displays L1, L2, etc.

5.   Swipe up to return to the main screen. Swipe up again to return to Lap View.

6.   Tap "Stop" when done.

7.   Tap "Reset" to begin a new set of recordings.

6.33 Timer

When you open the Timer app on your watch, swipe down to see options for one minute, three minutes, 20 minutes, 30 minutes, one hour, or two hours. To set a custom timer look at the instructions below. The Timer app remembers your custom timers. Custom timers are shown in the "Recents" screen. If you like, you can add the Timer complication to your watch face as outlined in Chapter 4. For multiple timers running at the same time, a third-party app like MultiTimer comes in handy.

1. On your **Apple Watch** press the side button.

2. Swipe and tap to open the "Timer" app.

3. Tap "Custom."

4. Swipe to adjust hours and minutes, or turn the Digital Crown.

5. Tap "Start."

Tip: Swipe up and down within the Timer app to see options.

6.34 Voice Memos

The "Voice Memos" app was introduced to the iPad with iOS 12 and is a welcome addition to the Apple Watch with watchOS 6. The "Transcribe" and "Otter" apps import and transcribe Apple Voice Memo recordings. I save my voice memos to iCloud and then import them to Otter. Third-party apps like Drafts with built-in transcription and powerful "actions" are covered in the next chapter.

6.35 Walkie-Talkie

The Walkie-Talkie app is an entirely new way to communicate around the world. The Walkie-Talkie app was introduced with watchOS 5 and redesigned in watchOS 6, including larger buttons.

The Walkie-Talkie app records a voice message when you press the "Talk" button. The message is instantly sent to your friend when you release the button. A gentle tap or sound alerts you to a conversation. Connections remain open for five minutes after you stop talking. After five minutes have elapsed, you must start a new conversation.

The Walkie-Talkie status icon is a stylized walkie-talkie radio. The icon appears on your watch face after you create a connection with a contact. The icon is yellow when the Walkie-Talkie is turned on and indicates your status in the Walkie-Talkie app is "available."

To use the Walkie-Talkie app check these settings.

- Apple Watch Series 1 or later with watchOS 5 or later.

- Both watches must have connectivity through a Bluetooth connection to the iPhone, Wi-Fi, or cellular.

- Both participants must mark themselves available in the app.

- Both watches must have the **FaceTime app** on their respective companion iPhone.

- Both participants must be logged in with a different Apple Id.

- On your Apple Watch open the Walkie-Talkie app and tap to add contacts. Swipe to set your status to available.

Invite a Friend

Before using the Walkie-Talkie app, follow these steps to connect with friends.

1. On your **Apple Watch** press the side button.

2. Swipe and tap to open the "Walkie-Talkie" app.

3. Tap "Add" (the plus symbol) to create a connection.

4. Swipe or turn the Digital Crown to browse through contacts. Contacts that already have Walkie-Talkie set up will appear at the top of the list in the "Suggested" section.

5. Choose a friend that has a compatible watch, and tap to send an invitation.

6. After your friend accepts the invitation, you can start a conversation.

Tip: Check your contact is set up with the correct Apple ID e-mail, on your iPhone in the Contacts app.

Start a Conversation

1. On your **Apple Watch** press the side button.

2. Swipe and tap to open the "Walkie-Talkie" app.

3. Tap a friend.

Figure 6.41   Start a Walkie-Talkie Conversation

4.   Touch and hold the "Talk" button. Release the button, and your friend instantly hears what you said.

Figure 6.42   Tap to Talk

Turn the Digital Crown to control volume while using the Walkie-Talkie app.

If you turn on Silent Mode, you can still hear chimes and your friend's voice. When Theater Mode is active, your Walkie-Talkie status is "unavailable." You can continue a conversation if you turn on "Do Not Disturb," but other calls are silenced.

6.36 Weather

The Apple Weather app is awesome. The Weather app Air Quality Indicator (AQI) and UV Meters were updated in watchOS 6. Weather information is dependent on the "Location Services" configured on your iPhone. I'd encourage you to try the app, and if you're not thrilled, you could try third-party apps like Dark Sky or Carrot Weather.

Example of Weather in Motion

Let's say you have the weather complication added to your watch face. Follow these steps to view the forecast, temperature, and rainfall.

1. On your **Apple Watch** face, tap to select the weather complication.

2. Turn the Digital Crown to see the hourly forecast, air quality, UV index, wind speed, wind direction, and the 10-day forecast.

3. Firmly press the screen to see rain percentage, conditions, and temperature.

To remove a city, tap the city name and firmly press the display, then tap "Remove."

6.37 Web Browser

While not the full-blown Safari app, you can use Siri to open a web browser with watchOS 6 to display web pages in Reader View. On your iPhone or iPad, Reader View is only available on some web pages and displays the page without ads. I appreciate the option to handoff my web browsing to my iPhone, as shown in Chapter 3. On your iPhone, when you press the home button to switch apps, the handoff banner is displayed at the bottom of your iPhone.

6.38 What's Next?

At this point, I'd like to point out the App Store showcases new third-party apps. We'll talk about a few interesting apps in the next chapter.

7. Third-party Apps

In this chapter we discuss

Calendar and Reminders

Grocery and Cooking Apps

Entertainment

Games

Health and Fitness

IFTTT

Photography and Video

Productivity

Schools

Smart Home

Sports and the Great Outdoors

Travel

Water Sports

Weather

What's Next?

Chapter 7

In April 2018 Apple began requiring that any updated app is based on watchOS 2 SDK or later. New apps had to use watchOS 4. This requirement ensured apps were native to the Apple Watch and paved the way for watchOS 6 apps that run independently of your iPhone. The advantage of a native app is data is not transferred back and forth to the companion iPhone.

Apple's decision was in response to complaints about sluggish apps. Unfortunately, in response to the requirement, companies like eBay and Instagram announced their apps for Apple Watch would no longer be available. In the long run, I'm hoping Google Maps and others will rejoin the fold.

While many third-party apps work with your Apple Watch automatically, sometimes you have to create a "widget" in the iPhone app. Often smart home apps that control many custom devices use widgets. The Philips HUE lighting app and the Hunter Douglas PowerView apps currently require you to create widgets for your smart home devices. We discuss widgets in the Smart Home section that follows.

Figure 7.1   Apple Watch HUE Widgets

Several third-party apps also provide "complications." A complication is information from an app that can be displayed on your Apple Watch Face, as discussed in Chapter 4.

Not only is it fun to search the internet for the latest "Apple Watch apps," browsing the "App Store" for new Apple Watch apps is a great way to see what's new. On your iPhone, launch "Apple Watch" and click on "App Store." The following pages present a few interesting third-party apps. The apps are organized by category to showcase the possibilities.

7.1 Calendar and Reminders

The CARROT To-Do app is available as a stand-alone app. The To-Do app is also part of the CARROT app bundle that includes CARROT Fit, the CARROT "Artificial Superintelligence" game, CARROT Weather, CARROT Alarm, CARROT Hunger, and CARROT Sticker Pack.

For calendars, lists, and reminders, take a look at these apps:

- CARROT To-Do
- Countdown Star
- Fantastical
- Things 3
- Tiny Calendar

7.2 Grocery and Cooking Apps

Consider using "To-Do Lists" or timer apps that remind you to check the food cooking on your grill. These recipe apps, shopping apps, and cooking apps are also helpful in the kitchen.

- CookCalc
- Cooking Time

- Grocery

- Shopper

- Vegan's Cook

- Yummly Recipes

Grocery

Grocery shopping moves to the next level with apps like "Grocery." The Grocery app complication for your watch face is perfect for grocery shopping. Tap the item as you shop to mark it complete. Firmly press the screen to "undo," "add," or switch to a different store. This app knows the route you take through the particular store and learns every time you shop.

The Grocery app uses iOS reminders lists to store your shopping list. With a combination of iOS "Family Sharing" and an IFTTT applet that automatically links my Alexa shopping list with my iOS reminder lists, I can easily add items to my grocery list with Alexa, Google Home, or Siri. With a simple tap on our watches, everyone in our family can access our family shopping list.

Add Items to the List

Add items to your shopping list in your Mac or iCloud "Reminders." If you're like me, you could use a digital assistant to add items to your shopping list. Simply say, "Siri, add corn to my "Family reminders."

If you use another digital assistant like Alexa, you can link your iOS reminders to the Alexa shopping list with an IFTTT applet, as shown below.

Enable Family Sharing

1. On your iPhone, open the Settings app and tap your name in the Apple ID banner.

2. Swipe and tap "Set up Family Sharing." Follow the prompts to invite contacts to join your family.

Share the List with Your Family

Family sharing is active on my iPhone. My "Family" reminder list is shared with both my husband and daughter.

1. On your iPhone, open the Reminders app and tap the "Family" list. Any list would work, but in this example, we're using the "Family" list.

2. Tap "Edit" and then tap "sharing." Select a contact and click Add (the plus sign) to send an invitation to join the family.

Use IFTTT to link iOS and Alexa

IFTTT will automatically sync your Apple reminder list when you add an item to your Alexa shopping list. First, enable the iOS and Alexa IFTTT services and link the services to your Apple and Alexa accounts. Second, create an IFTTT applet. Note that IFTTT also has services for other digital assistants like Google Home or Microsoft Cortana.

1. In a browser login to your IFTTT account.

2. Click on "Services." Search for the service "iOS Reminders" and follow the prompts to link your account. Repeat the steps to link your Alexa account to IFTTT.

3. Click on the button to create a **New Applet**. IFTTT stands for "If **This**, Then **That**." Begin creating the applet by clicking on "**This**."

4. Choose the **service** "Alexa." Click on "Item added to your shopping list."

5. Now you want to select the **trigger,** which is what you want to happen whenever an item is added to your Alexa shopping list. In IFTTT terms, ask yourself, when I add corn to my Alexa shopping list, do I want IFTTT to do "**that**?" Click on "**that**" and select "iOS Reminders."

6. Complete the trigger fields by selecting "Add Reminder to List." Type your iOS list name, in this case, "Family." Click Save.

7. Tap settings, the gear icon, to rename the IFTTT applet. Click Save.

7.3 Entertainment

Entertainment apps encompass music apps like **Shazam,** apps that read books aloud like **Audible,** or podcast apps like **Overcast.** Shazam is famous for listening to a song to identify the artist and now records song titles automatically in history.

Overcast is the award-winning podcast player. Features like voice boost, smart speed, and smart playlists give you complete control. Simply install the app on your iPhone, add a podcast, select an episode to download, and you're ready to go. I love the humor the developer added under the "Add a Podcast" button, that says "Otherwise, this may not be useful." In "Settings" tap "Sync to Watch" to enable "Auto-Sync to Watch."

Not just for workouts, Amazon's **Audible** app reads my books out loud while I go for a walk. I was going to say when I go for a run, but I decided to be honest about my exercise level. But still, how awesome is it to go for a walk and listen to the best selling book at the same time!

- Audible
- Elevate - Brain Training
- Fandango
- iHeartRadio
- Overcast
- Shazam
- Spotify
- TuneIn
- WJXT
- Video Call Santa

In November 2018 Spotify released its first app version for Apple Watch. The app also has a complication for your watch face. Launch the app on your iPhone, and then the Apple Watch is a remote control.

7.4 Games

Normally, I'm not a big fan of digital games, but I will admit Trivia Crack can be addictive. Check out some of these games.

- Nexus Tile
- Cylinders
- Egg
- Wordie
- Komrad
- Lifeline
- Pokémon Go
- Rules

- Runeblade
- Seedling Scavenger Bingo
- Trivia Crack
- Zombies, Run!

7.5 Health and Fitness

CARROT Fit motivates you with a glimpse into your no-exercise future and focuses on 7-minute workouts. The droll verbal abuse and sly humor are unique to this app; squats are called "Territory Markers." The Apple Watch extension adds real-time heart rate data.

Similar to Apple's "Breathe" app, the "Forest-Stay Focused" app has a unique approach to being mindful. **Forest** is hard to describe so I'd encourage you to check it out. There's a reason it's the #1 app in 113 countries. Headspace:Meditation is another app in this category. Recent research into the neuroscience of mindfulness shows deep breathing reduces stress and has long-term health benefits.

Featured by Apple in "New Apps We Love," **Gymatic** uses science to identify your exercises automatically, and count your repetitions. The LoseIt! app tracks exercise and calories. The "Utility" watch face has an option to add the "**LoseIt!**" complication. The complication shows me how many calories remain in my daily goal.

Lifesum has won many awards with its app focused on healthy living that includes diet, exercise, and healthy recipes. Do you have a loved one who forgets to eat regularly? Lifesum diligently reminds you to eat and drink water and warns when your energy level is too low. Lifesum also has complications for your watch face.

You may wonder why the following list of health apps includes Panera. In an interesting twist, when you order a meal from **Panera**, the calories of your meal are included in HealthKit apps.

The adorable characters in Standland make it a contender for the "Stand" activity.

- Calm
- Cardiogram
- CARROT Fit
- CVS
- Daily Yoga
- Forrest
- Gymaholic
- Gymatic
- Headspace (Meditation)
- Lifesum
- LoseIt!
- Map My Run
- My Fitness Pal
- Nike Run Club
- Paddle Logger
- Panera
- Pedometer
- Runkeeper
- Runtastic
- Seven
- Standland
- Streaks
- Strava
- Strong
- WorkoutDoors
- YogaGlo

Chapter 7

Strava is a social network created specifically for athletes. You configure devices like your Peloton bike within the Strava app. The next step is to configure the Strava app with your Apple Watch. Strava also has complications for your watch face.

1.   On your **iPhone**, launch the Strava app.

2.   Create an account.

3.   Follow the prompts to Connect a GPS watch or computer.

4.   To make changes, click the "More" button. Tap "Settings" and then tap "Applications, Services, and Devices."

5.   Select Apple Watch. The Strava app will walk you through the settings.

6.   In "Settings under Services," tap "Health" to connect with your Apple Health app.

In Chapter 9, I touch on the topic of Sleep. Although the Health app reminds you to set a consistent time to go to sleep, at this time, it doesn't monitor your sleep patterns. To track sleep today, you need a third-party app.

The benefits of quality sleep are you are more focused and have better blood sugar regulation. And most importantly, in my opinion - a fat-burning growth hormone is released while you sleep!

- Auto Sleep
- Sleep ++
- Sleepio
- Sleepmatic
- Sleepwatch
- Pillow

These sleep apps read your recorded health history. Once you have established a baseline of your sleep data, you can experiment with different apps to compare their insights.

7.6 IFTTT

As an Editors' Choice app with over 17,000 reviews and a 4.7 rating, you may wonder why is the IFTTT app so special. IFTTT is an acronym for If This happens, Then do That. If you've been searching for a watch app to no avail, chances are there is already an IFTTT applet that does what you need.

Thousands of cloud services, smart home device manufacturers, and app developers have IFTTT applets. IFTTT integrates systems for delivery information, weather, pollen counts, or location (geofencing). IFTTT also controls your smart home devices like lights, thermostats, or sprinklers. With IFTTT, you can also send e-mails, message notifications, or communicate with your digital assistant(s). Some popular IFTTT services include:

- Twitter
- Craigslist
- Amazon Cloud
- Facebook
- Logitech Harmony
- GE Appliances
- Google Drive
- eBay
- Whistle (Pet Tracker)
- Eve for Subaru

Figure 7.2   IFTTT Twitter Applet

Create IFTTT Widgets for your Apple Watch

The IFTTT iPhone app is used to configure Apple Watch widgets. These IFTTT widgets are then available on your watch.

1. On your **iPhone**, open the IFTTT app.

2. Tap the gear icon to open "Settings." Tap "Widgets," then tap "Get Widgets."

3. For example, tap "Quickly create events in Google Calendar," and then tap "Turn On."

4. When prompted, select your Google Calendar account.

5. Be sure the "Show on Apple Watch" switch is toggled on.

Create Your Own IFTTT Applets

When you visit the IFTTT web site, you can search for existing applets (recipes) you can reuse, or create your own. You'll see these common services used in many of the applets.

- Location
- Date and Time
- Calendars
- Notifications

The funniest applet I've seen was entitled, "Blink the lights when the cookie jar defenses are breached." I assumed it used a motion sensor attached to the cookie jar, but in actuality, it uses the "Manything" mobile app. The Manything app uses the camera on your smartphone or tablet as a surveillance device. Combined with a stand, you can catch the thief (or pet) in the act!

With IFTTT, you can easily create your own applets (pieces of code). When creating your applet recall that IFTTT stands for, "If **This**, then That."

1. Login to IFTTT and click on **New Applet**.

2. Choose a **service**.

3. Choose a **trigger**.

4. Complete the trigger fields.

5. Click on the **Plus** symbol to fill in "that." This is the **action**.

6. Choose an action service and save the applet.

Combine Several Actions

IFTTT has a Maker tier that allows you to combine multiple services and triggered actions. You can sign up for free at IFTTT.

1. Login to the Maker tier, or log in to IFTTT and select My Applets. Click on **New Applet**. There is a choice to **Build on the Platform** that takes you into the Maker tier.

2. Choose a **service**.

3. Choose a **trigger**.

4. Now fill in "that" – the **action**.

5. Complete the action fields.

6. Complete remaining action fields.

7. Repeat to add more triggers and actions. Then fill in a description and save your applet.

The Applet is private (only you can use it) until you click on **Publish**.

7.7 Photography and Video

Take your mobile photography to the next level with **ProCamera 8**. Synonymous with action photography, it's no surprise **GoPro** supports the Apple Watch and has complications for your watch face. Another app to explore is the ProCam app that captures stunning photos.

- Behance

- Camera+

- Cloud Baby Monitor

- EyeSpy

- GoPro

- Hydra

- infltr

- Moment - Pro Camera

- Opak - Photo Editor

- Photo Editor

- ProCam

- ProcCamera 8

- Video Editor

7.8 Productivity

The apps listed below are a bit varied. They include to-do lists, notes, counting, audio recording, e-mail, calculators, financial, and others.

- Bank of America
- Budget Boss
- Calcbot
- Calc Smart
- CARROT To-Do
- Cheatsheet (Quick Notes)

- Clicker (Counts When You Tap)
- Drafts
- Facebook Messenger
- Metronome
- Mint
- Noted (Recording with Time Tags)
- Otter Voice Memos
- Outlook
- Pcalc
- Pennies (Budget)
- Personal Capital
- Powerpoint
- Property Finder
- Recorder
- SIFT
- Slope - Finance Tracker
- Spark (e-mail)
- Streaks
- Tempo
- Transcribe
- Yelp

Drafts

The Drafts app is one of my favorite apps for dictation and note-taking. Another app in this space is Otter Voice Meeting Notes, which also imports Apple Voice Memos. Drafts actions go a step further than simple transcription with customizable actions. When an idea pops into my head, I tap the microphone to dictate a recording. The screen displays the transcription text of the recording as you are dictating. The Drafts app also works on my Apple Watch, so I always have it handy.

Another option to Drafts would be the Apple "Voice Memos" app with the "Transcribe" app.

On your iPad, open the Drafts app. From the main screen, tap the paper button in the top left corner of the screen to open the "Inbox" that lists your recordings. Tap a recording to see what actions are available. When a recording is open, in the top right corner, tap the "actions" button. Actions include Mail, Message, Share, Google Search, Calendar Events, List in Reminders, Print, and many more.

Actions are customizable and can be reordered. The first action in my app is "e-mail me," which opens an e-mail dialog with addresses I selected already entered.

Add a Custom Drafts Action

1. Open the Drafts app on your iPad. In the main screen, tap the actions button in the top right corner of the screen.

2. In the actions screen, tap the add button in the bottom right corner.

3. Tap the "Add New Action" button.

4. Tap the line under the "Identification" heading and enter a name for your action.

5. Swipe up and under the heading "Steps" tap the line that says "0 steps" to begin entering your steps or commands.

6. On the "Steps" screen tap the add button in the top right corner of the screen that looks like a plus symbol. Select "Step Type." For an e-mail action, select a contact. You can add a subject and

body text, or let the system generate it automatically from your recording.

7. In the top right corner, tap "Save & Exit."

Edit or Delete an Action

1. Open the Drafts app on your iPad. In the main screen, tap the actions button in the top right corner of the screen.

2. Tap to select an action and swipe left to right. Lift your finger, and the edit menu appears. Tap Delete.

3. To change the order of actions, tap to select an action, and drag it to a new location.

7.9 Schools

Some US Universities support Student ID cards in Apple Wallet. This integration combines the "eAccounts" education app with the secure logins provided by the "Duo Mobile" authentication app.

7.10 Smart Home

Many smart home apps like the Neato robot vacuum app and the Legrand **Light Control** app work perfectly on the Apple Watch. Legrand encompasses smart lighting as well as electrical outlets. The Honeywell **Total Connect Comfort** app for thermostats also supports the Apple Watch. Hunter Douglas PowerView shades, Neato, and Legrand all work with the Alexa digital assistant. I prefer tapping my watch compared to talking to Alexa in certain situations, especially if I'm trying to be quiet. For further information on smart home technology, check out our book, "Smart Home, Digital Assistants, Home Automation and the Internet of Things."

Although I love my robotic vacuum George, Jr., sometimes it's not a good time for him to vacuum. With a tap on my watch, I can direct George, Jr. to try again later. Our original **Neato** robot "George" didn't survive all the cat hair at our house. We're hoping George, Jr. has a long and productive life.

Figure 7.3   The Neato App

SmartThings is Samsung's solution for home automation. The SmartThings hub uses the ZigBee protocol to control lighting, security, sensors, sirens, and cameras, to name a few. In the SmartThings mobile app, select "More" and then click on "My Account" to create widgets for your Apple Watch.

An unusual smart app is "Eve for Subaru." Combined with an IFTTT applet, the Subaru app controls over 400 smart home devices.

Some third-party apps require you to create a "Widget" for your Apple Watch. In the figure below, I am creating a widget in the Hunter Douglas app "**PowerView**."

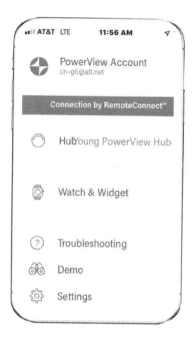

Figure 7.4   Creating a PowerView Widget

7.11 Sports and the Great Outdoors

Picture a beautiful, cool, sunny day. A gentle breeze blows as you prepare to tee off, but you're wondering just how far that green is. A glance at your Apple Watch, and you are all set. The Golf Shot AR has real-time distances to the green, hazards, and over 40,000 worldwide courses. The Golf Shot integration with your Apple Watch is like having a pro caddie on your wrist.

With Sky Guide on your Apple Watch, all you have to do is open the app and hold your watch to the sky. With the screen facing you, Sky Guide will automatically recognize the constellation patterns and orient the screen properly. Sky Guide will show you the constellations that have always been right in front of you, but you never knew existed. Sky Guide can send you a notification on your Apple Watch when an event is about to happen in the skies above your location.

There are so many apps in this category; I decided to break them down into sports and outdoor. This list of sports apps is the tip of the iceberg. I'd encourage you to search the app store for sports of interest to you.

- 365Scores
- College Hoops
- Cyclemeter
- DraftKings Fantasy Sports
- ESPN
- Football Live
- Golf Shot
- Komoot
- MLB at Bat
- MyScorecard
- NFL Sunday Ticket
- Onefootball - Soccer Scores
- PitchersPal
- Slopes
- The Score

The following is a brief list of apps that you may find interesting for outdoor activities.

- AllTrails
- Big Year Birding
- GAIA
- Gardenia
- History Here
- Santa Fe Botanical
- Sky Guide
- Sunrise Sunset
- Topo Maps
- Trails
- ViewRanger

7.12 Travel

When traveling third-party apps can handle activities like directions, currency exchange, reservations, translation, and locating local events and restaurants. Check out a few of these apps to see if they would fit your lifestyle.

- App in the Air
- BMW Connected
- Citymapper
- ELK
- ETA
- Glympse
- Hilton Honors
- Hotwire
- iTranslate
- Lyft

- Magic Guide to Disney World
- Marriott
- Microsoft Translator
- New York Subway
- Poison Maps
- Toyota Vehicle Remote

App in the Air includes airport maps, live updates, reminders when to head to your gate, wait times for security, and more.

7.13 Water Sports

Paddle Logger is an interesting app for those who like to be out on the water. I'm not sure what SUP and OC are, but I do like to Kayak! Sailors will appreciate Waterspeed, an app dedicated to water sports. Real-time speed, direction, distance, heart, weather, and stats make this a popular app.

Please keep in mind Apple's guidance on water resistance and avoid scuba diving, water skiing, or high-velocity water.

- Paddle Logger
- Sail Buddy
- Waterspeed

7.14 Weather

CARROT Weather frequently rates as one of the best weather apps. You can choose between an amusing "snark" version or a traditional "boring" announcer.

- CARROT Weather
- Dark Sky
- Night Sky
- Sunrise Sunset

7.15 What's Next?

Before we move on to real-life (the Day to Day chapter), I would encourage you to search online for Apple Watch apps related to your interests. There are hundreds of apps now, and more added every day.

8. Day to Day

In this chapter we discuss

Add Bluetooth Accessories

Charging Stands

Find Your Apple Watch

Find Your iPhone

Handoff and Continuity

Remote Control

Unlock Your Apple Watch

Unlock Your Mac

Theater and Sleep Mode

Watch Bands

Upgrade Your iPhone

Pair Your Watch to an iPhone

Update watchOS

What's Next?

This chapter covers those things that didn't fall into one of the previous categories. We'll also look at specific details for some common tasks.

8.1 Add Bluetooth Accessories

Low Energy Bluetooth is .3 Mbps, and classic Bluetooth is up to 2.1 Mbps. When selecting hearing aids and other devices, keep in mind Bluetooth speed impacts direct streaming.

Workout aficionados will appreciate wireless headphones, and I have to say Apple AirPods take it to the next level. Someone, or more likely several someones, put a lot of thought into engineering AirPods. Oprah's Favorite Things list for 2018 has both the Apple Watch Series 4 and AirPods. Airpods instantly turn on and connect to your iPhone, Apple Watch, iPad, or Mac. Double-tap to activate Siri to adjust volume, make a call, or change the song. The "Elgago" Silicone strap corrals AirPods to your Apple Watch.

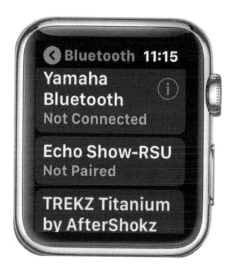

Figure 8.1   Pair Bluetooth Accessory

1.   Turn on pairing mode on your Bluetooth accessory.

2.   Press the Digital Crown on your **Apple Watch** to open the Dock.

3.   Tap the gear icon to open "Settings." If you don't see the gear, touch the watch face and move your finger until you locate the gear icon.

4.   Scroll and select "Bluetooth."

5.   Tap to select the Bluetooth accessory.

Hearing Aids

When choosing hearing aids, look for "Made for iPhone" or MFi hearing aids. Some models, like Phonak Audéo Marvel hearing aids, support direct Bluetooth streaming to both ears.

1.   Open your hearing aid's battery doors.

2.   On your **iOS device**, tap Settings > General > Accessibility > Hearing > MFi Hearing Devices.

3.   Close the battery doors of your hearing aid. Your iOS device will search for your hearing aid.

4.   Under "Devices," tap the name of your hearing aid.

5.   Tap Pair when you see the pairing request on the screen. If you have two hearing aids, you will get two requests. The pairing process could take up to a minute.

Once paired, the MFi Hearing Device screen has several options. By default "Control on Lock Screen" will be on. Leave it on to control your hearing aid from the Lock screen (using the Accessibility Shortcut,) or from Control Center. Chapter 10 has additional information on controlling MFi hearing aids.

Tap the audio status icon on your watch face, and turn the Digital Crown to adjust the volume on your Phonak Audéo Marvel hearing aids.

8.2 Charging Stands

After paying all that money for my Apple Watch, I want a safe place to charge it. I can imagine it falling off a table onto the porcelain tile. There are lots of designs available to choose from, ranging from styles where you loop the watch on the holder, to the elegant Apple Magnetic Charging Dock where the Apple Watch rests on the tray.

Most third-party docks leverage existing charging cables. The ClearGrass Amber box also has a power bank, which is ideal when traveling. It safely stores your Apple Watch and has a USB connection for charging other devices like your iPhone.

When your Apple Watch connects to the charging cable, a green lightning bolt symbol appears. The lightning bolt symbol is red when your watch needs charging. It may take a few minutes for the green lightning bolt symbol to appear if your battery level was low.

8.3 Find Your Apple Watch

Sign in to iCloud on your computer, or use the "Find My" app on your iPhone, to locate your Apple Watch. If you have an Apple HomePod, you can say, "Hey Siri, find my watch."

1. On your **iPhone**, open the "Find My" app and sign in.

2. Tap your Apple Watch to locate your watch on a map.

3. Tap "Actions" to play a sound, erase the Watch, or turn on lost mode.

8.4 Find iPhone

You may find the Control Center button "Find My iPhone" handy if you tend to misplace your iPhone as frequently as do I! Swipe up on your watch face and tap the button to sound an alert on your companion iPhone. The blue button has an iPhone with signal bars. At night touch and hold the button to **flash a light** on your iPhone.

1.   Swipe up on the **Apple Watch** face to open the Control Center.

2.   Swipe up and tap the Find My iPhone button.

8.5 Handoff and Continuity

Handoff is the ability to switch an application from one Apple device to another and is part of Apple's Continuity platform. For example, if you're reading mail on your iPad, you can continue reading the same message on your Mac or iPad. Continuity includes Handoff, the Universal Clipboard, Auto Unlock, the Continuity Camera, SMS and MMS, Cellular Calls, and Instant Hotspot.

The Apple Watch supports Continuity for Cellular Calls, Auto Unlock, and Handoff. Handoff is a way to seamlessly switch tasks between your Apple Watch, iPad, Mac, or iPhone. Wake up your Mac while wearing your Apple Watch and Auto Unlock gives you instant access to your Mac. The Universal Clipboard supports copying text, images, photos, or videos between Apple devices. The Apple Watch may include Universal Clipboard in the future. However, you can take screenshots of the Watch face, and they are saved to your iPhone photos, as outlined in Chapter 3.

Handoff From Apple Watch to iPhone

When the two devices are in range, the app appears on the other device. For example, when you have mail open on your Apple Watch, on your iPhone Mail appears in the app switcher, or as an "app banner" along the bottom of your iPhone screen.

Figure 8.2   Handoff Mail

Requirements

Each device must have these settings to use the handoff feature.

- Bluetooth enabled.

- Wi-Fi enabled.

- Signed in with the same Apple ID.

- Handoff turned on.

Enable Handoff on your Mac

1. On your **Mac**: Choose the Apple menu, System Preferences, then click General. Select "Allow Handoff between this Mac and your iCloud devices."

2. On your **iPhone, iPad**, or **iPod touch**: Go to Settings, General, Handoff, then turn on Handoff.

Enable Handoff on your Apple Watch

1. On your **iPhone**, open the Apple Watch app.

2. Swipe to scroll down to "Settings" and tap "General."

3. Scroll down and touch the "Enable Handoff" switch to toggle it on or off. The switch is green when on and white when off.

8.6 Remote Control

In Chapter 6, I discussed the Remote app for controlling your Apple TV or iTunes. I wanted to briefly mention these features here as a reminder of the possibilities. Make sure your Apple Watch, iPhone and computer are all on the same Wi-Fi network.

Apple TV

Once you pair your Apple Watch to your Apple TV, you tap or swipe your watch face to control the TV.

iTunes

At home, I play my iTunes music on a Yamaha amplifier connected to our whole house speakers. After pairing the Apple Watch remote app to my iTunes computer, I can control everything from my watch.

8.7 Unlock Your Apple Watch

When the auto-lock feature is enabled, you must enter a passcode to unlock your watch. You can also configure your iPhone to unlock your watch whenever you enter a passcode on your iPhone. The "Wrist Detect" feature will keep your watch unlocked as you move.

1. Open the **Apple Watch** app on your iPhone.

2. Tap the "My Watch" tab (bottom left).

3. Scroll down to "Passcode."

4. Scroll down and enable the setting.

8.8 Unlock Your Mac

Speaking of unlocking - did you know you can auto-unlock Mac mid-2013 or later computers with your Apple Watch? To see the version of your Mac, click on the Apple logo and then click "About this Mac." This "Continuity" feature also requires macOS Sierra or later, and that your Apple ID uses two-factor authentication. Bluetooth and Wi-Fi must be active on your Mac. Also, both devices must be signed in with the same Apple ID.

1. On your **Mac** from the Apple menu, select System Preferences.

2. Click "Security & Privacy," then select the General tab. Click the lock icon to allow changes.

3. Select "Allow your Apple Watch to unlock your Mac."

8.9 Theater and Sleep Mode

The first time I went to the movies my Apple Watch glowed with an alert; I was glad I had enabled the "Cover to Mute" option as I frantically covered my watch face with my palm. Right after that, I found "Theatre Mode." If I can remember to turn on Theatre Mode, I won't be that rude person that disturbs everyone around me.

1. Swipe up on the **Apple Watch** face to open Control Center.

2. Tap the icon for "Theatre Mode."

Silent Mode

1. Open the Apple Watch app on your **iPhone**.

2. Tap "My Watch," located in the left corner of the tab bar at the bottom of the screen.

3. Scroll down and tap "Sounds & Haptics."

4. Tap the "Silent mode" switch to toggle it on or off. The switch is green when on and white when off.

5. Press the side button on your **Apple Watch**.

6. Scroll down and tap "Settings."

7.   Scroll down and tap "Sounds & Haptics."

8.   Tap "Silent Mode."

8.10 Watch Bands

Changing watch bands seemed daunting to me at first, but after doing it one time, I realized how simple it is.

1.   Please your **watch** face down on a soft surface.

2.   Press the band release button on the back on the watch and slide the band left or right to remove it from the slot.

3.   Slide the new band into the slot until you feel and hear a click.

Figure 8.3   Release Buttons for the Watch Band

The end of the watch band that slides into the slot has a top and bottom. The top has three clips. The bottom has two clips on each end with a solid piece in the middle. If you reverse the top and bottom the band will not lock in place.

Apple Warns the Milanese Loop, Modern Buckle, and Leather Loop watch bands with magnetic clasps may cause magnetic interference with the Compass.

8.11 Upgrade Your iPhone

Backup your existing iPhone to your iCloud account, and restore the backup on your new iPhone. Your Health and Activity data is automatically stored in iCloud. The only requirement is that you sign in with the same Apple ID on all devices and run iOS 11 or later. Pair your Apple Watch to your iPhone as shown below.

8.12 Pair Your Watch to an iPhone

Normally if you hold your Apple Watch next to your iPhone, a notification will appear asking if you want to pair the iPhone to your Apple Watch. You can manually start the pairing process in the Apple Watch app on your iPhone. You can also pair your Apple Watch to additional iPhones.

1.   Open the Apple Watch app on your **iPhone**.

2.   At the top of the screen, tap your watch.

3.   Tap "Pair New Watch."

8.13 Update watchOS

When automatic updates are enabled, your Apple Watch will install updates whenever the battery level is at least 50%, and the watch is on its charger. Follow these steps to update the watchOS.

1. Ensure your Apple Watch battery level is at least 50%, and the watch is connected to the charging cable.

2. Open the Apple Watch app on your **iPhone**.

3. Open the Settings app. Tap "General" and then tap "Software Update."

8.14 What's Next?

Next up, we will look at Health and Fitness apps. I hope you agree I saved the best for last.

9. Health and Fitness

In this chapter we discuss

Basic Settings

The Health App

The Activity App

The Heart Rate App

The ECG App

GymKit

The Workout App

Sample Workouts

Additional Workout Apps

What's Next?

Chapter 9

When it comes to Health, Exercise, and Activity apps, Apple has covered all the bases with its HealthKit, GymKit, ResearchKit, and CareKit platforms. CEO Tim Cook said, "When you look back in a few years and ask, 'What was Apple's greatest contribution to mankind?' It will be about health."

The Apple Watch monitor, sensors, and health and fitness apps work together to meet your health and fitness goals. The Apple Watch features like an electrical heart rate sensor, built-in electrodes, optical heart sensor, accelerometer, and gyroscope are ideal for health and fitness apps. The accelerometer can differentiate between a walk and a run and enables features like "Running Auto Pause," to identify when you're taking an exercise break.

- Activity App
- Workout App
- Breathe (Mindfulness) App
- Health App
- ECG App
- Heart Rate App

Apple's HealthKit technology includes partners like the National Cancer Institute, the US Department of Veterans Affairs (VA), the National Heart Lung and Blood Institute, and the Mayo Clinic. So, if you're browsing "Vitals" and wonder what normal body temperature is, you will notice a citation from Mayo Clinic. Right now, there is a beta program underway designed to store your health data in one place - the Health app, of course. The list of companies supporting this feature includes LabCorp, Quest, and many hospitals and medical practices.

Third-party apps also link to medical devices with specific tasks like blood pressure monitoring or CGM (continuous glucose monitoring.) For example, the Dexcom system includes a sensor that connects to a transmitter, which communicates with a smart device. The Dexcom watch complication displays data on your Apple Watch.

9.1 Basic Settings

To ensure accurate activity logging, and accurate motion calibration and distance logging, configure these options.

- Fitness Tracking & Health
- Location Services (GPS)
- Motion, Calibration, and Distance
- Your Profile in the Health App

Motion & Fitness

1. On your **iPhone**, open Settings, and go to Privacy."

2. Scroll down and tap "Motion & Fitness."

3. Enable "Fitness Tracking."

4. Enable "Health."

After you enable the option for "Motion, Calibration, and Distance," Apple suggests you take a 20-minute walk outdoors away from Wi-Fi. This setting allows the watch to calibrate your movement with GPS location.

1. On your **iPhone**, open "Settings" and tap "Privacy."

2. Tap "Location Services" and scroll to the bottom and tap "System Services."

3. Enable "Motion, Calibration, and Distance."

Location Services

To view your location on your watch face or in the workout app set it up on your iPhone. Location is also helpful with distance calibration.

- On your **iPhone**, open Settings, and go to "Privacy."

- Enable "Location Services."

- Scroll down to the list of apps, and select "Apple Watch Faces" and "Apple Watch Workout."

- Set both options to "While Using the App."

Heart Rate Alerts

Set heart rate alerts in notification settings.

- On your **iPhone**, open the Apple Watch app.

- Tap "Notifications."

- Tap "High Heart Rate" or "Low Heart Rate" and set the threshold.

Setup the Health App

Your Apple Watch uses your personal information: height, weight, gender, and age to calculate metrics for daily activity. It also asks your activity levels. Activity levels are light, moderate, or active. Enter your personal information, as shown in the topic "Health Account" that follows.

9.2 The Health App

The Health app on your iPhone is the focal point for your health data and health account settings. With iOS 13 and later, a dynamic Summary View displays health data, including Highlights. The Health app displays metrics for Activity, Workout, Mindfulness, Cycle Tracking, Heart Rate, and more. The Heart Rate app also shows insights into your heart rate, such as your Heart Rate Recovery results.

When linked to other health apps, the Health app displays body measurements, health records, lab results, and vital statistics in one place. The Health app also provides personalized encouragement and coaching.

iOS 12.1.1 introduced blood pressure monitoring, Electrocardiogram monitoring, and irregular rhythm notifications. iOS 13 added Cycle Tracking, Highlights, and a dynamic Summary View to the Health app. Apple also began using machine learning with iOS 13 to focus on relevant topics based on your interactions. For example, if you routinely weigh yourself, your Highlights may show data related to weight loss.

Your Health Account

Your Account data in the "Health Profile" screen displays your personal information and has the options shown below. In the Privacy section, you can control which health records each app or device can read or write to your health data at a granular level.

- Health Profile
- Medical ID
- Organ Donation
- Health Records
- Privacy (Apps & Devices)

Chapter 9

Your Health Profile

Your vital statistics in your Health Profile are used by app algorithms to ensure your health and activity data is accurate. I'd encourage you to enter this information in the Health app. Fitness, exercise, health, and other third-party apps use your personal health information. For example, the Fitzpatrick Skin Type Scale measures how susceptible your skin is to the sun's rays. In combination with weather apps, this information is used to predict the effects of the daily UV index.

- Birth Date

- Sex

- Blood Type

- Fitzpatrick Skin Type

- Wheelchair

Edit Your Personal Informational

1. On your **iPhone**, open the "Health" app.

2. In the top right corner of the screen, tap the "Account" icon that looks like a person. If you don't see the icon, swipe down.

3. In watchOS 6, swipe up and tap "Health Profile."

4. In the top right corner of the screen, tap "Edit."

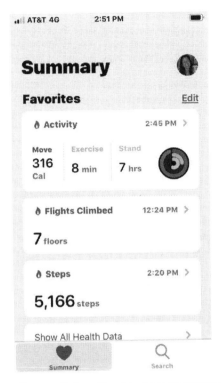

Figure 9.1   Health App Summary Page

Wheelchair Mode

While "Wheelchair" mode is active, the "stand goal" in the Activity app changes to a "roll goal," and the "steps" counter changes to "pushes." Two new workouts take into account different pushing conditions with varying speeds and terrain. To ensure you receive the Weekly Summary report on Monday, be sure to change the "Wheelchair" mode to "Yes" or "No." If "Wheelchair" is "Not Set," it could affect Activity Logging.

Configure Medical ID in the Health App

1. On your **iPhone**, open the "Health" app.

2. In watchOS 6 or later, in the top right corner of the screen, tap the "Account" icon that looks like a person. If you don't see the icon, swipe down.

3. Swipe up and tap "Export All Health Data."

Prioritize Data Sources

To conserve battery power, you could use an external heart rate monitor instead of the sensor on your Apple Watch. Set the external heart rate monitor as the preferred data source, as shown below.

1. On your iPhone, open the "Health" app.

2. In the bottom tab bar tap "Browse."

3. Swipe up to see Health Categories and Health Records. For example, Tap "Health" and then swipe to tap "Heart Rate."

4. Swipe up and tap "Data Sources & Access." Drag the external heart rate monitor to the top of the list.

Health Data Backups

In case you replace or upgrade your iPhone, note that if you use iCloud and your iPhone has iOS 11 and later, iCloud already has your Health and Activity data. Data is automatically kept up to date on devices where you've signed in with the same Apple ID.

The Health Data Screen

In watchOS 5, the Health Data screen has four categories: Activity, Mindfulness, Nutrition, and Sleep, and you could tap the Activity button to see your daily and weekly logs. watchOS 6 introduced a Summary page and a Search feature. Open the Health app and tap "Search" in the bottom tab bar to see the categories shown below.

Data for some of these categories will come from a variety of sources. Some data comes from third-party apps. For example, sleep tracking data logged by the Pillow app. Apple partners like the VA, Labcorp, or hospitals also add health data. Smart devices may record blood pressure or glucose data. The Apple Watch automatically records Heart and Activity data. Finally, you can enter data yourself, such as Body Measurements, Cycle Tracking, Nutrition, Vitals, and more.

- Activity

- Body Measurements

- Cycle Tracking

- Hearing

- Heart

- Mindfulness

- Nutrition

- Other Data

- Respiratory

- Sleep

- Vitals

- Health Records: Allergies

- Health Records: Clinical Vitals

- Health Records: Conditions

- Health Records: Immunizations

- Health Records: Lab Results

- Health Records: Medications

- Health Records: Procedures

- Heart

Data Sources indicate apps linked to your Health data. For instance, my sleep app reports my sleep analysis in the "Sleep" category.

1. On your **iPhone**, open the "Health" app.

2. In the bottom tab bar tap "Browse."

3. Swipe up to see Health Categories and Health Records. For example, Tap Activity and then swipe to tap "Workouts." In the top right corner of the screen, tap "Edit" to add data. Only some activities have an "Edit" option.

On the Health Data tab, you can add accounts like Quest, LabCorp, hospitals, and other supported medical providers. After account linking you can see LabCorp diagnostic reports on the "Results" screen as shown below.

Figure 9.2 Health Data

View Heart Rate Data

The Health Data tab is also where you can view data from the "Heart Rate" app.

1. On your **iPhone**, open the "Health" app.

2. In the bottom tab bar tap "Browse."

3. Swipe up and tap "Heart." Tap "Heart Rate" to see details.

4. Tap a letter at the top of the screen to move between hours, days, weeks, months, or years. Tap anywhere on the graph to

view the day, time, minimum, and maximum information. Swipe left or right on the graph to change the time frame.

Add Lab Records

You can add lab or hospital records to your Health app.

1. On your **iPhone**, open the "Health" app.

2. In the top right corner of the screen, tap the "Account" icon that looks like a person. If you don't see the icon, swipe down.

3. Scroll down and tap "Health Records."

4. Tap "**Add Account**" and browse to select a company.

Explore Recommended Apps

In each Activity category, Apple includes a section called "Recommended Apps." Tap on the app you are interested in, and it opens in the App Store.

Although the Health app reminds you to set a consistent time to go to sleep, at this time, it doesn't monitor your sleep patterns. To track your sleep patterns, install a third-party app such as one shown below, or explore the recommended apps. Sleep affects diet, motivation, energy levels, muscle growth, and tissue repair. Proper sleep means you are more focused and have better blood sugar regulation. And most importantly, in my opinion, a fat-burning growth hormone is released while you sleep!

- Auto Sleep
- Sleep ++
- Sleepwatch

● Pillow

Export Health Data

Not only can you save your health data, but you can also export the data to XML files and e-mail or message to anyone. The new ECG app has an option to "Export a PDF for Your Doctor." No more fudging our answers when your doctor asks how much you exercise a week!

As far as I know, there isn't a handy app to interpret the XML files at this time, but you can export them following these instructions.

1. On your **iPhone**, open the "Health" app.

2. In the top right corner of the screen, tap the "Account" icon that looks like a person. If you don't see the icon, swipe down.

3. Scroll down and tap "Export Health Data."

9.3 The Activity App

The Activity app ensures you are getting enough exercise every day, and will send you reminders to stand, move, or exercise. Activity Trends introduced in watchOS 6 provide a long term look at your activity goals. In addition to notifications and reminders, special challenges, and daily coaching options encourage you to meet your goals. We'll look at sharing and competitions in the next topics.

The Activity app has three goals: move, stand, and exercise. Apple calculates your exercise and stand goals for you, but does allow you to change your move goal. The goals change weekly, adapting to your lifestyle. Goals will be attainable or a challenge that is within your reach. My goal is to be active enough that I'm not embarrassed to turn on "Activity Sharing Notifications" with my nieces and nephews. Activity sharing works with friends who also have an Apple Watch.

Activity Trends introduced in watchOS 6 provide a long term look at your activity goals, as shown below.

Set Activity Settings

1.   Open the Apple Watch app on your **iPhone**.

2.   Tap "My Watch," located in the left corner of the tab bar at the bottom of the screen.

3.   Swipe up and tap "Activity."

4.   Tap the "Stand Reminders" switch to turn off. The switch is green when on.

Share Activity with a Friend

Activity Sharing is a great way to find out just how serious your friends, or husband, feel about winning. In hindsight, working out with my husband wasn't one of my better ideas. For friends who also have an Apple Watch, you can share your activity. The information listed below is shared. Personal information is not shared.

- The day's activity rings which include exercise and stand minutes.

- The number of active calories you burn throughout the day.

- Workout information, including type and duration.

- Daily step counter.

Enable Sharing

You can share your activity with up to 40 friends. Use preset replies to lend encouragement, or choose a "smack talk" reply.

1.   On your **iPhone**, open the "Activity" app.

2.   In the tab bar along the bottom of your screen, tap "Sharing."

3.   Tap the "Add" icon in the top right corner of the screen. The icon looks like a red plus sign.

4.   Tap "Add" again to select a contact, or simply type the e-mail address.

When your friend accepts your request, the next time you open the Activity app, you can accept the invitation.

Accept a Sharing Request

Seriously, you may want to think twice before accepting an invitation from a friend (or spouse). If you want to go forward, this is how to accept the invitation.

1.   On your **iPhone**, open the Activity app.

2.   Tap the "Sharing" tab.

3.   Tap the account icon at the top of the screen.

4.   Tap, Accept, or Ignore.

View Your Friend's Progress

1.   On your **iPhone** or **Apple Watch**, open the Activity app.

2.   Tap the "Sharing" tab.

3.   Tap the name of your friend to see their progress.

Chapter 9

Enable Activity Sharing Notifications

1. Open the Apple Watch app on your **iPhone**.

2. Tap "My Watch," located in the left corner of the tab bar at the bottom of the screen.

3. Swipe up and tap "Activity."

4. Tap the "Activity Sharing Notifications" toggle to turn on. A green switch indicates the switch is on.

Move, Exercise, & Stand Rings

The Activity app has three rings: move, exercise, and stand. The idea is to close your rings every day. When the rings overlap, you've exceeded your goal. While "Wheelchair mode" is active, the "stand goal" in the Activity app changes to a "roll goal," and the "steps" counter changes to "pushes."

Move Ring

The Move ring tracks steps or "pushes." Each week your Apple Watch displays a weekly summary and suggests a new weekly Move Goal based on your daily average for the week. Tap the plus or minus symbols, and then tap "Set Move Goal."

Figure 9.3   The Weekly Goal

Exercise Ring

Your personal exercise goal is calculated based on your vital statistics. Set vital statistics like age and sex in the Health app outlined in the next section.

Stand Ring

The Stand goal is one minute every hour, for twelve hours a day.

Change the Move Goal

Follow these steps to change your Move Goal in the app.

1. On your **Apple Watch,** press the Side Button.

2. Scroll and tap the Activity app.

3. Firmly press the screen and tap "Change Move Goal."

4. Use the symbols or turn the Digital Crown to adjust your goal.

5. Tap "Update."

Trends

Trends are located in the bottom tab and average the past 90-days of physical activity, and then compare it to the past 365 days. Arrows show whether you are trending up or down for the Move goal, Exercise, the Stand goal, Distance, Flights climbed, and your Walking Pace.

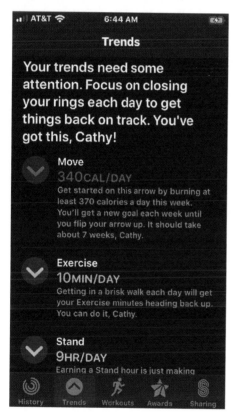

Figure 9.4 Trends

It can be an eye-opener to see how much of a lifestyle change you've had, instead of what I thought was a gradual decline. The personalized coaching and guidance is based on your results and will help get you back on track if needed.

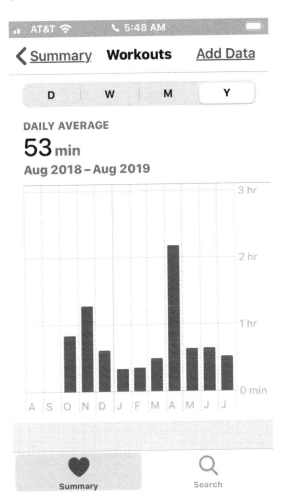

Figure 9.5   Workouts

Trends in the Activity app and Highlights in the Health app are new in iOS 13. The Highlights also displays a map of your exercise route, as shown below.

Figure 9.6   Highlights

Challenge a Friend

For a little friendly competition, challenge a friend. During a 7-day competition, you both earn points by filling your Activity rings. You can earn up to 600 points a day. When you share an Activity with a friend, you can reply to notifications with a "challenge." In the Activity app, you can also issue a challenge at any time.

1.   On your **Apple Watch**, open the "Activity" app.

2.   Swipe left, tap a friend, then tap "Compete."

While I have yet to experience the phenomenon, Apple did announce watchOS 5.1.2 and later included animated celebrations when you achieve the maximum daily points in an Activity competition. I obviously need to challenge a new set of friends if I'm ever going to achieve this goal.

VO2 max Metric

VO2 max is a measure of your cardio fitness. You can view VO2 max on the Activity tab in the Health app. Merriam-Webster defines VO2 max as the maximum amount of oxygen the body can use during a specified period of usually intense exercise that depends on body weight and the strength of the lungs. You'll need to work out at your maximum intensity for 20 minutes for Apple Watch to record a VO2 max metric.

Hearing Metrics

The Noise app in watchOS 6 includes a Decibel Level complication and updates to the Health app. The Health app Hearing metric shows sound levels and your 7-Day Exposure. The Health app displays Charts and information about the risks of high noise levels over time. I think the Headphone Audio Level metric is particularly interesting.

History, Weekly Summary & Details

On Monday morning, your watch displays a weekly summary, along with a new Move goal suggestion. When the weekly summary is displayed, tap the plus or minus symbols, and then tap "Set Move Goal."

Workout and Activity History

1. On your **iPhone**, open the "Activity" app.

2. In the bottom tab bar tap "Summary" or "Search."

3. Swipe up to see activities like Steps, Distance, and Flights Climbed.

4. Select an Activity. Tap a day, and then swipe up to see details.

Weekly Summary or Activity Details

1. On your **Apple Watch** open the "Activity" app. Force touch the dial (press firmly and hold) to open the options.

2. Select "Weekly Summary."

3. Scroll up to see calories, steps, distance, and flights climbed.

Activity Reminders

1. On your **iPhone**, select Settings, and scroll to Notifications.

2. Tap "Activity," and then tap "Allow Notifications."

Manually Add a Workout or Activity

Sometimes I forget to record a workout or want to manually add calories or some other data to my Health record. The following steps apply to the various data points, but this example is specifically for workouts.

1. On your **iPhone**, open the "Activity" app.

2. In watchOS 6, in the bottom tab bar on the right, tap: Search.

3. Tap "Activity." Swipe to scroll and tap "Workout."

4.   In the top right corner of the screen, tap "Add Data."

9.4 The Heart Rate App

The Heart Rate ⬤ app displays your current, resting, and walking average heart rate. iOS 12.1.1 and later includes blood pressure monitoring, electrocardiogram monitoring, and irregular rhythm notifications. The optical heart sensor uses photoplethysmography (PPG) to detect your heart rate. The Apple Watch green LED lights, paired with light-sensitive photodiodes, detect the amount of blood flowing through your wrist based on green light absorption.

1.   On your **Apple Watch,** press the Side Button.

2.   Scroll and tap the "Heart Rate" app.

3.   Swipe or turn the Digital Crown to see your "Resting Rate" and your "Walking Average" heart rate.

When you open the Heart Rate app on your Apple Watch, it measures your heart rate every five seconds. To measure your heart rate every second, touch your finger to the Digital Crown. When you lift your finger, the Heart Rate app goes back to measuring your heart rate every five seconds.

The Health app also records your Heart Rate Recovery after a workout. watchOS 4 first introduced Heart Rate Recovery. Heart Rate Recovery measures your heart rate when you end a workout, and compares it to your heart rate two minutes later. So for instance, depending on your age, a heart rate recovery over 60 would be considered very good. Search the internet for the latest information on heart rate recovery and see where you stand. There is scientific evidence that suggests a low heart rate recovery indicates heart problems. Check out the "Heart Rate" app in Chapter 6 for instructions on how to view your "Heart Rate Recovery."

9.5 The ECG App

The Apple ECG app arrived with watchOS 5.1.2 and iOS 12.1.1. The app provides heart rate monitoring similar to an electrocardiogram (EKG). The FDA granted the app the De Novo classification in the U.S. for the ECG and atrial fibrillation detection features. The ECG app works by measuring your heart rate on your wrist while you touch the opposite hand to the electrode in the Digital Crown, creating a circuit.

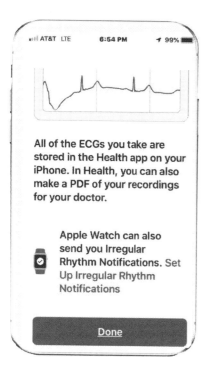

Figure 9.7   ECG App

Install the latest watchOS software to see the ECG icon on your watch. Follow these steps to check if you have the latest watchOS software on your iPhone.

1.   Update your **Apple Watch** to the latest watchOS version.

2.   On your **iPhone**, open the "Health" app. The app will prompt you to set up the ECG app.

3.   Tap "Browse" located in the tab bar at the bottom of the screen.

4.   Swipe up and tap "Heart."

5.   Swipe up and tap "Electrocardiograms."

Figure 9.8   Take an ECG

9.6 GymKit

Recently you may have noticed elliptical or treadmill equipment compatible with Apple's new GymKit platform. Tap your watch against the machine's NFC reader at any time during your workout. Your Apple Watch pairs with the machine, and the "Workout" app opens on your watch. Look for the green logo "Connects to Apple Watch."

For those who regularly use gym equipment, you're familiar with entering your age and weight to gauge your optimal heart rate and calculate calories burned. Until now, you had two options; enter information every time you work out, or create an account and log in. The GymKit interface automatically connects with a tap of your Apple Watch, and your workout data syncs with the Health Kit app automatically. Manufacturers supporting GymKit include:

- Life Fitness (Elevation, Integrity, Discover)

- TechnoGym

- Matrix Fitness

- StarTrac

- Stairmaster

- Schwin

- Nautilus

9.7 The Workout App

The workout app is quite sophisticated and encompasses several different components. The workout app includes walking, running, cycling, hiking, swimming, and yoga workouts, to name a few. If you don't see the workout you want, the "other" category allows you to record a workout and then give it a custom name. watchOS 6 allows you to review elevation and summary data on your Apple Watch during a workout, and shuffle your workout playlist.

First, we will look at the mechanics of a workout: starting a workout, viewing progress, pausing, and stopping. Recording a workout is effortless with the Apple Watch. The watch is engineered with an accelerometer and gyroscope to correctly identify your movements, and pause workouts when you stop moving. The app even asks if you want to end the workout when it detects a change in your movements.

To help the time pass, Apple provides entertainment in the form of podcasts, music, or Audible books. Lastly, for motivation, Apple hasn't overlooked the social aspect of workouts. The watchOS 5 and later include challenges and sharing your Activity data.

Next, we will look at the mechanics of a workout: starting a workout, viewing progress, pausing, and stopping a workout.

Running Auto Pause

Thanks to the Apple Watch accelerometer, your workout will automatically pause when you take an exercise break. Workouts automatically resume when you start moving again. Enable this feature in the Apple Watch App, as shown below.

1. On your **iPhone**, open the Apple Watch App.

2. Tap "My Watch," located in the left corner of the tab bar at the bottom of the screen.

3. Tap "Workout," then toggle on "Running Auto Pause."

Metrics

Each workout has its own set of metrics, which you can reorder and customize to your personal preferences. Metrics vary by workout and may include the items listed below. So for example, the hiking workout uses pace, heart rate, and elevation gain.

- Duration
- Active Calories
- Heart Rate
- Average Pace

- Current Pace

- Distance

- Current Cadence

- Average Cadence

- Total Calories

- Elevation Gain

- Rolling Mile

Cadence is your steps per minute. Elevation gain ensures you will get credit when hiking those tough hills. We recently biked up a mountain in Acadia National Park, and I like knowing I get credit for that since it almost killed me. While working out, you can view metrics when you raise your wrist and turn the Digital Crown.

1. On your **iPhone**, open the Apple Watch app.

2. Tap "My Watch," located at the left corner of the tab bar at the bottom of the screen.

3. Tap "Workout."

4. Make sure "Workout View" is set to "Multiple Metric."

5. In the "Workouts" section tap the workout you are interested in, for example, "Outdoor Walk."

6. The top of the list displays included metrics. To remove a metric tap "Edit" in the top left corner of the screen.

7. Drag the three horizontal bars to reorder the items. Swipe left to delete.

Scroll down to the "Do Not Include" section to add metrics.

Start a Workout

1. On Your **Apple Watch**, press the Side Button to open the Dock.

2. Swipe and tap "Workout."

3. Swipe to find your workout, and then tap to start the workout.

4. watchOS 6 added the ability to review your workout data on your Apple Watch. Alternatively, you can view data in the Health app on your iPhone.

Tip: When running at night – for safety, try turning on the strobe flashlight. Swipe up on the Apple Watch face, tap the flashlight, and then swipe left.

Set a Goal

On your **Apple Watch**, select a workout as outlined above, and tap "More." The more icon looks like an ellipsis. The More Settings are also where you can set a pace alert. Goals include Calories, Distance, or Time. When you reach your goal, the workout automatically ends.

Figure 9.9   Workout Options

Add to Your Workout

To add another type of workout without ending your session, open the Workout app, swipe right, then tap the "Add" icon that looks like a green plus symbol.

Track Your Progress (View Metrics)

Raise your wrist and turn the Digital Crown to highlight a metric.

Listen to Music While You Workout

When working out with your Apple Watch, swipe left to play music.

Watch a Podcast or Tune in a Show

1. On our **Apple Watch**, open the "Podcasts" app.

2. Tap "Podcasts" in the top left corner of the screen. Tap on "iPhone" or "Library."

3. Tap Listen Now, Shows, Episodes, or Stations.

To play podcasts stored on your Apple Watch, in the Podcasts app, turn the Digital Crown to scroll and tap a podcast.

Pause Your Workout

On Your Apple Watch, press the Digital Crown and the side button at the same time. Press both buttons again to resume your workout.

End Your Workout

On Your **Apple Watch**, swipe right, then tap the red X.

Name Your 'Other' Workout

At the end of an "Other" workout, you can choose a name for the workout such as Barre, Core, Cross Training, Kickboxing, Dance, Badminton, Table Tennis, Tennis, Archery, AUS Football, Baseball, Basketball, Bowling, Boxing, Climbing, or Cricket. I have to admit; initially, I didn't understand why my daughters wanted to go to a barre class. I asked them, "Why do you have to learn how to drink?" I'll probably never live that one down.

1. On your **Apple Watch**, open the "Workout" app.

2. Tap "Other."

3. Complete your workout.

4. Swipe right and tap "End."

5. Tap "Name Workout," then tap Save.

Workout and Activity History

WatchOS 6 added Trends to the tab bar.

1. On your **iPhone**, open the "Activity" app.

2. In the bottom tab bar, tap History, Trends, Workouts, or Awards.

9.8 Sample Workouts

The Apple Workout app includes these workouts: yoga, hiking, cycle, stair stepper, rower, run, walk, strength training, elliptical, or interval training. You can also expand your workouts, utilizing third-party apps. You may find the following list of some of the features related to workouts of interest.

- Listen to podcasts or Audible books. Install the apps on your Apple Watch, as shown in Chapter 6.

- Set custom metrics for each workout. See the earlier section for specifics on Metrics. While working out, you can view metrics when you raise your wrist and turn the Digital Crown.

- At night turn on the strobe flashlight. Swipe up on the Apple Watch face, tap the flashlight, and then swipe left.

Running

Since I have specially fitted running shoes, I have no excuse not to run. But I don't. I find running really difficult. For those of you amazing people who have mastered the experience, I have listed a few ideas for your running workout.

- Listen to podcasts or Audible books. Install the apps on your Apple Watch as shown in Chapter 6.

- Enable the metrics for average and current cadence, or average and current pace. While working out, you can view metrics when you raise your wrist and turn the Digital Crown. See the earlier section for specifics on Metrics.

- At night turn on the strobe flashlight. Swipe up on the Apple Watch face, tap the flashlight, and then swipe left.

- Enable "Running Auto Pause." On your **iPhone**, open the Apple Watch App. Tap "Workout," then toggle on "Running Auto Pause."

- The option "Set Pace Alert" ensures you're not running too fast or too slow. When starting an Outdoor workout, tap the "More" icon (that looks like an ellipse). Then swipe up and tap "Set Pace Alert." There is an option for minutes per mile.

Swimming and Water Sports

The Workout app has an option for "Open Water Swim" or "Pool Swim" workouts. Third-party apps like Paddle Logger or "Waterspeed," are ideal for water sports. Real-time speed, direction, distance, heart, weather, and stats make this a popular app.

Please keep in mind Apple's guidance on water resistance and avoid scuba diving, water skiing, or high-velocity water while wearing your Apple Watch.

Turn on Water Lock

1. On your **Apple Watch**, swipe up from the bottom of the screen to open Control Center.

2. Tap the water lock icon. It looks like a drop of water.

When your workout is over, turn the Digital Crown to unlock the screen and clear water from the speaker.

Yoga

There is a Yoga Workout available with Apple Watch. To avoid bumping your watch during a workout, you could change the watch orientation, or turn on Water Lock.

Workout Playlist

Whenever you start a workout, you can automatically play music from a workout playlist you configure in your iPhone Apple Watch app.

1.   On your **iPhone**, open the Apple Watch app.

2.   Swipe to scroll down and tap "Workout."

3.   Swipe up and tap "Workout playlist" to select a playlist for your workouts.

If you haven't already added music to your Apple Watch, check out Chapter 6 (Watch Apps, Music), or follow these steps.

1.   On your **iPhone**, open the Apple Watch app.

2.   Swipe to scroll down and tap "Music."

3.   Tap the playlist or album you want to add.

9.9 Additional Workout Apps

There are third-party workout apps geared toward specific activities like sailing, kayaking, or climbing. Social networking and entertainment apps add a little fun into your workout, and apps like Forest and Breathe promote mindfulness. Check out these and other apps in Chapter 7.

- Audible
- Gymatic
- Lifesum
- Music
- Paddle Logger

- Podcasts
- Pokémon
- Runtastic
- Seedling Scavenger Bingo
- Strava
- Strong

Strava is a social network created specifically for athletes. You can configure devices like your Peloton bike with Strava. The next step to complete integration is to configure the Strava app with Apple Watch.

Entertainment apps like Music, Podcasts, and Audible help your workout pass by quickly. Amazon's "Whispersync" technology allows you to listen on one device like your Apple Watch, and then seamlessly continue reading on your Kindle. How awesome is it to go for a run and listen to the new number one bestseller? Honesty compels me to point out I didn't say when "I" go for a run since my exercise level is more along the lines of a brisk walk. I also want to add a shameless plug here for my books: "Smart Home, Digital Assistants, Home Automation and the Internet of Things," and as soon as Amazon accepts it this book will also be available on Audible.

Don't limit yourself to boring gym workouts. Why not do something fun for exercise? Although I don't even know what the Pokémon game is, when I read sessions can be logged as workouts and traveling certain distances for egg hatching counts as steps, I thought, "Why not?"

A few years back, National Geographic had a scavenger hunt in grocery stores. I find it amazing how many countries are represented at my local grocery store. Anyway, the App Store has scavenger hunt games like Seedling Scavenger Bingo. Seedling Scavenger Bingo works on an Apple Watch or smartphone so that most everyone can play. This app would have been simply awesome for sleep over parties when my daughter was younger, or for rainy afteroons when the kids are bored and driving you out of your mind. Oops, did I just say that? Let me try the politically correct version. I loved raising my daughter, but it came with challenges.

Nature and sports enthusiasts will appreciate these apps that are available today for your Apple Watch. Several of these apps also have complications for your watch face.

- AllTrails
- Big Year Birding ABA
- Gaia GPS
- Gardenia
- Golf Shot
- Komoot
- Scavenger
- New York City Museums
- Paddle Logger
- Santa Fe Botanical
- Trails

Similar to Apple's "Breathe" app, the "Forest-Stay Focused" app has a unique approach to being mindful. Forest is hard to describe so I'd encourage you to check it out. There's a reason it's the #1 app in 113 countries.

Explore Apps

Why not search the App Store today for your favorite hobby, or try searching for sailing, hiking, nature, botany, or birding? Another option is to explore "Recommended Apps" in the Health app. Simply tap on the app you are interested in, and it opens in the App Store.

1.   On your **iPhone**, open the "Health" app.

2.   In the bottom row, tap "Health Data."

3.   Tap Activity, Mindfulness, Nutrition, or Sleep.

4.   Scroll down to the "Recommended Apps."

5.   Tap the app.

9.10 What's Next?

After reviewing all the health features in this chapter, I hope you can find a place for at least some of them in your life. Now let's take a look at the accessibility features in Chapter 10.

Chapter 9

10. Accessibility

In this chapter we discuss

The Accessibility Shortcut

The Taptic Engine

Customize App Notifications

Vision

Workout App

Hearing

Bluetooth Accessories

Messaging

The Walkie-Talkie App

What's Next?

In earlier chapters, we briefly mentioned haptic alerts and other accessibility features unique to the watchOS operating system. In this chapter. I wanted to recap and expand on those topics. Apple has an accessibility site that showcases these features.

The work Apple has done for accessibility is outstanding. In fact, in November 2018, Apple won the prestigious Eleanor Roosevelt Humanitarian Award from the Center for Hearing and Communication for its accessibility features. The Apple Watch, watchOS, and Apple Apps work together to provide accessibility in three areas.

- Vision

- Hearing

- Physical and Motor Skills in the Workout App

watchOS 6 added Accessibility options to the Settings app on your Apple Watch. In the next sections, we will discuss haptic alerts (wrist touches), accessibility settings, app integrations, wheelchair settings, and workouts.

10.1 Accessibility Shortcut

The "Accessibility Shortcut" uses the Digital Crown to turn on "Zoom" or "VoiceOver" with a triple-click.

1. Open the **Apple Watch** app on your **iPhone**.

2. Tap My Watch and go to "General."

3. Tap Accessibility, then tap "Accessibility Shortcut."

4. Choose "VoiceOver" or "Zoom."

10.2 The Taptic Engine

The Taptic Engine encompasses "Haptic" wrist touches to alert you to an activity or message. For example, haptic alerts in the Map app gently vibrate to indicate an upcoming turn. Taptic Touch is a useful accessibility feature for deaf or hard of hearing drivers.

- On your **iPhone**, open the Apple Watch app.

- In the Haptics section, tap the "Haptic Alerts" switch to toggle Haptic Alerts on or off. The switch is green when on and white when off.

To ensure you receive alerts, check that "Notification Center" is configured to your preferences.

Enable the Notification Indicator

1. On your **iPhone**, open the Apple Watch app.

2. Tap "Notifications."

3. Enable the "Notifications Indicator." When enabled a red dot at the top of your watch face indicates you have unread notifications.

10.3 Customize App Notifications

Some apps allow you to customize notification options. There is also a choice to "Mirror my iPhone," to use the same notification settings on your iPhone and Apple Watch. These are the notification choices.

- Allow Notifications
- Send to Notification Center
- Notifications Off

To set app notification options, follow these steps.

- On your **iPhone**, open the Apple Watch app.
- Tap "Notifications."
- Tap an app and select the option.

10.4 Vision

As outlined in Chapter 3, there are several settings on the "Accessibility" screen to accommodate vision. Visual enhancements include these "General" settings as well as an X-Large watch face. A complication on the X-Large watch face fills the entire screen.

- Bold Text
- Reduce Motion
- Reduce Transparency
- Side Button Click Speed
- VoiceOver
- Zoom
- On/Off Labels
- Grayscale

VoiceOver

VoiceOver is a built-in screen reader. As you move your finger over the display, each item is announced. The VoiceOver feature has

37 supported languages and works with all native apps, including mail, calendar, maps, or messages.

During the initial setup process, press the Digital Crown three times to activate "VoiceOver." There is also a setting to toggle the Accessibility Shortcut on, as mentioned earlier.

Siri excels at toggling VoiceOver on or off. Press the Digital Crown to wake up Siri and say, "Turn on VoiceOver." Siri responds with "VoiceOver on." If you prefer, you can turn on VoiceOver in "Settings."

1.   On your **Apple Watch**, press the Side Button.

2.   Tap Settings, and then tap General.

3.   Swipe to select "Accessibility."

4.   Tap "VoiceOver" to toggle on or off.

Tap twice to open an app. "Tap twice" works in place of any single tap action. To go back to the last screen-swipe a "Z" on the screen. While using VoiceOver, there is a "Screen Curtain" setting to turn off the Apple Watch display for privacy.

Set the Reading Rate

The reading rate is controlled by "Accessibility" settings.

1.   On your **Apple Watch**, press the Side Button.

2.   Tap "Settings," and then tap "General."

3.   Swipe to select "Accessibility."

4.   Drag the slide bar to adjust the reading rate.

Zoom

The Zoom magnification is fifteen times the native size. Turn the Digital Crown, or pinch the screen with two fingers, to control the zoom level.

On/Off Labels

The "On/Off Labels" setting will display additional label information when toggled on.

Grayscale

The "Grayscale" settings assist users where the color might impair visibility. Grayscale is a system-wide setting.

10.5 Workout App

The Workout app is optimized for wheelchair users. Two wheelchair-specific workouts take into account varying speeds, terrain, and pushing conditions. There is also a new "Time to Roll" notification. While "Wheelchair mode" is active, the "stand goal" in the Activity app changes to a "roll goal," and the "steps" counter changes to "pushes."

In the Health app toggle the "Wheelchair" switch on or off. To ensure you receive the Weekly Summary report on Monday, be sure to change the "Wheelchair" setting to "Yes" or "No." If "Wheelchair" is "Not Set," it could affect Activity logging.

1. On your **iPhone**, open the Apple Watch app.

2. Tap "My Watch" located in the left corner of the tab bar, at the bottom of the screen.

3. Swipe up, then tap "Health."

4. Tap "Edit" in the top right corner of the screen.

5. Tap Wheelchair, and choose an option at the bottom of the screen.

10.6 Hearing

If you're deaf or hard of hearing in one ear, you may miss some stereo audio or alerts. The "Mono Audio" setting plays both audio channels in both ears. You can also adjust the balance for greater volume in either ear. Toggle the "Mono Audio" switch on the "Accessibility" screen and use the slider to adjust the volume for the left or right side.

1. On your **Apple Watch** press the Side Button.

2. Tap "Settings," and then tap "General."

3. Swipe to select "Accessibility."

4. Tap the "Mono Audio" switch to toggle the switch on or off.

5. Drag the slider bar to adjust the volume for the left or right side.

10.7 Bluetooth Accessories

Low Energy Bluetooth is .3 Mbps, and Classic Bluetooth is up to 2.1 Mbps. If you are using hearing aids, look for those that are "Made for iPhone" or MFi. Some models, like Phonak Audéo Marvel hearing aids, support direct Bluetooth streaming to both ears. Chapter 8 discusses how to add Bluetooth accessories.

Hearing Aids

With watchOS 6 you can pair Bluetooth hearing aids to your Apple Watch in the Settings app, as shown below. You can also control hearing aid volume with the Digital Crown.

Figure 10.1   Connected Bluetooth Hearing Aids

In addition to regular Bluetooth hearing aids, MFi, or Made for iPhone, hearing aids have additional options on the Hearing Device screen. By default "Control on Lock Screen" will be on. Leave it on to control your hearing aid from the Lock Screen (using the Accessibility Shortcut) and from Control Center. The list below shows MFi options.

- Play Ringtones
- Audio Routing
- Control Nearby Devices
- Audio Handoff
- Control on Lock Screen

Hearing Aids that support Classic Bluetooth with speeds up to 2.1 Mbps are better for direct audio streaming. For innovative hearing aid designs, check out the 2019 CES Innovation Awards for accessibility products.

With Audio Routing you select the default device for audio playback. Audio Handoff allows you to continue listening with your hearing aid when you switch between your iOS devices.

The "Control Nearby Devices" applies to iOS devices. Your iOS device will adjust hearing aid settings when devices are on the same Wi-Fi network and connected to your iCloud account.

1. Open your hearing aid's battery doors, or power rechargeable hearing aids off.

2. On your **iPhone**, tap Settings > General > Accessibility > Hearing > MFi Hearing Devices.

3. Close your hearing aid's battery doors, or turn on your rechargeable hearing aid. Your iOS device will search for your hearing aid.

4. Under Devices, tap the name of your hearing aid.

5. Tap Pair when you see the pairing request on the screen. If you have two hearing aids, you will get two requests. The pairing process can take up to a minute.

Control your MFi Hearing Aid

Control the volume of your Phonak Audéo Marvel hearing aid with your Apple Watch. Tap the audio status icon on your watch face, and turn the Digital Crown to adjust volume.

Use your iOS device to see your hearing aid's battery life, turn on Live Listen, and more. To configure your hearing aid, use "Settings" or the Accessibility Shortcut on your iPhone. Tap your hearing aid name for these options.

● View battery life.

● Unpair your hearing aid.

- Adjust volume levels for either or both hearing aids.

- "Live Listen" options (Basic, Restaurant, Outdoor, Party.)

10.8 Messaging

Text messaging is a great alternative to close-captioned phone calls. Unfortunately, Facetime is not available on your watch at this time.

10.9 The Walkie-Talkie App

WatchOS 5 introduced the Walkie-Talkie app. The new Walkie-Talkie app simplifies conversations. Apple Watch Series 1 or later watches with watchOS 5 or later can use Walkie-Talkie. To instantly start a conversation, press the side button. Release the side button to listen. Communicate with anyone who has a compatible Apple Watch. Both devices must have connectivity through a Bluetooth connection to the iPhone, Wi-Fi, or cellular. A gentle tap or sound alerts you to a conversation.

Tip: The "Tap to Talk" setting for the Walkie-Talkie app is also found under the General, Accessibility screen.

*10.10 iPhone Voice Control**

Enabling Voice Control will download Voice Control files to your iPhone so that you can use Voice Control even when you're not connected to the internet. Check out the YouTube video, "Introducing Voice Control on the Mac and iOS," to see voice control in action.

Set up Voice Control in the "Settings" app on your iPhone, as shown below. Once Voice Control is configured, you can say, "Hey Siri, turn on Voice Control."

1.   Open the "Settings" app on your **iPhone** and tap on "Accessibility."

2.   In the section "Physical and Motor" tap "Voice Control" then tap "Set up Voice Control."

Tip: When you initially set up Voice Control instructions, common phrases are displayed. At any time, you can say, "Show me what to say."

While dictation doesn't always work perfectly the first time, with iPadOS 13 your can make corrections and apply rich text editing features as you dictate when you turn on Voice Control.

While dictating say, "Correct" and the word you want to change. In the following example, say "Correct" to replace a word with an emoji.

A few common phrases for Voice Control follow.

- Show Grid

- Show Numbers

- Show Names

- Long Press

- Tap Item Name

- Click Share

- Next Field

Chapter 2, "Touch Gestures," lists several common phrases like Tap or Long Press. Search the internet for Apple's "Human Interface Guidelines" to see other phrases.

*Add Custom Words on your iPhone**

For specific words used in the medical, legal, or other areas, iPadOS 13 allows you to add custom words, as shown below.

1.   Open the "Settings" app on your **iPhone** and tap on "Accessibility."

2.   In the section "Physical and Motor" tap "Voice Control" then tap "Vocabulary."

3.   In the top right corner, tap the plus symbol to add a word.

10.11 What's Next?

Just in case something goes wrong with your Apple Watch, or you have unanswered questions, the next chapter outlines basic troubleshooting steps. A few specific examples are also included.

11. Troubleshooting

In this chapter we discuss

What's Wrong?

Apple Pay Not Working

Battery

Calendar & Contacts

Complications Not Available

Can't Connect to iPhone

Connectivity

Digital Crown Not Responding

Force Restart

Forgotten Passcode

Home Screen Views

How Much Space is Available

Mickey Won't Announce the Time

Notifications

Reset, Restore and Backups

Chapter 11

Screen Settings

Siri Doesn't Respond

Walkie-Talkie App

Watch Not Responding

Watch Will Not Wake

watchOS Version

Weekly Summary

Why is My App Not Showing on My Watch?

My lazy guide to troubleshooting would be to turn your watch off and back on. A reset often fixes the problem. This chapter gathers a few of the problems I've come across in one place to save you time searching the Internet.

In the worst-case scenario where I'm on my own to find the cause of the problem, I start with a few basic questions.

- Has it ever worked?

- When did the problem start?

- When was the last day I added something new?

- Is the cellular network or Wi-Fi OK?

- Did I unpair and repair the watch as outlined in Chapter 2.

- Did I **force restart** my Apple Watch?

- Am I running the latest version of the watchOS?

11.1 What's Wrong?

If you don't know what the problem is, it can be hard to look up an answer in a particular category. This section should really be entitled, "What the heck is going on?" This topic covers those odd problems that are hard to describe.

When the screen seems locked and won't respond to anything, check if the water lock icon is displayed at the top of the screen. Turn the Digital Crown to "unlock" the screen.

When the screen display looks wonky, with impossibly large text, turn the Digital Crown to zoom out. Turn off "Zoom" on your iPhone in the Apple Watch app, as outlined in Chapter 3.

The bright white light on your screen is actually the flashlight. Press the Digital Crown to turn off the flashlight.

11.2 Apple Pay Not Working

Apple Pay is unavailable if you turned off the passcode on your Apple Watch. Follow these instructions to enable a passcode.

1. Open the Apple Watch app on your **iPhone**.

2. Tap "My Watch" located in the left corner of the tab bar, at the bottom of the screen.

3. Scroll down to "Passcode."

4. Touch the "Unlock with iPhone" switch to toggle the Passcode on or off.

Check the Status of the Apple Pay System

Apple maintains a system status page for all their apps. Check out https://www.apple.com/support/systemstatus/.

11.3 Battery

Several things affect battery life, such as installed apps, screen colors, and connectivity. Although battery life is better on the Apple Watch Series 4 and Series 5 compared to previous models, the following are a few suggestions to improve battery life.

- Choose a dark watch face.

- Remove favorite apps from the Dock.

- Remove apps from your Apple Watch.

- Use Accessibility, Grayscale.

- Turn off unnecessary push notifications.

- Force quit an unresponsive app.

- Turn off, "Wake Screen on Raise."

- Turn on iPhone Bluetooth.

- Use a Bluetooth chest strap for heart rate monitoring and disable the heart rate alerts.

- Turn off, "Hey Siri."

Check Your Battery

Swipe up on the **Apple Watch** face to open Control Center, then swipe to see battery life. When in "Nightstand Mode you can tap the green lightning bolt icon to see battery life.

Battery Not Charging

When your Apple Watch connects to a charging cable, a green lightning bolt symbol will appear. The lightning bolt symbol is red when your watch needs charging. It may take a few minutes for the green lightning bolt symbol to appear if your battery level is low.

To troubleshoot charging try these suggestions.

1. Completely remove any plastic wrap from both sides of the charger.

2. Plug the charger into a different cable or power outlet.

3. Reset your watch.

Check Cellular Data Usage

Checking cellular data usage for apps provides a picture of how much battery power the app is using. Usage is shown for the current period, as well as for each app.

1. On your **iPhone**, open the Apple Watch app.

2. Tap the My Watch tab, then tap "Cellular."

3. Swipe to see cellular data usage for apps.

Remove Favorite Apps From the Dock

The Dock can have up to 10 favorite apps. Apps using background services over cellular networks drain your battery. Location Services, alerts, and health data syncing all drain your battery. For this reason, I remove apps I don't regularly use. In Chapter 6, I explain two methods for removing Apple Watch apps on your iPhone.

1. Open the **Apple Watch** app on your iPhone.

2. In the section "Installed on Apple Watch," tap the app you want to remove.

3. Ensure "Show App on Apple Watch" is not enabled. The slide bar should be white.

Turn on Grayscale

Grayscale is a system-wide setting to assist users with difficulty viewing colors. Grayscale has the added benefit of reducing battery power.

1. On your **Apple Watch**, press the Side Button.

2. Tap Settings, and then tap General.

3. Swipe to select "Accessibility."

4. Tap the "Grayscale" switch to toggle Grayscale on or off.

Turn Off Notifications

1. On your **iPhone**, open the "Apple Watch" app.

2. Tap "Notifications."

3. Tap each app and set notification options for that particular app.

Power Reserve

Your Apple Watch will automatically ask if you want to turn on Power Reserve when power drops to 10%. With Power Reserve active, you can press the side button to see the current time, but you can't access any other watch features. Power Reserve mode saves power by displaying only the time. Other apps are not available when power reserve mode is active.

Turn on Power Reserve

1. Swipe up on the Apple Watch face to open "Control Center."

2. Tap the battery percentage.

3. Drag the Power Reserve slider to the right, then tap "Proceed."

Turn off Power Reserve

On the Apple Watch, press and hold the side button until you see the Apple logo. In a few seconds, the logo will appear. Your watch will restart.

Turn Off Siri

1.   On your **Apple Watch** press the Side Button.

2.   Tap "Settings," and then tap General.

3.   Scroll down and tap "Siri."

4.   Disable "Hey Siri." The slider is green when enabled and white when disabled.

Turn Your Watch Off and Back On

1.   On your **Apple Watch**, press and hold the side button until the menu appears.

2.   Touch the "Power Off" slider and drag to the right to turn off your watch.

3.   Press and hold the side button to turn your watch back on.

11.4 Calendar & Contacts

When your contacts or calendar are not syncing try a reset.

1.   On the **iPhone**, open the Apple Watch app.

2.   Tap "My Watch," located in the left corner of the tab bar at the bottom of the screen.

3.   Tap "General" and then tap "Reset."

4.   Tap "Reset Sync Data."

11.5 Complications

Occasionally I've noticed that a complication won't show as available in the Apple Watch app on the iPhone. However, it is still possible to add the complication on the Apple Watch itself.

1. On your **Apple Watch**, press the Digital Crown to go to the Watch Face.

2. Firmly press the display and then tap "Customize."

3. Swipe to display the highlighted area to customize.

4. Turn the Digital Crown to change the highlighted feature or select an app "Complication."

Strangely, the complication will then show in the Apple Watch app on your iPhone, but only for that particular watch face.

11.6 Can't Connect to iPhone

It doesn't happen often, but sometimes your watch won't connect to the companion iPhone. The Control Center displays the connection status. A red iPhone icon with a slash indicates the connection is broken.

Figure 11.1   iPhone Connection Status Icon

On your **Apple Watch face**, swipe up to open Control Center. When your watch and phone are paired, a green phone icon is displayed in the top left corner of the screen, as shown in Figure 11.1.

When your Apple Watch loses its connection to your iPhone, these troubleshooting steps might fix the problem.

- Disable Airplane mode on both devices.
- Restart your Apple Watch and iPhone.

11.7 Connectivity

There is no setting on your Apple Watch for Bluetooth. It is always on unless you enable Airplane Mode. If you are experiencing trouble with a Bluetooth device, check the settings on that device. To fix other basic connectivity issues, try these steps.

1.   On your **Apple Watch**, swipe up on the watch face.

2.   Tap to enable "Airplane mode," then tap again to disable Airplane Mode.

3.   On your iPhone, go to the "Settings" and disable Bluetooth, then Re-enable it.

Am I Connected to Cellular?

The Cellular button turns green when you have a connection. The green dots show the signal strength. Four green dots indicate the Apple Watch is connected to a cellular network.

Figure 11.2   Cellular Connection Status

Am I Connected to Wi-Fi?

The Cellular button turns white when your cellular plan is active, but your watch is connected to your iPhone or Wi-Fi.

Figure 11.3   Wi-Fi Connection Status

Global Cellular

There are two separate models for Apple Watch, optimized for the country of purchase. The LTE and UMTS bands used around the world are supported by the corresponding model.

Wi-Fi Won't Switch to Cellular

If you experience problems switching between Wi-Fi and LTE networks, these suggestions may help.

- Restart your watch.
- Install the latest watchOS.
- Check your cellular connection.

11.8 Digital Crown Not Responding

When the Digital Crown does not respond, try to isolate if it is a software or hardware issue. When the Digital Crown turns, and nothing happens, it is a software problem.

A hardware issue is when the Digital Crown will not turn. Try cleaning your watch according to Apple's instructions.

11.9 Force Restart

If your Apple Watch is not responding, you should try a "**force restart**".

1.   On your **Apple Watch** press and hold the Digital Crown and side button for 10 seconds.

2.   Release both buttons when you see the Apple logo.

11.10 Forgotten Passcode

There are two ways to access your Apple Watch if you forget your passcode.

Unpair the Apple Watch from the corresponding iPhone. Then set up your watch again. When prompted, you can restore your watch from a backup to recover your settings.

Reset your Apple Watch and pair it once again with your iPhone.

1.   Open the **Apple Watch** app on your iPhone.

2.   Tap "My Watch."

3. Scroll down to "General."

4. Tap "Reset."

11.11 Home Screen Views

If you are unable to switch between grid and list view on the Home screen, turn off your watch and turn it back on.

Switch Between Grid or List View

With the Home screen open, firmly press the screen and then tap either "Grid View" or "List View."

11.12 How Much Space is Available

To free up space, you could remove Apps, photos, or Music as outlined in Chapter 6.

How Much Total Space is Available

The "About" information includes these items.

- The count of songs on your watch.

- The count of photos on your watch.

- The number of applications on your watch.

- The total capacity.

- The available capacity.

1. On your **iPhone** open the Apple Watch app.

2. Swipe to scroll down and tap "General."

3. Tap "About" to see available capacity.

Figure 11.4   About - Capacity

11.13 Mickey Doesn't Announce the Time

Try these steps when Mickey or Minnie Mouse doesn't announce the time.

1. Check "Tap to Speak" is enabled in "Sounds & Haptics," as outlined in Chapter 2.

2. Make sure "Silent Mode" is not active in "Sounds & Haptics."

3. <u>Turn off</u> your Apple Watch and turn it back on. (Press and hold the side button.)

4. Try a "**force restart**." On your Apple Watch press and hold the Digital Crown and side button for 10 seconds. Release both buttons when you see the Apple logo.

11.14 Notifications

If you don't see notifications check your paired iPhone is connected, and the Apple Watch is not locked.

1. On your **Apple Watch**, press the Digital Crown to open the Home screen.

2. Swipe up from the bottom to open the Control Center.

3. In the top left corner verify the companion iPhone icon is green.

4. Ensure Wi-Fi is enabled.

5. Make sure "Do Not Disturb" is disabled.

Troubleshooting Message Notifications

There are a few things to check when you are not receiving message notifications.

1. In the Apple Watch app on your **iPhone**, check if the setting "Mirror My iPhone" is enabled. In the Watch app open "Notifications" and then tap "Messages."

2. On your **iPhone**, disable "Allow Notifications" and "**force restart**" your iPhone. Enable "Allow Notifications." Try turning on "Badge App Icon" and "Show on Lock Screen."

3.   Check if "Mute" or "Do Not Disturb" is enabled.

4.   Unlock your watch screen.

5.   **Force restart** your watch. Press the side button and Digital Crown for three seconds until the Apple logo appears.

6.   Check connectivity. Swipe up on your watch face to open the Control Panel.

7.   Check your settings for iMessage. iMessage allows you to send to an e-mail address if that contact has an Apple device. On your **iPhone** in Settings open "Messages." In the section "Send & Receive," verify your Apple ID and SMS phone number.

8.   A basic test involves sending a test SMS message by typing in a phone number in the "To" section of the message.

11.15 Reset, Restore & Backups

The reset option will unpair your Apple Watch from the corresponding iPhone. After reset, set up your Apple Watch again as outlined in Chapter 2, and restore from backup to recover your settings. You can reset your Apple Watch with the watch controls, or from your iPhone.

1.   On your **Apple Watch**, press and hold the side button until you see "Power Off."

2.   Firmly press the power off slider, and then release your finger.

3.   Tap "Erase all content and settings."

Turn Your Watch Off and Back On

1.   On your **Apple Watch**, press and hold the side button until the menu appears.

2.   Touch the "Power Off" slider and drag to the right to turn off your watch.

3.   Press and hold the side button to turn your watch back on.

Backups & Restore

Your Apple Watch settings are automatically backed up to your iPhone. Whenever you backup your iPhone to iTunes or iCloud, your Apple Watch settings are automatically included. Backups do not include Bluetooth pairings, Apple Pay cards, or your passcode.

11.16 Screen Settings

At night you may not want the screen to light up when you move your wrist. The solution is to turn off "Wake Screen on Wrist Raise" or turn on Silent Mode.

1.   On your **Apple Watch** press the Side Button.

2.   Tap "Settings," and then tap General.

3.   Scroll down and tap "Wake."

4.   Scroll down to the selection "Wake Screen on Wrist Raise."

Reset Home Screen Layout to Factory Default

1.   On the **iPhone**, open the Apple Watch app.

2.   Tap "My Watch," located in the left corner of the tab bar at the bottom of the screen.

3.   Tap "General" and then tap "Reset."

4.   Tap "Reset Home Screen Layout."

11.17 Siri Doesn't Respond

If Siri doesn't respond with a vocal prompt check "Voice Feedback" is toggled on.

- On your **iPhone**, follow the steps in Chapter 9 to turn Siri off and back on.

- On your **Apple Watch**, open "Settings" and tap "Siri." Toggle "Voice Feedback" on, and adjust the volume.

- On your **Apple Watch**, follow the steps to turn Siri off and back on, as shown below.

- Turn off your Apple Watch and turn back on. (Press and hold the side button.)

Check your internet connection. Wi-Fi and Bluetooth should both be active on your iPhone. To check your Apple Watch, press the Digital Crown to go to your watch face. Swipe up to see Control Center and the status of connectivity.

1. On your **Apple Watch** press the Side Button.

2. Tap "Settings," and then tap General.

3. Scroll down and tap "Siri."

4. Touch the "Hey Siri" slider and continue holding the slider as you move it to disabled. The slider is green when enabled and white when disabled.

Check if the Siri System is Available

Apple maintains a system status page for all its apps. Check out https://www.apple.com/support/systemstatus/.

11.18 Walkie-Talkie App

To use the Walkie-Talkie app check these settings.

- Apple Watch Series 1 or later with watchOS 5 or later.

- Both watches must have connectivity through a Bluetooth connection to the iPhone, Wi-Fi, or cellular.

- Both participants must mark themselves available in the app.

- Both watches must have the **Facetime app** on their respective companion iPhone.

- Both participants must be logged in with a different Apple Id.

- On your Apple Watch open the Walkie-Talkie app and tap to add contacts. Swipe to set your status to available.

The Walkie-Talkie app behaves differently when you turn on Silent Mode, Theater Mode, or Do Not Disturb. Swipe up on the watch face to open Control Center to check the status.

Silent Mode: You can still hear chimes and your friend's voice.

Theater Mode: Your Walkie-Talkie status is "unavailable."

Do Not Disturb: You can continue a conversation if you turn on "Do Not Disturb," but other calls are silenced.

11.19 Watch Not Responding

If your Apple Watch is not responding, try a **force restart**.

1. On your **Apple Watch** press and hold the Digital Crown and side button for 10 seconds.

2. Release both buttons when you see the Apple logo.

11.20 Watch Will Not Wake

If your Apple Watch doesn't wake when you lift your wrist, check the settings for wrist and digital crown orientation.

1. On your **iPhone**, open the Apple Watch App.

2. Tap the "My Watch" tab located in the bottom left corner of the screen.

3. Scroll down to "General."

4. Under "Watch Orientation," select the left or right wrist.

11.21 watchOS Version

Yes, I am one of those people whose OS and app versions are usually out of date, simply because I like to control what's installed. If it works OK and there is no security issue I'm happy, and I tend to ignore update alerts. However, installing the latest version does fix some issues or security risks, so when your watch notifies you it's time to update your watchOS, follow these instructions.

1.   Make sure your Apple Watch is on the charger.

2.   On your **iPhone** open the Apple Watch app.

3.   Tap "General" and then tap "Software Update."

11.22 Weekly Summary

In case you don't receive the Weekly Summary from the Activity app on Monday mornings, check your wrist orientation and wheelchair settings.

1.   On your **iPhone** open the Apple Watch app.

2.   Tap "Passcode."

3.   Swipe up, then tap "Wrist Detection." A green slider bar indicates Wrist Detection is on.

4.   Change the "Wheelchair" setting to "Yes" or "No."

1.   On your **iPhone** open the Apple Watch app.

2.   Tap the "My Watch" tab located in the bottom left corner of the screen.

3.   Swipe up, then tap "Health."

4.   Tap "Edit" in the top right corner of the screen.

5.   Tap Wheelchair, and choose an option at the bottom of the screen.

11.23 Why is My App Not Showing on My Watch?

If you don't see an app on your Apple Watch, check Content & Privacy Restrictions. These settings apply to Mail, Safari, FaceTime, Camera, Siri & Dictation, Wallet, AirDrop, and CarPlay.

Also check the app was not deleted from your iPhone. I noticed after I deleted the Podcasts app from my iPhone, it was not available on my Apple Watch. I reinstalled the Podcasts app on my Apple Watch using the Watch App Store, and the app was still not displayed on my Watch. After reinstalling the app on my iPhone, it was instantly available on my Apple Watch.

Screen Time: Content & Privacy Restrictions

1.   On the **iPhone**, open the Settings app.

2.   Swipe up and tap "Screen Time."

3.   Swipe up and tap "Content & Privacy Restrictions."

4.   Tap "Allowed Apps" and enable "Camera."

Chapter 11

Conclusion

In the course of writing this book, I discovered gaps in my knowledge and many useful features. Hopefully, you too, have found new benefits. Thank you for reading along with me through both the interesting topics, as well as the less than thrilling subjects. If the end result is you have mastered new features, it was worth it! I'd love to hear the cool things you're doing with your watch, so please don't hesitate to leave comments in a review.

Chapter 12

Visual Index

Camera Effects. Messages or Facetime.

Shapes, Camera Effects.

Text Label, Camera Effects.

Filters, Camera Effects, Camera, Screen Effects.

Camera

Front or Rear Camera.

Live Photos, Camera.

Focus, Camera.

Brightness and Contrast, Camera.

Folders

Trash

Settings, Safari.

More.

Crop

Color Adjustment

Brightness

Black and White, Camera.

Favorite

Rotate, Camera.

Silent Mode

Rotate, Camera.

Airplane Mode.

Reply, Mail.

Do Not Disturb

New Message, Mail.

AirPlay

Mailboxes, Mail.

AirDrop

Location

Wi-Fi

Activity (Send), Camera, Screen Effects

Noise

Sliders, Camera Effects & Photo Editing

The Home App

Animated GIFs, Messages.

Volume

Undo

iCloud

Download from iCloud

Digital Touch. Messages.

Family Sharing. iCloud.

More. Photos app.

Send

Apple TV

Stickers. Messages.

App Store

Microphone. Messages.

Books

Bluetooth

Calendar

Carrot

Home (Smart Home) App.

Clock

iTunes Store

Contacts

Mail

Drafts

Maps

Grocery

Messages

Visual Index

Music

Reminders App

Reminders App

Safari (Web Browser)

Philips Hue

Settings

Photos App

Shortcuts App

Podcasts

Wallet

Siri

Transcribe

Voice Memos

Refresh, Safari

Back, Safari

Forward, Safari

Bookmark, Safari

Flag, Mail

Index

A Quick Look at Watch Controls, 2.3
Accept a Sharing Request, 9.3
Accessibility, 3.13, 10
Accessibility Shortcut, 3.13, 10.1
Accounts and Passwords, 2.10
Activate Credit Cards on Your Watch, 6.3
Activity App, 9.3
Activity Reminders, 9.3
Add a Calendar Event, 6.8
Add a Complication to Your Watch Face, 4.6
Add a Custom Drafts Action, 7.8
Add a Reminder or Show Completed Reminders, 6.27
Add a Workout Playlist, 6.22
Add an Alarm, 6.2
Add an App to The Dock, 2.13
Add Apple TV, 6.28
Add Bar Code Tickets with PassU, 6.3
Add Bluetooth Accessories, 8.1
Add Cards and Passes to Apple Wallet, 6.3
Add Items to the List, 7.2
Add or Remove a Favorite Contact, 4.6, 6.24
Add the World Clock Complication, 6.10
Add to Your Workout, 9.7
Add World Clock Complication, 4.7
Additional Workout Apps, 9.9
Adjust Alert Volume, 5.8

Adjust Volume, 2.19
Airplane Mode, 2.15
Alarms, 6.2
Always-on, 1.2, 2.18
Am I Connected to Cellular?, 11.7
Am I Connected to Wi-Fi?, 11.7
Answer a Call, 6.24
Apple HomeKit Automation Platform, 6.17
Apple ID & iCloud, 3.12
Apple Pay & the Wallet App, 6.3
Apple Pay Not Working, 11.2
Apple Resources, 2.21
Apple TV, 8.6
Apple Watch Series 5, 1.2
Arrival, 6.15
Ask Siri a Question, 6.29
Ask Siri to Send Cash in a Message, 6.3
Ask to Buy, 3.12
Astronomy, 4.2, 4.7
Audio Output, 2.15
Audiobooks, 6.4
Auto Launch the Now Playing App, 3.6
Automatic App Install, 3.4
Automation, 6.17
Backups & Restore, 11.15
Band Release Buttons, 2.17
Basic Settings, 9.1
Basics, 3
Battery, 11.3

Battery, 2.15
Battery Not Charging, 11.3
Bluetooth Accessories, 10.7
Books, 6.5
Breathe, 6.6
Breathe Watch Face, 4.7
Brightness & Text, 2.18
Buy Books, 6.5
Calculator, 6.7
Calendar, 6.8
Calendar & Contacts, 11.4
Calendar and Reminders, 7.1
Calendar Notifications, 5.7
Calendar Sync Issues, 6.8
Call a Favorite Contact, 6.24
Camera Remote, 6.9
Camera Remote and Timer, 6.9
Can't Connect to iPhone, 11.6
Cellular, 2.15
Challenge a Friend, 9.3
Change Notification Delivery, 5.4
Change Passcode Options, 2.10
Change the Move Goal, 9.3
Change the Time Shown, 2.20
Change Volume With the Digital
    Crown, 6.22
Changing the Watch Face Style, 4.3
Charging Stands, 8.2
Charging the Watch, 2.5
Check Available Space, 6.22
Check Cellular Data Usage, 11.3
Check if the Siri System is Available,
    11.17
Check the Status of the Apple Pay
    System, 11.2
Check Your Battery, 11.3
Clear Website Data, 2.10
Clock, 6.10
Collections, 6.20
Color, 4.7
Combine Several Actions, 7.6
Compass, 6.11
Complication Not Showing on iPhone,
    4.6
Complications, 11.5
Complications, 4.6
Configure Emergency SOS, 3.3, 6.14
Configure Medical ID in the Health
    App, 3.2, 6.14, 9.2
Configure Rooms and Devices for

Apple Watch, 6.17
Configure the World Clock Time
    Zones, 4.7, 6.10
Connectivity, 11.7
Contacts, 6.12
Continuity & Handoff, 3.14
Control Audio Volume, 2.15
Control Center, 2.15
Control your MFi Hearing Aid, 10.7
Cooking and Kitchen, 4.7
Cover to Mute, 2.19
Create a Message, 6.21
Create a Photo Album on your
    iPhone, 4.7
Create a Shortcut, 6.30
Create an Audio Clip, 6.21
Create IFTTT Widgets for your Apple
    Watch, 7.6
Create Your Own IFTTT Applets, 7.6
Customize App Notifications, 5.7,
    10.3
Customize Calendar Notifications, 6.8
Customized Samples, 4.7
Customizing a Watch Face, 4.4
Cycle Tracking, 6.13
Day to Day, 8
Decline a Call, 6.24
Delete a Watch Face, 4.3
Delete an Alarm, 6.2
Delete an E-mail, 6.19
Delete Apps, 2.12
Dictate, 6.21
Digital Crown Not Responding, 11.8
Digital Touch, 6.21
Disney, 4.7
Display Calendar Month View, 6.8
Do Not Disturb, 2.15
Do Not Disturb, 2.19
Download Music to Your Apple Watch,
    6.22
Drafts, 7.8
ECG App, 9.5
Edit Complications, 4.6
Edit General Settings, 3.1
Edit or Delete an Action, 7.8
Edit Your Personal Informational, 9.2
Emergency Phone Call, 6.24
Emergency SOS, Fall Detection, &
    Medical ID, 6.14
Enable Activity Sharing Notifications,

9.3
Enable Emergency Bypass, 6.12
Enable Emergency SOS, 6.14
Enable Emergency SOS on your
    Watch, 3.3
Enable Family Sharing, 3.12
Enable Family Sharing, 6.27
Enable Family Sharing, 7.2
Enable Handoff on your Apple Watch,
    8.5
Enable Handoff on your Mac, 8.5
Enable Haptic Notifications, 5.5
Enable Raise to Speak, 6.29
Enable Screenshots, 3.15
Enable Sharing, 9.3
Enable Siri on Your Apple Watch, 6.29
Enable Siri on Your Watch, 6.29
Enable the Notification Indicator, 5.6
Enable the Notification Indicator, 10.2
End Your Workout, 9.7
Entertainment, 7.3
Example of Weather in Motion, 6.36
Exercise Ring, 9.3
Explore Apps, 9.9
Explore Recommended Apps, 9.2
Explore the Digital Crown, 2.14
Exploring Interactive Watch Faces,
    4.2
Export a PDF for Your Doctor, 9.5
Export Health Data, 9.2
Family Sharing, 3.12
Favorite Shortcuts, 6.30
Find an Address for a Contact, 6.20
Find iPhone, 8.4
Find My, 6.15
Find My iPhone, 2.15
Find My, Share My Location, 3.12
Find Your Apple Watch, 8.3
Find Your Apple Watch, 2.10
Fire, Water, Liquid Metal, and Vapor,
    4.7
Flag Style, 6.19
Flashlight, 2.15
Force Restart, 11.9
Force Touch, 2.1
Forgotten Passcode, 11.10
Forward, Mark, Notify Me, Move, or
    Delete an e-Mail, 6.19
Games, 7.4
Get Location Notifications, 6.15

Global Cellular, 11.7
Gradually Wake Your Watch, 2.14
Gradually Wake Your Watch, 3.6
Grayscale, 10.4
Grocery, 7.2
Grocery and Cooking Apps, 7.2
GymKit, 9.6
Handoff and Continuity, 8.5
Handoff From Apple Watch to iPhone,
    8.5
Haptic Alerts, 2.19
Haptics, 2.19
Health and Fitness, 7.5
Health and Fitness , 9
Health App, 9.2
Health Data Backups, 9.2
Hearing, 10.6
Hearing Aids, 10.7
Hearing Aids, 8.1
Hearing Metrics, 9.3
Heart Rate Alerts, 9.1
Heart Rate App, 9.4
Heart Rate Recovery, 6.16
Heart Rate Sensors & Electrodes,
    2.16
High or Low Heart Rate Alerts, 5.9
History, Weekly Summary & Details,
    9.3
Home - Grid or List View, 2.12
Home Automation, 6.17
Home Screen Views, 11.11
How Much Space is Available, 11.12
How Much Total Space is Available,
    11.12
Human Interface Guidelines, 2.2
iCloud Backup, 3.12
iCloud Drive, 3.12
iCloud Keychain, 3.12
iCloud Photo Stream, 3.12
IFTTT, 7.6
Install & Delete Apps on your Apple
    Watch, 6.1
Integration with Third-Party Calendar
    Apps, 6.8
Invite a Friend, 6.35
Invite People to Join Your Home, 6.17
iTunes, 8.6
Kaleidoscope, 4.7
Keynote, 6.18
Language and Region, 3.8

Laps, 6.32
Lift Your Wrist to Wake Your Watch, 3.6
Listen to Music While You Workout, 9.7
Location Services, 9.1
Log Data, 6.13
Magnetometer, 6.11
Mail, 6.19
Mail Notifications, 5.7
Mail Settings - Inboxes, 6.19
Make a Call, 6.24
Manually Add a Workout or Activity, 9.3
Map Notifications, 5.7
Map Notifications, 6.20
Maps, 6.20
Message Alerts, 6.21
Message Notifications, 5.7
Messages, Digital Touch, & Apple Pay, 6.21
Messaging, 10.8
Metrics, 9.7
Mickey Won't Announce the Time, 11.13
Monogram, 6.10
Motion, 4.7
Motion & Fitness, 9.1
Move Ring, 9.3
Move, Exercise, & Stand Rings, 9.3
Music and the Now Playing App, 6.22
Mute an e-mail Conversation, 6.19
Name Your 'Other' Workout, 9.7
Name, Phone Numbers, E-mail, 3.12
Navigating Complications, 4.6
Navigation, 6.20
New Apps, 1.3
New Features, 1.3
Nightstand Mode, 3.7
Notifications, 5, 11.14
Notifications, 5
On/Off Labels, 10.4
Open the Notification Center, 5.2
Options, 6.21
Organize Books in Collections, 6.5
Organize Your Watch Faces, 4.5
Pair Your Watch & iPhone, 2.7
Pair Your Watch to an iPhone, 8.12
Parked Car, 6.20
Passcode & Security Features, 2.10

Password & Security, 3.12
Pause Your Workout, 9.7
Pay a Merchant on Your Watch, 6.3
Phone, 6.24
Photography and Video, 7.7
Photos, 6.25
Play Music, 6.22
Podcasts, 6.26
Power Reserve, 11.3
Privacy & Location Services, 3.10
Productivity, 7.8
Read a Message, 6.21
Read and Reply to an e-mail, 6.19
Rearrange Icons in the Control Center, 2.15
Reminders, 6.27
Remote Control, 8.6
Remote Control, 6.28
Remove an App from the Dock, 2.13
Remove Apps, 6.1
Remove Apps from the Home Screen, 6.1
Remove Apps Using iPhone Storage, 6.1
Remove Complications, 4.6
Remove Favorite Apps From the Dock, 11.3
Rename Your Watch, 2.8
Reorder Cards in the Wallet, 6.3
Reorder the List of Apps, 2.13
Reorder Watch Faces, 4.5
Reply to a Message, 6.21
Requirements, 3.14
Requirements, 8.5
Reset Home Screen Layout to Factory Default, 11.16
Reset Home Screen Layout to Factory Default, 2.12
Reset, Restore & Backups, 11.15
Return to Last Activity on Screen Raise, 3.6
Review Photos, 6.9
Running, 9.8
Running Auto Pause, 9.7
Safari Apple Pay and Apple Watch, 6.3
Sample Workouts, 9.8
Schools, 7.9
Screen Settings, 11.16
Screen Time: Content & Privacy Re-

strictions, 11.23
Screen Time: Content & Privacy Re-
  strictions, 3.11
Screen Time: Content & Privacy Re-
  strictions, 6.9
Scribble, 6.21
Search, 6.20
Search for Apps to Install, 6.1
Search Here and 'Transit Map', 6.20
Set a Goal, 9.7
Set Activity Settings, 9.3
Set an Alarm, 3.7
Set Mail Options, 6.19
Set Mail VIPs, 5.7
Set the Reading Rate, 10.4
Set VIPs, 6.19
Setup & Getting Started, 2
Setup Cellular Service, 2.9
Setup the Health App, 9.1
Share a Reminder List, 3.12
Share a Reminder List, 6.27
Share Activity with a Friend, 9.3
Share Calendars, 3.12
Share the List with Your Family, 7.2
Share Your Location with a Friend,
  6.15
Shuffle, Repeat, Source and Output,
  6.22
Side Button & Dock, 2.13
Sign in with Apple, 2.10
Silent Mode, 2.15
Silent Mode, 2.19
Silent Mode, 8.9
Siri, 3.9
Siri, 4.7
Siri, 6.29
Siri Doesn't Respond, 11.17
Siri Doesn't Respond, 6.29
Siri Phrases, 6.29
Siri Shortcuts, 6.29
Siri Shortcuts, 6.30
Smart Home, 7.10
Smart Replies, 6.21
Sounds & Haptics, 2.19
Sports and the Great Outdoors, 7.11
Stand Ring, 9.3
Start a Conversation, 6.35
Start a Workout, 9.7
Status Icons, 5.1
Status of the Apple Pay System, 6.3

Stocks, 4.7
Stocks, 6.31
Stopwatch, 6.32
Subscriptions & Purchase History,
  3.12
Suggested Shortcuts, 6.29
Suggested Shortcuts, 6.30
Swimming and Water Sports, 9.8
Switch Between Apps, 2.14
Switch Between Grid or List View,
  11.11
Switch Between Grid or List View,
  2.12
Take a Screenshot, 3.15
Taptic Engine, 10.2
Teach Siri about You, 6.29
The 'My Faces' Screen, 4.5
The Apple Watch App Store, 6.1
The Default Type of Audio Response,
  6.21
The Digital Crown, 2.14
The Display, 2.11
The Favorite Complication, 4.6
The Health Data Screen, 9.2
The Heart Rate App, 6.16
The Home App, 6.17
The Home Screen, 2.12
The Noise App, 6.23
Theater and Sleep Mode, 8.9
Theater Mode, 2.15
Third-party Apps, 7
Timelapse, 4.7
Timer, 6.33
Track Your Progress (View Metrics),
  9.7
Transfer a Call to Your iPhone, 6.24
Transit Cards, 6.3
Travel, 7.12
Trends, 9.3
Troubleshooting, 11
Troubleshooting Message Notifica-
  tions, 11.14
Troubleshooting Message Notifica-
  tions, 5.7
Troubleshooting Notifications, 5.10
Turn Alarm Off or Snooze, 6.2
Turn App Notifications Off, 5.3
Turn Off, 2.6
Turn Off Notifications, 11.3
Turn off Power Reserve, 11.3

Turn Off Siri, 11.3
Turn off Water Lock, 2.15
Turn on Find My Watch, 2.10
Turn on Find My Watch, 3.12
Turn on Grayscale, 11.3
Turn On or Wake, 2.4
Turn on Power Reserve, 11.3
Turn on Water Lock, 2.15
Turn Your Watch Off and Back On, 11.15
Turn Your Watch Off and Back On, 11.3
Two-Factor Authentication, 2.10
Unlock Your Apple Watch, 8.7
Unlock Your Mac, 8.8
Update watchOS, 8.13
Update Your Watch Face, 4.1
Updated Apps, 1.3
Upgrade Your iPhone, 8.11
Use Apple Pay to Send & Receive $, 6.21
Use Audio Output With Apple Watch, 6.22
Use IFTTT to link iOS and Alexa, 7.2
View a Message Timestamp, 6.21
View and Rerecord Shortcut Phrases, 6.30
View Heart Rate Data, 6.16, 9.2
View Medical ID or Call Emergency Services, 3.3, 6.14
View Your Friend's Progress, 9.3
Vision, 10.4
Voice Memos, 6.34
VoiceOver, 3.13, 10.4
VOmax Metric, 9.3
Wake Screen, 3.6
Walkie-Talkie, 2.15, 6.35, 10.9, 11.18
Watch a Podcast or Tune in a Show, 9.7
Watch Apps, 6
Watch Bands, 8.10
Watch Faces, 4
Watch Not Responding, 11.19
Watch Orientation (Wrist), 3.5
Watch Will Not Wake, 11.20
watchOS and iOS , 1.3
watchOS Version, 11.21
Water Lock, 2.15
Water Sports, 7.13
Waze, 6.30

Weather, 6.36, 7.14
Web Browser, 6.37
Weekly Summary, 9.3, 11.22
What Can Siri Do?, 6.29
What's Wrong?, 11.1
Wheelchair Mode, 9.2
Which Device Determines Your Location?, 6.15
Why is My App Not Showing on My Watch?, 11.23
Wi-Fi, 2.15
Wi-Fi Won't Switch to Cellular, 11.7
Workout and Activity History, 9.3, 9.7
Workout App, 9.7, 10.5
Workout Playlist, 9.8
Workout Reminders, 5.7
World Traveler, 4.7
Wrist Detection, 2.10
Yoga, 9.8
Your Apple Watch Device Info, 3.12
Your Contact Card, 6.12, 6.29
Your Health Account, 9.2
Your Health Profile, 9.2
Your Photo, 4.7
Zoom, 3.13, 10.4

Index

Index

Index

Apple Watch Series 5

Beginner to Advanced, a Complete Guide

Trademarks

All terms mentioned in this book that are known to be trademarks have been capitalized. All other trademarks are the property of their respective owners. Apple® Watch, Apple® iPad®, Apple Watch® and Apple® iPhone® are trademarks of Apple Inc., in the U.S. and other countries.

Warning and Disclaimer

The information provided in this book is on an "as is" basis. The author is not responsible or liable to any person or entity with respect to any loss or damages arising from the information contained in this book. The author makes no representations or warranties, express or implied, as to the condition, quality, merchantability or fitness of any product mentioned.